How to write law essays and exams

D0418648

How to write law essays and exams

Third Edition

S I Strong, PhD (Cantab), **DPhil** (Oxon), **JD** (Duke)

Solicitor, Supreme Court of England and Wales
Attorney, New York and Illinois

OXFORD
UNIVERSITY PRESS

OXFORD
UNIVERSITY PRESS

Great Clarendon Street, Oxford OX2 6DP

Oxford University Press is a department of the University of Oxford.
It furthers the University's objective of excellence in research, scholarship,
and education by publishing worldwide in

Oxford New York

Auckland Cape Town Dar es Salaam Hong Kong Karachi
Kuala Lumpur Madrid Melbourne Mexico City Nairobi
New Delhi Shanghai Taipei Toronto

With offices in

Argentina Austria Brazil Chile Czech Republic France Greece
Guatemala Hungary Italy Japan Poland Portugal Singapore
South Korea Switzerland Thailand Turkey Ukraine Vietnam

Oxford is a registered trade mark of Oxford University Press
in the UK and in certain other countries

© S I Strong 2010

The moral rights of the author have been asserted
Database right Oxford University Press (maker)
Crown copyright material is reproduced with the permission of the Controller,
HMSO (under the terms of the Click Use Licence).

First published 2003

All rights reserved. No part of this publication may be reproduced,
stored in a retrieval system, or transmitted, in any form or by any means,
without the prior permission in writing of Oxford University Press,
or as expressly permitted by law, or under terms agreed with the appropriate
reprographics rights organization. Enquiries concerning reproduction
outside the scope of the above should be sent to the Rights Department,
Oxford University Press, at the address above

You must not circulate this book in any other binding or cover
and you must impose the same condition on any acquirer

British Library Cataloguing in Publication Data
Data available

Library of Congress Cataloging-in-Publication Data
Strong, S I
  How to write law essays and exams / S.I. Strong.—3rd ed.
  p. cm.
  Includes index.
  ISBN-13: 978–0–19–953357–2
  ISBN-10: 0–19–953357–1
  1. Legal composition. 2. Law—Great Britain—Language. I. Title.
  KD404.S77 2010
  808'.06634—dc22
                                        2010001497

Typeset by MPS Limited, A Macmillan Company
Printed in Great Britain by Ashford Colour Press Ltd, Gosport, Hampshire

ISBN 978–0–19–953357–2

10 9 8 7 6 5 4 3 2 1

Preface to the third edition

This is a book for law students, so it is only appropriate that I first thank all the students with whom I have worked over the years. Without their enthusiasm and individuality, I would not have enjoyed teaching them as much as I have, nor would I have learned as much about the qualities of good writing. In particular, I would like to thank Alison Cole of New Hall, Cambridge, for suggesting that I write this book. Without her inspiration, the CLEO method might exist only in seminar form. I would also like to acknowledge the fine work of my research assistants, Charles Clarke, Mark Davison, Mark Higgins, Neshan Minassian, Marcus Pollard and Justin Simon. Their contributions to this book have been most welcome.

I would also like to thank my former colleagues at Cambridge and Oxford, as well as my current colleagues at the University of Missouri, for all of their assistance. I have found their company enlightening and invigorating, and I appreciate all the wisdom that they have shared with me. I particularly wish to thank Dr Rosy Thornton of Emmanuel College, Cambridge, for her unwavering support and encouragement over the years. She is a fine scholar, an inspiring educator and a wonderful writer, and I appreciate all that she has done on my behalf. She has been a friend as well as a mentor.

Due credit must also be given to those with whom I worked during my years in private practice, both at Weil, Gotshal & Manges and Baker & McKenzie. I wish to thank each of them, including the many wonderful trainees, for their advice and input on this project.

I also wish to thank Sarah Viner at Oxford University Press. Over the years, I have had the privilege of working with her on several books, and I have always found her to be a great source of support, assistance, ideas and good cheer. I appreciate all that she does.

Finally, I wish to acknowledge the encouragement and support of my friends and family. Special thanks go to Ann Wagner, who kindly offered her marvellous proof-reading services, and Hannah Waine, who provided expert assistance on chapter eight. All errors of course remain my own.

S I Strong
August 2009

Contents

Guide to the Online Resource Centre

Students often worry about their writing skills, thinking that first-class essays need big words, flowery phrases and metaphors that would make Shakespeare stand in awe. In fact, anything too tricky often backfires. If you keep your writing simple, succinct and clear, you'll do much better. This book helps you attain those goals by giving you an analytical structure that works in a variety of different circumstances as well as a wealth of general writing tips.

online resource centre
www.oxfordtextbooks.co.uk/orc

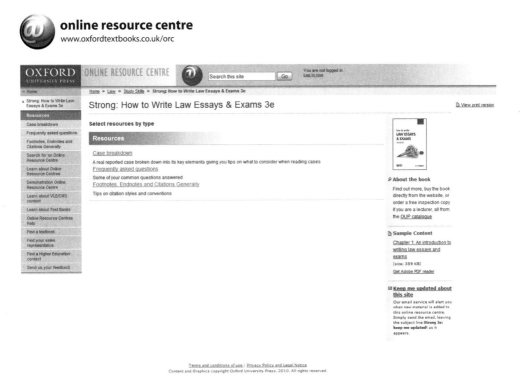

This book is now accompanied by an Online Resource Centre, which can be found at www.oxfordtextbooks.co.uk/orc/strong3e/ and offers additional features to provide further assistance in the writing of law essays.

Discussion of citation styles – provides guidance on citation style and how to reference your work correctly

Breakdown of a case – this feature highlights the various elements of a written case, to help students read and assess cases accurately and efficiently

FAQ – provides answers to students' frequently asked questions about many aspects of writing law essays and exams, and is a quick reference to some of the material covered throughout the book

An introduction to writing law essays and exams

1.1 Why the need for a special approach to law essays and exams?

Most people who choose to study law are bright, motivated and hard-working. They know that law is a very competitive field, and they are prepared to do whatever is necessary to do well. Why, then, do so many able and intelligent students fail to achieve the marks they deserve in their university or professional examinations? Once they have left their studies behind, why do so many find their first years of legal practice so difficult? The answer is simple: they have been given insufficient guidance regarding how to demonstrate their knowledge of the law in written form. By the time they reach vocational training and legal practice, they are assumed to have been taught the requisite skills and so find themselves in even more trouble as they struggle to produce professional quality work without knowing the rudiments of legal writing and analysis.

Students are not to blame for the current state of affairs, but they are the ones who suffer as a result of it, both in terms of their health – which can be affected by overwork and stress – and their careers. Good legal writing in essays and examinations leads to good marks at university and vocational school, and good marks lead to good jobs. If a student is unfortunate enough not to be able to guess what constitutes effective legal writing or to have a lawyer in the family who can give some helpful advice, then that student will find it difficult to compete at the top level.

Fortunately, good legal writing skills are not a matter of luck or genetic predisposition. Effective writing techniques can be learned. Once you have mastered those skills, you are more likely to receive good marks at university. You will also find the transition to professional writing easier than it otherwise would have been.

You might wonder why, if good writing is so important, it doesn't appear on the syllabus. Quite simply, no one feels that it's their job to teach good writing. Schools believe that 'legal writing' is beyond their competence and that they have enough to do teaching basic writing skills. Universities believe that students should have already acquired basic instruction in good writing by the time they arrive at university and the duty of a university lies in teaching the substantive law, not in teaching writing and analytic skills. Of course, this approach ignores the fact that students come unprepared to the study of law, since it is qualitatively different from the study of other A-level subjects. Professional schools also take the view that they should not have to spend their time teaching writing, except to the extent that their courses introduce the specialised forms of writing (such as pleadings, legal opinions, etc) undertaken by legal practitioners.

While this kind of mutual finger-pointing presents one type of problem, there is a deeper issue, namely that most teachers and educational institutions don't know how to teach legal writing. Because most legal academics were never offered any special assistance in this area, they don't know how to instruct their students. Therefore, the feedback that's given on written work tends to focus on either substance (ie missed cases or statutes) or on style (ie misplaced commas, passive voice, etc). While these sorts of comments are very helpful, they don't help students learn how to structure an argument or how to present information in an effective manner. The CLEO method is intended to help you learn how to analyse questions in law, particularly problem questions, and write strong, effective, well-structured essays in response.

1.2 Hallmarks of a good essay in law

It is difficult to produce a first-class essay if you don't know the criteria examiners use when marking your work. Every university or vocational school has its own guidelines which describe what constitutes a first-class, second-class and third-class essay or examination. If those guidelines are not made available to you as a matter of course, you should ask to see them so that you can know the standard by which you are being judged. If you know what you are aiming to achieve, you are more likely to succeed.

However, there is some consensus in the academic community about what constitutes a good essay in law. For example, most instructors would agree that the basic elements of a first-class essay include:

> ✳ **NOTE**
>
> A first-class essay stands out on a variety of levels.

- close attention to the question as it is asked;
- detailed knowledge of the topic addressed, as well as a deeper understanding of the context in which that topic exists;

- superlative coverage of the question, including both breadth and accuracy, with no or almost no significant errors or omissions relating to the law at issue;

- identification of at least some of the less obvious points of law;

- outstanding clarity of structure, argument and writing style;

- excellent use of supporting information and ideas;

- use of more than one possible line of argument; and

- presentation of theoretical arguments concerning the subject, significant critical analysis and thoughtful personal perspective on the debate.

It may seem that it is impossible to demonstrate all these qualities within a single essay and, indeed, this is a very high standard of performance. However, most people fail to achieve first-class marks not because they are deficient in their understanding of the subject matter, but because they do not present their knowledge of the law in the best possible light. The CLEO method of legal writing and analysis is designed to teach you how to integrate elements of a first-class essay into your work so that you can win full marks for your understanding of the substantive law.

As you would expect, a good second-class mark falls slightly below the first-class standard and includes most of the following qualities:

* **NOTE**

A good second-class mark falls slightly short in some or all of the various areas of evaluation.

- attention to the question as it is asked;

- a good and relatively detailed knowledge of the topic addressed, as well as a good understanding of the context in which that topic exists;

- good coverage of the question, including breadth and accuracy, with few significant errors or omissions relating to the law at issue;

- strong organisational structure, argument and written style;

- good use of supporting information and ideas;

- use of more than one possible line of argument; and

- some degree of familiarity with theoretical arguments concerning the subject and a significant degree of critical analysis.

A low second-class mark falls slightly below a good second-class mark in most or all areas of achievement and includes the following attributes:

* **NOTE**

A low second-class mark conveys some understanding and analytic skill but lacks detail and insight.

- attention to the subject matter asked but not necessarily precise treatment of the particular question as it is asked;

- satisfactory knowledge of the topic addressed as well as understanding of the context in which that topic exists;

- acceptable coverage of the question, with reasonable breadth and accuracy, though possibly marred by some substantial errors or omissions relating to the law at issue;

- a reasonably organised structure, argument and written style; and

- satisfactory use of supporting information and ideas, albeit with a weak or deficient theoretical or critical approach.

Finally, a third-class or passing mark demonstrates significant short-comings in most areas of evaluation and includes:

- discussion of the relevant area of the subject, even if there is a lack of attention to the question as it is asked;

- some knowledge of the topic addressed as well as some understanding of the context in which it was placed, despite some weakness in accuracy or breadth and possibly including significant errors and omissions in the law relating to the issue;

- some structure, argument and ability to express one's thoughts; and

- some ability to use supporting information and ideas, even if they are somewhat unclear or inappropriate and offer little theoretical or critical analysis.

> **✳ NOTE**
>
> A third-class mark signifies an essay that demonstrates a minimal understanding of the question and issues.

Knowing your examiners' criteria is the first step in achieving higher marks, but you must move on to the second step, namely learning how to meet those criteria. This book teaches you how to do just that. For example, the CLEO method of legal writing described in this book will provide you with a strong structural and analytical framework for your arguments. By presenting your ideas in an organised manner, you demonstrate the kind of clarity of thinking and expression that examiners appreciate. This book will also teach you how to identify relevant topics of discussion, compile the best possible supporting material and craft sophisticated arguments that contain detail, insight and relevance to the question asked. Finally, the CLEO method will teach you how to present your ideas quickly and efficiently, which will give you more time to write your answers and thus increase the breadth and depth of your discussion.

> **WRITING TIP** 🖉
>
> *Make a list of all the qualities of a first-class essay. Compare this list with your finished work before you hand it in. Have you fulfilled the criteria necessary to earn top marks?*

1.3 What is CLEO?

> CLEO primarily addresses problem questions, but can also apply to 'discuss' questions and legal practice.

CLEO is a four-step method of legal analysis and writing that provides a practical and proven method of answering law school essay and examination questions. The CLEO technique focuses primarily on problem (ie 'fact pattern') questions but is equally applicable to 'discuss' questions and legal practice. Each of the four steps requires you to exercise a different kind of analytical skill. If you implement the CLEO method in your essays, your marks should improve dramatically, since you will be showing the examiners precisely those qualities they want to see.

For example, in the first step of a CLEO analysis, you identify the **claim** at issue. Here, you show how you can spot legal controversies, construct multiple lines of argument and respond to questions as they are asked. The second step in the CLEO system involves the presentation of the applicable **law**. In this section, you identify the relevant legal authority regarding each of the legal issues discussed in the first step of your essay. The 'L' step allows you to demonstrate the depth and breadth of your legal knowledge as well as the quality of your legal reasoning skills. CLEO's third step requires you to **evaluate** the facts of the problem in light of the legal authority presented in the second step. Here, you illustrate your powers of analysis and persuasion as you discuss the extent to which the facts in your particular question live up to the general legal standard identified in your discussion of the law. CLEO's fourth step requires you to identify the **outcome** of your argument. In so doing, you finally weigh up the different strands of legal thought, decide which of your arguments are most compelling and introduce any relevant theoretical points, to the extent you have not done so already. If you adhere to this analytical framework, your overall structure and arguments will be clear and easily understandable, thus increasing your reader's comprehension throughout.

> CLEO provides a four-step framework for analysis and stands for:
> Claim;
> Law;
> Evaluation; and
> Outcome.

The CLEO system is not a panacea. It cannot replace time spent attending lectures and reading up on the law. Nevertheless, it will help you to present your knowledge in the best possible light. If you read the four chapters describing the CLEO system (chapters three through six) carefully, you will gain an excellent understanding of the ways to craft a legal argument and support it with legal authority. Read chapter seven to learn how to adapt CLEO to 'discuss' questions, then go on to chapter ten to see further examples of CLEO essays and obtain additional hints on how to formulate your responses.

Writing good essays involves more than a sound analytical structure, however. You need to understand the substance of the law before you can analyse it, which is why this book contains a chapter on how to read, understand and summarise legal materials (see chapter two). Once you know the law and how to structure your arguments, you need to be sure not to obscure your thoughts with poor writing. For that reason, this book includes a chapter containing various tips on legal writing (see chapter eight).

Finally, this book recognises that many, though of course not all, law students intend to go on to practise law. After spending several years perfecting your CLEO essay style, it would be unfortunate if CLEO were only applicable to academic law. However, because the CLEO method is built on a litigation model (more on that in subsequent chapters), it is eminently adaptable to legal practice. Therefore, when you are ready to begin your pupillage or traineeship, you can consider the tips contained in chapter nine.

Having set out the basic outlines of the book and of the CLEO method, it is time to move into the substantive discussion. The following chapter will therefore focus on the first skill set a law student needs to acquire: the ability to read, understand and summarise legal materials.

Building the necessary foundation: reading, understanding and summarising legal materials

CLEO provides you with a framework for analysing and answering essay and examination questions. However, applying the CLEO methodology will not, by itself, result in top marks if you lack a proper understanding of the substantive law. Knowing the underlying legal principles constitutes the raw material or building blocks for a sound essay; CLEO provides the blueprint for putting those materials together. If you don't have the building blocks – ie the understanding of the relevant legal authority – then you cannot create anything worthwhile. You may have a fabulous structure and a flawless prose style, but if you don't have anything substantive to say, then you cannot receive good marks for your work. The best organisation and writing style in the world cannot overcome a lack of knowledge.

NOTE

Good content leads to good structure.

You will also find that the more you have to say as a substantive matter, the better your organisation and writing become. When you don't quite know what points you want to make, you spend a lot of time on vague generalities and common-sense (but not necessarily legal) comments. All of your statements may be true as a matter of law, but they may not be as sophisticated, insightful or relevant as your examiners would like them to be. You may also spend a lot of time qualifying your remarks or resorting to 'lawyerly' language to hide your lack of knowledge. Some students take great pride in the belief that they can fool their instructor into thinking that they know more about the law than they actually do. While it is impossible to say that no law tutor has ever been misled in this way, it is much harder to bluff your way through an examination in law than it is in other subjects. You either know the relevant law or you don't. While there

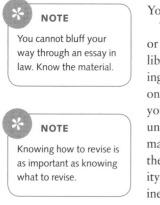

NOTE

You cannot bluff your way through an essay in law. Know the material.

NOTE

Knowing how to revise is as important as knowing what to revise.

WRITING TIP

Don't rest on your laurels. Every step up the educational ladder requires you to improve your writing that much more.

is room for argument and persuasion – points that will be covered in later chapters – a complete lack of knowledge cannot be disguised. You need to know the material, in detail, to do well.

This book does not purport to teach substantive principles of law or provide shortcuts to students who want to spend less time in the library. Learning the law is hard work. There is no substitute for reading the texts, attending lectures and thinking about the legal concepts on a daily basis. However, spending a lot of time in the company of your textbooks does not guarantee that you will gain a sophisticated understanding of the law. Many times the people who receive the top marks are not the ones who spent the most time reading and revising their notes. These hard-working students are not lacking in the ability to understand the material; it is just that they are using their time ineffectively.

Just as learning to write a law essay is a learned skill, so too is the ability to read, understand and summarise legal materials. While there is no way to avoid putting in the necessary time, there are techniques to help you use your time wisely. This is not to say that you either must or should change your revision habits completely. The mere fact that you have made it into a law programme at university or into a vocational course demonstrates that you are intelligent and have good revision skills. However, the study of law is qualitatively different from the study of other subjects, and you will need to supplement your approach to reading and revision to take that difference into account.

It is also true that the leap from school to university or from university to vocational education signifies a change in what people will expect of you. A university student is expected to be more focused, more capable and more motivated than someone in school. Similarly, someone undertaking professional education is expected to have the desire and the ability to perform at a professional level of competence. Those who understand these heightened expectations will be better able to fulfil them.

Finally, there are differences in the way that you will use the material you have learned as well as a basic difference in the type of materials that you will be using to support your arguments. As will be discussed in more detail in later chapters, A-level students are taught to craft their arguments with broad brush strokes, focusing on the big ideas and overarching themes. While there are times when law students can and should use broad, sweeping statements, it is necessary first to delve into the details of the materials, parsing carefully through the cases and statutes to identify the important language. This detailed information constitutes the evidence which will support your larger arguments. If you jump straight to the conclusions that you have reached – ie the big themes – then you have failed not only to demonstrate your understanding of how legal arguments are constructed and your detailed knowledge about the content of the materials, but you have also failed to persuade your reader that your perspective is correct. Since persuasion is an important part of law essays, you must be able to demonstrate why yours is the best course of action. You cannot do so, however, without a detailed understanding of the underlying legal authorities.

> **NOTE**
>
> Show, don't tell – put all your reasoning onto the page.

WRITING TIP

*Support your arguments. If someone says, 'X is true', but doesn't say **why** X is true, you are unlikely to agree with the statement. If, on the other hand, the person says, 'X is true **because** Y and Z show it to be true', you have a basis for understanding. In law essays, the detailed discussion of legal materials indicates why yours is the best course of action.*

There are three types of legal materials with which you must become familiar in the course of your studies: (1) statutes, (2) cases and (3) legal commentary, which includes textbooks, treatises and legal articles. Statutes and cases constitute 'binding' legal authority, whereas legal commentary constitutes merely 'persuasive' legal authority. The distinction between the two types of authority becomes important when you have to decide how to use the various legal materials in support of your argument. Chapter four discusses that point extensively. However, the distinction is not important to the immediate and preliminary question of how to understand and summarise the materials. Each of the three types of materials is discussed separately below, since each requires a different approach to learning and revision.

2.1 Statutes

In the context of this discussion, the term 'statutes' includes not only laws enacted by Parliament for domestic application but also refers to European legislation and international instruments such as treaties or conventions. It is beyond the scope of this book to discuss whether and to what extent international instruments apply within the UK or the different ways courts can interpret statutory materials (ie either purposively or literally). However, some suggestions can be made regarding the way you should read and use statutes in your work.

Students often overlook the importance of statutes, when in fact statutes are the first source of law that any lawyer – even a common law lawyer – should consider when faced with a legal problem. Remember, the UK embraces the concept of Parliamentary supremacy; therefore,

> **NOTE**
>
> When doing legal research, first look to see if any statutes apply.

statutes constitute the supreme law of the land. However, because the UK is a common law jurisdiction, the study of law focuses largely on cases which supplement or elucidate statutes or which define the law in the absence of a statute. By focusing so heavily on case law, instructors and textbook writers can accidentally trick students into thinking that statutory law is not as important as the common law in this jurisdiction. However, because cases can never replace or supersede a statute, students should learn to look first to see whether a statute applies to the question at hand and then identify the extent to which case law can and should apply.

2.1.1 Reading statutes

In some ways, the importance of statutory law is disguised as a result of the way statutes are presented in the course materials. Most students are introduced to a new subject through lectures and a textbook. The textbook may contain excerpts of cases and statutes (and thus be called a casebook, rather than a textbook) or may simply para-phrase important legal principles, using detailed footnotes to point students to the relevant sources of binding legal authority. While this approach gives a fluid, cohesive introduction to the subject, it can mislead the student, particularly with respect to the treatment of statutory materials, since neither textbooks nor casebooks will include the relevant statutes in their entirety. Instead, the text will cite or excerpt one or two sections from the statute, suggesting to students that they need only know those sections.

Nothing could be further from the truth. Statutes must be read in their entirety if one is to understand their purpose and their applicability to a legal question. At the very least, you should skim the section headings to see how the statute works together as a whole. Full-text statutes can be found in Halsbury's Statutes or on various online computer databases. Excerpted student statute books provide another alternative. While some aspects of the statute may be lost during the excerpting process, editors generally do a good job in identifying the relevant legislation and the relevant portions of each individual statute for students.

Pay particular attention to the definitions contained within a statute, since a word in common usage may be given a technical definition in the statute. Note the extent to which a defined term differs (if at all) in one statute as compared to another. Note also how one statute may define a term by reference to a definition in another enactment.[1]

> **EXAMPLE**
>
> Section 11 of the Unfair Contract Terms Act 1977 has a very precise definition of 'reasonableness', for instance.

---

[1] For example, see section 1(1)(c) of the Unfair Contract Terms Act 1977, which incorporates by reference the common duty of care imposed by the Occupiers' Liability Act 1957 and the Occupiers' Liability Act (Northern Ireland) 1957.

Your lecturers and textbook will help you identify those sections of the statute that are particularly important, so you will, of course, focus on those aspects in your studies. When you read cases discussing a piece of legislation, be sure you know which statute or portions of the statute are at issue; it usually doesn't help you, for example, to cite a case discussing the Occupiers' Liability Act 1957 when the question is directing you to an analysis of the Occupiers' Liability Act 1984. You must pay particular attention to the precise language of a statute, even more so than in a judicial opinion. While judicial opinions can and do use terms of art, language is especially important in statutory analysis because Parliament has spent a great deal of time debating the language of the statute. Therefore, avoid paraphrasing statutes and instead use the exact terms in your notes as well as in your essays and examination papers (though see the caution against lengthy quotations in chapter four).

2.1.2 Summarising statutes

One benefit of using a statute book is that many law faculties allow students to bring statutes into the examination room. Check with your tutors before you begin your course, since each university varies in its approach. Differences may also arise within the same faculty as to the availability of materials in the examination room. For example, students may be permitted to use a statute book in their criminal law examination but not in their tort examination. Universities also take different opinions about the extent to which a student may mark up a statute book prior to an examination. Sometimes underlining or highlighting is permitted, sometimes it is not. Check before you spend an entire term making extensive notations in your book, only to find that only unmarked books are allowed in the examination room.

2.1.3 Revising statutes

Marking up your statute book (or your photocopy of a statute) is a useful way of understanding the important aspects of a statute. Attention to the precise language of the statute is important, and highlighting and underlining important passages saves you the trouble of having to rewrite everything into your notes. However, the mere act of marking up your copy of the statute does not mean that you understand (or will remember) why those phrases are highlighted. You must supplement your mark-ups with notes (in your book or elsewhere) describing (1) why those phrases are important, (2) how they are interpreted or applied by courts and (3) how they interact with other sections of the statute or with other statutes.

There are two reasons why it is important that you undertake this sort of analysis and cross-referencing. First, strict memorisation of the relevant passages will not lead you to a sophisticated understanding of the issues involved. At most, you will be able to repeat what you have heard or read about that particular section of the statute. It will be difficult for you to apply your knowledge in an exam situation, since you don't really understand the importance of that aspect of the statute. Part of the art of reading a question involves knowing what issues and controversies are being raised. If you don't really understand the underlying law, you won't be able to break down the question appropriately and will end up answering a question that wasn't asked or providing a pre-prepared treatise on the law regarding subject matter X. As is discussed further in chapters three and four, neither of these two approaches wins you high marks. To do well, you must answer the question asked and, to answer the question, you must understand the question. Examiners want to see how well you integrate different aspects of the statute and the relevant cases. They are not primarily interested in how well you can repeat back the language of the statute. The language of the statute is the foundation of your essay; you must build upon it rather than leave it bare.

Second, imposing your own organisational structure on the various statutes and cases means that you will remember them better. Research into the intricacies of human memory demonstrates that people remember facts better if those facts are organised into groups of related information. Individual facts (or, in the study of law, individual cases or statutes), standing by themselves, are difficult to remember. While it can be useful to work from an organisational structure that is given to you, the best way of ensuring that you will remember the relevant material is to organise it yourself. Part of the reason why this approach works best is because you are forced to spend a significant amount of time with the material and think about how the different pieces interact with one another. Beyond that, however, the process of creating a mnemonic structure ingrains the information into your brain. How you organise your material is up to you – some people prefer a traditional outline, whereas other people swear by 'spider charts', where a central idea is surrounded by supplementary points. The method doesn't matter – what matters is that you do the work.

You should try to complete these first two steps – ie understanding the material at a deeper level and organising it – as you progress through your course, well before you begin your revision period. By the time you get to the revision stage (and this applies to all three types of legal materials), you have two additional tasks to undertake. First, you must cull down a large amount of information into something that is more manageable. While you should have been discriminating in your note-taking as you

EXAM TIP

Simply parroting statutory language will not earn you a first-class mark. You must be able to manipulate the statute to address the question asked.

EXAM TIP

Start organising your revision materials early.

went along, now is the time to be ruthless in discarding those elements that are interesting but ultimately tangential to your main purpose. At this point, you have seen the course as a whole and have the judgment necessary to decide which facts are important and which are not. You will no doubt recognise that it is impossible to remember everything. Therefore, you must focus your attention on those parts of the syllabus that are most important, at least for the purpose of your essays and examinations.

WRITING TIP

Students worry that the information that they discard may turn out to be central to an exam question. It is altogether possible that you may inadvertently discard something that turns up on the examination or that should have been included in your essay. That is to be expected from time to time. You cannot expect to exercise perfect judgment as a student, nor, indeed, as a practitioner. Errors will occur. However, more errors will occur if you try to achieve too much by remembering everything in great detail.

The second important revision task involves committing the information to memory. You must be familiar enough with the material that you not only know what each of the statutes (or cases) says, but also how you can apply that material to legal problems. If you can repeat the language of a statute or the facts and outcome of a case, you have made good progress but are only halfway to your goal. You must know the material well enough to be able to manipulate it for use in novel situations. If you are at all dubious about the barebone facts, then this higher level of analysis will be more difficult in an exam or essay scenario.

2.1.4 Example

It may help to see an example of one way to analyse a statute. Your other instructors may have additional ideas that you find helpful. While you may not need to get into this amount of detail for all of the statutes that are mentioned in your lectures and reading materials, you should take at least a cursory glance at the original language of any statute that is mentioned in your studies. There may be limitations on the applicability of the statute or cross-references to other areas of law which do not become immediately apparent from an excerpted text or passing reference.

For our example, we will look at the Unfair Contract Terms Act 1977. As most of you know, the 1977 Act will play a significant role in both your tort and contract courses. Therefore, it definitely merits close examination. The following discussion will show you how to go about identifying important aspects of this or any statute and how to make your own notes to help you analyse statutory materials.

The analysis of any statute should include the following steps:

(1) an analysis of the applicability of the statute to your coursework;

(2) an analysis of any defined terms within the statute;

(3) the identification of contentious areas within the statute; and

(4) the identification of case law supplementing or clarifying the statute and of other statutes that may influence the application of the enactment.

Under this analytical approach, your first task is to get an overview of the relevant statute and figure out which sections are most applicable to your coursework. This step incorporates three different analytical elements. First, you need to see whether the statute contains a section that broadly defines the scope of applicability of the statute. In the case of the Unfair Contract Terms Act 1977, that description is contained in section 1, which is usefully entitled 'Scope of Part I'. However, section 1 notes that the scope of the 1977 Act is further limited or affected by certain other provisions in the Act: for example, Part I is subject to Part III (see section 1(2)) and, in relation to contract, is also subject to the exceptions made by Schedule 1 (although that limitation only applies to sections 2 to 4 and 7 (see section 1(2)). Therefore you will have to look at each of these different sections and parts to learn the scope of application of the 1977 Act. Section 1(3) makes further qualifications to the scope of applicability in relation to cases arising in contract and tort. You need to work through each of the subsections to identify the circumstances in which the Act applies.

The Unfair Contract Terms Act 1977 provides a somewhat complex example, but not extraordinarily so. In a simple statute, it may be sufficient to mark up your copy of the statute so that you will remember to take note of the scope of application when it's time to revise. When you deal with a statute like the 1977 Act, however, mere highlighting is not going to help you. You need to make your own notes outlining the types of situations to which the Act applies and the types to which it does not. It may be that a problem question turns on the applicability of the Act and your detailed knowledge of its scope makes the difference between a first- and second-class mark.

EXAM TIP

Look at the full text (or the text reprinted in a student statute book) of every statute mentioned in your coursework. There's no better way to understand a statute than by seeing it in context.

Second, you should skim through the body of the statute to see if there are any further limitations in scope buried within the substantive provisions. In the case of the 1977 Act, you can see that some sections contain their own scope provisions, either limiting the application of the Act in whole or in part (for example, see section 5(3), noting the inapplicability of that section of the Act to contracts in which possession of goods passed) or expanding the application of the Act in whole or in part (for example, see section 6(4), which notes that the liabilities discussed in that section include not only the business liabilities discussed in section 1(3), the main provision on scope, but also those arising under any contract of sale of goods or hire-purchase agreement). Again, the Unfair Contract Terms Act 1977 is more complex than most of the statutes you will be asked to consider, and it may very well be that you can disregard a number of these details, since they arise in sections that do not apply to your coursework. For example, if your syllabus does not include sale and hire-purchase agreements, then you will not need to worry about section 6 and thus about the scope provision in section 6(4). However, you should use this technique to identify limitations or expansions on the scope of applicability of any particular statute.

Third, you will need to skim through the headings of the statute to see which sections bear the most substantive applicability to your coursework. This will allow you to ignore sections of the statute which do not relate to you. For example, as noted above, you may decide not to focus on section 6 of the Act because your course does not include sale and hire-purchase agreements. Alternatively, you may decide that you are unlikely to be examined on guarantees of consumer goods and can thus ignore section 5 of the Act. However, reading through the section headings at least once does more than indicate which sections are not applicable to your work. In reading through the statute, you will also get a better idea of how the statute is laid out and how it operates. If you look only at single sections of a statute, you never really understand the overall purpose and application of the statute. By reading through the statute, even cursorily, you have the opportunity to figure out how the various sections work together substantively, something that is not always clear from lectures or textbooks.

The second major step in your analysis of a statute involves the identification of any particularly defined terms. As you know, terms like 'fraud' or 'misrepresentation' may have a common definition and a legal definition. Sometimes that legal definition arises through case law and sometimes through statutory law. Your task, when analysing a statute, is to see if any of those unique definitions exist in your statute.

Looking at the Unfair Contract Terms Act 1977, you will see that important definitions exist in several different sections of the Act. Section 1, which broadly describes the scope of the Act, defines 'negligence' in section 1(1). Section 14, which relates to the interpretation of Part I, also includes several important definitions. Often you will find important definitions contained in the first few or the last few sections of a statute, so always check both those places. However, you may also find important definitions within the substantive provisions.

WRITING TIP

It's okay to use an excerpted student statute book when you read through a statute 'in whole', since a statute book will give you an overall idea of the statute. Just don't rely on the excerpts found in textbooks or casebooks. Those references are too short to help you.

For example, the 1977 Act defines 'reasonableness' in section 11² and 'dealing as a consumer' in section 12. This Act makes finding definitions particularly easy, since the terms appear in the section headings, but sometimes you may find definitions hidden within the text of the section. Be careful.

In a simple statute, it may be enough to highlight the key definitions in your copy of the statute. In a complex statute, such as the Unfair Contract Terms Act 1977, such highlightings may not be useful, since there are so many exceptions and cross-references, and it may be better to make a separate list of the key defined terms. If the definition is short, you can transcribe it into your notes, but remember you do not want to make a habit of copying a statute into your notes. It may be enough to make a list of the terms and note where their definitions exist in the statute. That way you're aware of the potential areas of dispute and can go and refresh your memory as to the precise language during your revision period.

The third step in your statutory analysis requires you to identify the contentious areas within and relating to the statute. Here, you will be led by your lecturers, tutors and reading materials to focus on substantive concerns. For example, you will learn from your lectures and reading that the Unfair Contract Terms Act 1977 applies to both your tort and contract courses and that the definition of 'reasonableness' has been disputed from time to time. You will therefore take particular note of section 11 and related aspects of the Act, such as the scope of application. You will also identify the content of those substantive disputes, since that is as important as knowing that the disputes exist.

Finally, you will identify any cases that discuss or clarify the application or content of the statute in question, again relying on your lecture notes and reading materials to point you in the right direction. You also need to know the extent to which other acts relate to the statute in question. For example, the Unfair Contract Terms Act 1977 incorporates, by reference, the concept of the common duty of care under the Occupiers' Liability Act 1957 and the Occupiers' Liability Act (Northern Ireland) 1957 (see section 1(1)(c)). The 1977 Act also relates to obligations arising under the Sale of Goods Act 1979 and the Supply of Goods (Implied Terms) Act 1973 (see section 6(1)). However, a statute need not refer to another statute specifically to bring it into the sphere of influence (see, for example, section 11(4) of the 1977 Act).

---

² Note also that the definition of 'reasonableness' will be affected in some circumstances by the guidelines contained in Schedule 2 to the Unfair Contract Terms Act 1977. This is not an aspect you would necessarily know if you did not look at the statute as a whole. However, attention to this kind of detail is what raises an essay mark from a good 2:1 to a first.

Again, in a simple statute, the cross-referencing to other enactments may be easily identifiable. In those cases, you would simply highlight the cross-references. You would not need to make a separate list of the potential areas of statutory overlap, as you would do with a complex statute such as the Unfair Contract Terms Act 1977. However, no matter how complex your statute is, it is always good to make a single list of the cases which discuss your statute and the statutes/sections to which they relate. Compilation of a single list is necessary because you may learn about the cases at different points over the term. It is astounding how much more easily you can remember a series of cases if you have them all listed in a single place.

As you can see, the emphasis is on consolidating your knowledge about the statute and relevant cases. Although some of the steps appear to be primarily mechanistic, you need to use your discretion throughout this process, since you want to include neither too much nor too little detail. It is hard to know in advance what will be relevant later, but you need to start developing your legal judgment, otherwise you will have too much information to review when it comes time to revise.

If you implement the four steps described above, you will be well on your way towards understanding the important points about any statute. Although some statutes can be quite complex, the majority are straightforward and easy to apply, as long as you are aware of their constituent elements.

EXAM TIP

Constantly strive to consolidate your notes. Cross-reference different aspects of the course and make sure overarching structures are clear.

2.2 Cases

As important as statutory law is, the vast majority of your time will be spent reading and analysing case law. Cases are important to the student and practising lawyer for three reasons. First, statutes cannot, and are not intended to, cover every possible situation. Instead, they are often supplemented by case law that describes how the statute is to be applied in particular circumstances. You must know and describe pertinent clarifying cases whenever you think the statute is relevant to your problem.

Second, statutes sometimes retain common law definitions or principles within the language of the enactment. Discussing a statute without the accompanying case law or the case law without the accompanying statutory language gives the court an incomplete – and thus incorrect – description of the law.

Finally, in a common law jurisdiction, there will be instances where no statute applies. Instead, the law will be embodied in all of the various cases that have grown up over time. You must identify those

EXAMPLE

Section 1(2) of the Occupiers' Liability Act 1957 explicitly retains some elements of earlier case law.

cases that pertain to the legal question at hand. As discussed further in chapter four, there will seldom be but one case relevant to your problem.

Many students become nervous when faced with the task of reading and taking notes on case law. Part of the fear arises from the concern that their initial understanding of the case will be inaccurate or incomplete. Students intuitively know that if they don't comprehend the material in the first place and thus fail to note the important aspects, then their revision will be built on a faulty foundation. In this, they are correct. You must have the proper building blocks if you want to do well in your written work.

Unfortunately, those who worry about their ability to distinguish between relevant and irrelevant facts often end up taking notes that are too voluminous to be helpful at the revision stage. These people are also less than discriminating when it comes to highlighting their textbooks and cover their books in fluorescent yellow ink. One can certainly understand why these people act this way: they worry that there is one important detail that will save them in an exam scenario, and they are adamant that they are not going to overlook anything that might be helpful. However, once they understand that one's ability to analyse a question and construct a strong legal argument is not entirely based on the ability to remember minute details about every case that has been decided since 1066, then they will be less likely to overcompensate in their note-taking. Remember, good lawyers demonstrate their judgment as much by what they don't say as by what they do say, a point that will be discussed further in chapter four. Note-taking is all about cutting down the information you've been given to a manageable quantity. If, at the end of the day, you still have too much information to process easily, you are not exercising enough discretion at the initial stage.

Some students have the opposite problem. These are the students who have relied on excellent short-term memories to get by in the past or who overestimate their understanding of the materials and hence fail to take sufficiently detailed notes at first. Later, they find they can't remember as much as they thought they could, which means they must go back and re-read the original materials when they should be focusing on organisation and memorisation of facts. People who fall into this category may also worry about doing too much work before they understand the entirety of the course and thus wasting time on less-than-fruitful inquiries. In fact, the process of figuring out what the important points are and why is what learning law is all about.

As you have no doubt figured out by now, the study of law at university and vocational school is far more reading-intensive than anything you did at school. You simply have too much information to allow you either

---

WRITING TIP

Note-taking is all about cutting down the material to a manageable size. Be ruthless.

✳ NOTE

Too often, laptop users transcribe lectures nearly word for word. Be careful about that – you need to practise discernment in your note-taking.

to re-read the material just before the examination or wait until the last minute to organise your notes. You must do the work as you go. At the end of the day, students who take too many notes and students who take too few notes both fear that their initial note-taking method is flawed and exhibit a reluctance to exercise their judgment as they progress through their course. In fact, the students who do the best in their examinations are those who don't just take notes as if they're on automatic. Instead, they engage their brains during each and every step of the learning process. Instead of waiting for good legal judgment to descend upon them from on high, they acquire good legal judgment by hard work. By the time the revision period comes around, they are ready to focus on the tasks of cross-referencing the material and organising it in a useful manner rather than doing what should have been done during the first stage of the note-taking process: cutting down the material to a manageable amount.

✳ NOTE

Don't take notes by rote. Think about what you're doing as you do it.

Obviously, the dilemma of note-taking is finding the right balance: neither too much detail nor too little. If you take the view that there is one objectively right way to take notes, you will make yourself unnecessarily anxious. Dismiss from your mind the notion that there is one tiny, hidden nugget of information that will save you on an examination. While you will need to know some detail, memorising every detail is impossible and is not your end goal. You need to see the big picture, too, and if you spend too much time on the nuances you will miss the overall themes. Trust that the important information will be reinforced through both reading and lectures and that it will be given a good deal of attention in both contexts.

In the end, the 'right' way of taking notes is whatever works for you. However, if you follow the suggestions discussed below on how to read and summarise a case, you should gain more confidence in your note-taking skills and in your ability to exercise your legal judgment as your course progresses.

2.2.1 Reading cases

The first obstacle you must surmount involves learning to read cases. Students facing case law for the first time often come to the conclusion that many – if not all – learned members of the judiciary purposefully intend to make their opinions unclear. While single opinions can be deciphered eventually, cases involving multiple opinions seem unfathomable. Whose opinion controls? Which aspect of the controlling opinion is most important? Must I read the whole 60-plus page decision?

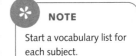

✳ NOTE

Start a vocabulary list for each subject.

To learn to read cases, you must first learn the language of the law. Lawyers use special vocabulary known as 'terms of art', which refers either to language that is unique to the law (for example, 'ex post *facto*' or 'fee simple') as well as language that is used in ordinary conversation but which has a special additional meaning when used in legal contexts. For example, someone might say that a term of a contract is 'unfair', but that does not mean the term is unenforceable under the Unfair Contract Terms Act 1977. While it is easy, in some instances, to work out the meaning of a term in the context of a judicial opinion, it is equally easy to forget the meaning of the term as soon as you see it out of context. Therefore, you should start a vocabulary list for each subject at the beginning of each term. Doing so will help solidify your learning and help you when it comes time to write an essay, since you will then be able to frame your answer in a succinct and lawyerly manner.

Vocabulary is a relatively simple matter. What is more difficult is parsing out the important aspects of a case, particularly when there are several conflicting opinions. This is particularly important if your course requires you to locate and read the original opinions rather than allowing you to rely on casebook excerpts. Different universities take different approaches to case law research, and you may not have to spend much time working with the original materials. Alternatively, you may find reading cases to be too much work and instead rely on the various shortcuts available (headnotes, casenotes in scholarly journals, lecture notes, etc). While this may seem preferable in the short term, it means that you will miss out on the nuances and intricacies of argument that make the study of law most interesting. It will also make your transition to legal practice that much harder, if you decide to go into law professionally. Practitioners have no choice but to work with the original materials, and there will be less room for forgiveness of error if you have to learn case law research from scratch at that point.

How, then, should you go about reading a judicial opinion? Your textbook or lecturer will give you some initial indications about the important aspects of any particular case, so you will be sure to look out for those points when you read through the opinion. However, the next place to go is to the headnotes, which briefly summarise the facts and salient legal points. Because headnotes are presumptively assumed to be correct in this jurisdiction (something that is not the case in other countries, such as the US), many students rely only on the headnotes and go no further in their research. That sort of approach takes a mistakenly short-term view of legal education. It is based on a belief that to do well in the law (either in academia or in practice), one need only know the facts and the outcome of a particular decision. In fact, the most valuable, interesting and important aspect of a legal education is learning how to reason. Law, like

WRITING TIP

Avoid colloquialisms and slang in legal writing. Many of your readers will be older than you and will not appreciate that sort of informality.

life, is seldom clear-cut. Both exist in shades of grey, rather than in black and white. If you take the view that every legal question can be answered by one case or statute, you are not only ensuring that you will not win top marks but are adding to the stress in your life – in that you assume that you must find the 'one case' that will answer your question – and missing much of the fun in law. Anyone who has ever participated in moot arguments or observed in a courtroom (particularly an appellate court, where the arguments are based on law, not on fact) will know that the realm of law applicable to any particular set of facts is relatively narrow. Both sides have to rely on the same legal authority. The difference is in how they argue their points by downplaying those cases and statutes that are detrimental to their cause and emphasising those that are helpful. Practising lawyers are under an ethical obligation not to mislead the court, so they cannot ignore troubling cases. To do so would be tactically unwise in any case, since it would give the court the impression that a particular argument could not be rebutted. While students have no ethical obligation to inform their examiners of every relevant case – and are indeed limited by time and the nature of legal education – they should argue both sides of an issue to demonstrate a good facility with the legal materials as well as a sophisticated understanding of legal reasoning and analysis.

Reading only the headnotes will not teach you how to undertake sophisticated legal reasoning, nor will it give you the building blocks to do so. The only way to understand how to manipulate cases in your favour is to see it done in practice. Because many judges recount counsels' arguments in their opinions – and, indeed, some legal reports include their own summaries of counsels' arguments – students who read only the headnotes rob themselves of an excellent opportunity to learn how to construct legal arguments. In addition, the best legal arguments are not based on the facts of earlier cases or on a one-line recitation of the major ratio (ie the information you will find in the headnotes). They are instead based on a complex understanding of why the court ruled as it did in that circumstance and what theories and arguments the court found unpersuasive. That information is found in the body of the case, either in the portions where the judges discuss counsels' arguments or the sections where the judges discuss each others' opinions. Reading the headnotes will give you an idea of which aspects of the judges' reasoning is most important, but to understand how and why the judges concluded as they did, you have to get into the case itself.

You should, however, be aware that many judges' opinions cannot be taken as models of good legal writing. For example, some judges

WRITING TIP

The best way to learn how to craft a legal argument is to read judicial opinions in their entirety.

CAUTION

Not all judges write well.

spend several pages on a point that turns out to be irrelevant (or *obiter*) to the outcome of the case.[3] Do not adopt a similar approach yourself; stick to the determinative points. In addition, some judges spend an inordinate amount of time discussing the facts of earlier cases.[4] You do not have that kind of luxury and should limit yourself, in most instances, to a line or two that puts your legal discussion in context. How to write the legal portion of your essay is discussed in more detail in chapter four.

NOTE

Learn how to harmonise and distinguish cases.

The most important reason to read legal opinions in their entirety is because it is the best way to learn how to distinguish and harmonise cases. 'Distinguishing' a case requires you to identify how and why an earlier case differs from the situation presented in your immediate problem. You might be able to argue that the facts are sufficiently dissimilar from yours and that the case shouldn't apply for those reasons. Alternatively – and this is the more sophisticated approach – you may claim that the reasons supporting the legal holding – ie the ratio – in the precedent can't be applied in the problem currently under discussion. You should always pay attention to the level of the court which handed down the earlier opinion, since later courts will be more deferential to the Supreme Court (formerly the House of Lords), and the Court of Appeal than to trial-level courts. You should also be aware of when a case was handed down so that you can get an idea of how a particular line of analysis is evolving. Ancient precedents are still followed, but a more recent case may be more persuasive.

'Harmonising' a line of cases requires you to look at a number of different decisions and explain the direction in which the law is moving. Harmonisation can be especially difficult when you have seemingly contradictory opinions that have no apparent distinguishing rationale.[5] Whereas distinguishing cases usually focus on individual precedents, harmonising cases usually focus on a sequence of cases. Very often examiners will pose questions that require you to distinguish and/or harmonise cases, since that (1) invites you to introduce more than one case into your essay (an invitation many people decline, to their detriment) and (2) allows you to demonstrate a sophisticated understanding of the intricacies of the cases

---

[3] For example, see the opinions of Lord Clyde and Lord Browne-Wilkinson in *Panatown Ltd v Alfred McAlpine Construction Ltd* [2000] 4 All ER 97.

[4] Again, see *Panatown Ltd v Alfred McAlpine Construction Ltd* [2000] 4 All ER 97.

[5] For example, a man who caused an accident whilst suffering a stroke was liable in negligence (*Roberts v Ramsbottom* [1980] 1 All ER 7), whereas a man who caused an accident whilst suffering from a bout of hypoglycaemia was not (*Mansfield v Weetabix Ltd* [1998] 1 WLR 1263). These cases are difficult to reconcile.

as you argue why the precedents should or should not be followed. Therefore, when your lecturers or textbooks indicate a split in authority on a certain matter, make a note of it as a potential area for examination.

It may sound like reading law is a lot of work, and it is. However, you can tailor your workload to suit your own purposes. Many cases are decided on a number of different points. For example, a case may contain the seminal discussion on causation in negligence but also contain a lot of procedural information on the injunctive powers of the court. By reading the headnotes, you identify the relevant portions of the case and where they are located in the opinion. Focus your detailed reading on those parts of the case; skim the rest of the opinion, by all means, but don't spend a great deal of time on legal points that are outside the syllabus.

The headnotes will also help you figure out which opinions are most important in an appellate decision with multiple opinions. For example, the headnotes will indicate who sided with whom and whether any of the opinions are dissenting in whole or in part. While some dissents are given great weight by later courts, most are not. Those dissenting opinions that are most influential will be highlighted by your textbooks and lecturers.[6] You can read those opinions with some attention to detail to get an idea of the interplay of concepts, but for the most part you can spend less time on dissents.

Reading opinions in their relevant entirety has other benefits. First, it will reinforce other aspects of your learning, since you will be working within the same line of cases, albeit in different contexts. Therefore, you will remember cases and statutes more easily. Second, you will begin to get a better idea of the relative weight of precedent. A case

---

Why read cases in the original?

- It teaches you how to undertake legal reasoning
- It teaches you how to distinguish and harmonise cases
- It teaches you how to manipulate cases to suit your purposes
- It reinforces your learning by repeating important points
- It indicates the relative weight of precedent
- It makes the study of law more interesting, since you are learning to argue creatively and not merely memorising facts

---

[6] For example, Lord Atkin's dissent in *Liversidge v Anderson* [1942] AC 206 is now considered the most influential opinion in that case.

that is referred to again and again is obviously more important than a case that pops up just once.

2.2.2 Summarising cases

Once you have read your cases, you need to make notes to ease the revision process. As was said earlier in this chapter, revision is all about culling down the material and organising it in a helpful manner. Case law will constitute the major portion of your legal materials, so you need to have an efficient and effective manner of summarising and organising the opinions.

Some students photocopy the headnotes for all the cases they are supposed to know. While this approach ensures that you have the relevant information in your possession, it will be somewhat over-inclusive, since the headnotes will contain information irrelevant to your course. In addition, photocopying something is not the same as learning it. To understand and remember the material, you must manipulate it in some fashion. Therefore, you should consider compiling your own short case summaries.

A good case summary gives you a snapshot of the case and why it is important. It also contains enough information to allow you to look up the reference in case you need to refer back to some particular point. Therefore, you should include the following information in your case summary:

- Case name (ie *Smith v Jones*)
- Full citation (ie [1998] 4 All ER 200)[7]
- Court (ie Court of Appeal)
- Facts (one to two sentences at most)
- Ratio (the legal rationale supporting the outcome; be sure to know what the outcome was as well)
- Relevant *dicta* ('*dicta*' refers to any statement by the court that is not necessary to decide the outcome of the case (these statements are also referred to as being made '*obiter*'); however, *dicta* can be highly persuasive in later cases, so note it when it's important)
- Queries (these can be questions to ask your tutor or to bandy about with your peers; alternatively they might be points you want to remember as you continue your reading in that area of

---

[7] You could delete the citation in your notes if the citation shows on your syllabus or in the case index of your textbook. If you delete the citation, however, be sure that you indicate when the case was handed down, since the timing of a decision can affect its precedential value.

law. Having a 'queries' section starts you thinking about the larger philosophy of law, how different cases work together and what questions might appear on an examination)

A case summary is a quick, standardised way to help you remember the important elements of a judicial opinion so that you can apply those elements appropriately to later fact patterns.

A case summary does not include all points of fact or law. Focus on the important bits. Include key quotes, if appropriate. If you don't exclude some points, you diminish the value of the summary. Both students and practitioners summarise cases to prepare for meetings with supervisors, clients or the court. At first this method may slow you down slightly, but you will save time in the long run, since you will not be forced to re-read entire cases and reconstruct your analyses of the relevant issues when revising for exams.

> *** NOTE**
>
> Case summaries are very short.

2.2.3 Examples

Following are some examples of case summaries in the area of tort. Look at the original decisions and see which elements have been noted and which elements have been discarded. There is no right or wrong when it comes to case summaries; there is only what is helpful to you and what is not helpful to you.

Daly v Liverpool Corporation [1939] 2 All ER 142	
COURT:	Liverpool Hilary Assizes
FACTS:	69-year-old woman claimant hit by bus. Defendant bus driver said he did not know she was old and could have missed her had she been young.
RATIO:	(Stable J) Drivers of buses have two irreconcilable duties: (1) to keep to schedules and (2) to avoid pedestrians/others. However, '[o]ne must take people as one finds them. There is no hypothetical standard of care.' Standard of care for drivers: 'very high indeed'. Driver negligent despite two irreconcilable duties: fact that woman was not as fast/clever as younger person irrelevant.
DICTA:	Equates driving to surgery/other difficult tasks
QUERY:	Note this case was decided in 1939 – what concerns about driving were in place then? [note bit about cars as 'lethal weapons'].

	Nettleship v Weston [1971] 3 All ER 581
COURT:	Court of Appeal
FACTS:	Defendant asked friend (claimant) to teach her to drive in her husband's car. Defendant crashed car, injured claimant.
RATIO:	(Denning) Criminal law standard is objective – skilled, experienced and careful driver. Civil standard of care is: (1) [*obiter*] objective toward things/pedestrians outside car; (2) [*obiter*] same standard of care to passengers – though contributory negligence may reduce damages, it does not alter standard of care; (3) [ratio] same standard of care due to instructors, unless there's an implicit or explicit agreement to waive claim for negligence. Knowledge of risk insufficient; claim will still lie (no defence of *volenti non fit injuria*). However, instructors may be contributorily negligent if they let students take control too early. This holding does NOT apply to professional instructors. The standard of care 'is measured objectively by the care to be expected of an experienced skilled and careful driver'.
(Salmon)	Does not see that insurance has any impact, but agrees standard to other road-users is same as Denning.
(Megaw)	Sees standard of care to passenger v pedestrian as the key query – too confusing to have multiple standards, so must have single objective standard.
QUERY:	How to harmonise with *Daly*? Both drivers held to high duty of care; however note that *Daly* had an inexperienced/old plaintiff while *Nettleship* had an inexperienced defendant.

	Mullin v Richards [1998] 1 All ER 920
COURT:	Court of Appeal
FACTS:	Claimant and defendant were 15 years old, playing with rulers. One ruler snapped and went into claimant's eye. Trial judge looked at foreseeability (whether a similar injury could occur and whether at 15 they could appreciate the danger).

RATIO:	(Hutchison) The standard of care is 'whether an ordinarily prudent and reasonable 15-year-old schoolgirl in the defendant's situation would have realised as much'. States age-appropriate standard of care is well agreed. Decided there was no one legally responsible for the injury, since there was no evidence why the ruler broke or that there was culpable behaviour.
(Butler-Sloss)	Cites Australian case *McHale v Watson* stating that age is relevant and that courts should not have one standard of 'normal' behaviour for all.
QUERIES:	Is this case implicitly affected by the absence of insurance (see *Nettleship*)? What about the commonality of practice (evidence existed that ruler fencing was common)? What about the absence of a statute addressing this behaviour (see *Nettleship*, Road Traffic Act)? Why else is the result different from *Nettleship*? Also, do children get special treatment because everyone can see they are children? In *Daly*, it was harder to see that the plaintiff was old. What happens if children look older or are on the brink of adulthood? [compare statutory rape with tort's sliding scale of reasonable behaviour].

These are just some suggestions on how you might want to summarise cases in tort. Your notes might emphasise different details and will probably contain your own abbreviations and shorthand. For example, you might summarise the facts in *Mullin* as 'ruler fight – 15-year-olds'. That might be enough to jog your memory. Be sure, however, to write down important judicial language about legal standards, using the exact words if possible. For example, in *Mullin* it is important to note that the standard relates to an 'ordinarily prudent and reasonable' child of the defendant's age and circumstances.

These examples are merely intended to give you an idea of how to summarise the cases you read. You should feel free to develop your own approach on the advice of tutors and others whose opinion you respect.

2.2.4 Revising cases

Once you are past the initial note-taking stage, you must organise your notes into a workable format. Some people use traditional step outlines, whereas others prefer spider charts or other, less rigid, structural tools. The important thing is that you make an effort to group individual cases together in some logical manner. As was stated earlier in this chapter, the human brain is more likely to remember facts when they are linked in together some way. A string of independent, unrelated facts is easily forgotten.

Because you are new to the law, it would be difficult for you to come up with an independent organisational approach. Perhaps the easiest way to organise your thinking is to rely on the table of contents in your textbook or on your lecturers' course outline. Break down each major topic (for example, consideration in contract) into several sub-headings (for example, definitions of consideration, functions of consideration, motive and consideration, scope of the doctrine of consideration, etc), then start listing the cases and statutes that relate to that sub-heading. Prioritise your notes by putting statutes and leading cases first, followed by cases that flesh out the parameters of that particular legal issue. The statutes and leading precedents will give you the general legal rule, whereas the later or less important cases will describe how the basic legal principle should be applied in particular circumstances. As the legal language suggests, you are trying to identify a line of cases rather than a series of unrelated decisions. When it comes to time to introduce the legal principles in your essay or examination (discussed in chapter four), you will always mention the broad general principles of law, but will only mention those minor cases that are relevant to your question. You will not list each and every case that touches on the subject – that would demonstrate a lack of judgment in deciding what was relevant.

In your outline, you should pay particular attention to conflicts or shifts in the law, since these are fruitful areas for discussion and hence for examination. If you are presented with the opportunity to distinguish conflicting cases, you should rejoice (rather than groan), since that's an excellent opportunity to show off your legal talents. Obviously those areas of law that have experienced reform or a radical change are very likely to form the basis of an examination or essay question, so you should also make particularly detailed notes of those lines of cases. Be sure to know how and why the change has occurred.

In your notes, you should indicate to yourself how the different areas of law relate to each other. For example, you may discover that many cases about the existence of a duty of care in tort could also relate to questions about the standard of care, a question that is more often considered as relating to whether the duty of care has been breached. However, because the duty of care question is a legal issue that may be taken up as a preliminary matter, courts reframe the dispute to suit their purposes. As will be further discussed in the next

EXAM TIP

Use external aids to help you appreciate the overall structure of the course. Don't lose the forest for the trees!

chapter, this type of cross-referencing will help you spot the relevant areas of controversy in a question and will allow you to undertake a more sophisticated analysis.

As you go through this process, you will see that some cases fall under several different outline headings. This is as it should be. Undergraduate and vocational courses are designed to reinforce students' learning rather than tax their ability to memorise long strings of cases. Also, many leading cases instituted change in several different areas of law or created a new relationship between those areas of law: that's why they are leading cases. Because a case could stand for several different propositions, it is important to indicate in your essay why you are citing it. This technique will be discussed in more detail in chapter four, but it bears mention here, since you will first start to see which cases stand for which ideas when you are structuring your knowledge into a coherent whole.

WRITING TIP

Always say why you are citing a case.

For the most part, you should focus your efforts on organising your materials in terms of legal relevance, since that is how the cases will be presented to you. However, you should not disregard factual similarities. For example, you may have a number of tort cases involving children. Some of these cases will stand primarily for propositions relating to the existence of a duty of care, whereas others will primarily discuss breaches of a duty. Alternatively, you may have a series of cases involving motor accidents. The cases may not necessarily hang together, but you may want to lump them together at some point in your notes, since one of the ways to identify fruitful areas of discussion is to consider the factual similarity of your question to cases that you have learned (for further explanation of this point, see chapter four).

Therefore, your goal during your revision is to create lines of cases that relate to one another legally and, to a lesser extent, factually. You should cross-reference cases and issues between different sections of your outline as far as possible. For example, issues relating to third-party rights under a contract may come up not only with respect to remedies but also to modification and variation of a contract, or possibly even with respect to creation of a contract.

You should also be aware of how different fields of law overlap. For example, tort and contract interact in several important ways, such as, for example, the ability to limit liability for negligence by contract. While you will not indulge yourself in a lengthy discussion of tort law in a contract essay or examination (or vice versa), you can (and in some cases, should) note in passing how the problems associated with the overlap are handled by lawyers.

Proper revision is a time-consuming process. As such, you should not leave it to the last minute. Many people find it helpful to start creating their outlines as they go along; others find the pressure of work

EXAM TIP

Spread your revision out over time. You'll learn the material better.

during term so heavy that they leave it to the end. While you should do whatever works best for you, don't underestimate the time it takes to integrate notes you have made from different sources and, more importantly, to integrate the ideas across the breadth of the course. People learn best when they stretch it out over a period of time, particularly when they are working with deep conceptual issues rather than simple facts. Scientific research on how memory works suggests that sleeping on a problem – literally – improves results. While you are asleep, your brain is organising the material you just read. This suggests that even though last-minute cramming may seem to be an effective method of revision, it will be of limited use in helping you see the larger connections between different areas of law. Since those larger connections often yield the most sophisticated analysis, leaving your revision until the last minute may be counter-productive to those who want to win top marks on their essays and examinations.

2.3 Textbooks, articles and treatises

Many people find their first – and possibly only – introduction to law through the use of non-binding legal materials such as textbooks, casebooks, articles and treatises. Depending on your course, you may or may not be required to find and read binding legal materials, meaning statutes and cases. Despite their status as non-binding or 'secondary' (as opposed to 'primary') materials, textbooks, casebooks, articles and treatises have their uses and benefits.

As mentioned earlier in this chapter, a textbook contains paraphrases and occasional quotes from primary legal materials (cases and statutes) and relies on editors to give an overview of the legal issues in their own words. Textbooks are helpful in giving a student a broad perspective on the subject and in using language that is readily accessible to the student reader. Even if your programme relies heavily on the case method of legal education (which involves the students being given long lists of cases and being told to find and read them), you may still find a textbook useful in helping you prioritise the importance of the cases on your reading list and in filling in the gaps in your learning. The case method of legal education gives students great depth of understanding and (ideally) a facility with binding legal materials in their original form. However, most tutors will also recommend a textbook to round off their students' education.

A casebook contains far less editorial discussion and instead provides heavily edited versions of cases and articles (and statutes to a far lesser degree). A casebook forces students to do more work in parsing out the important aspects of the material, since the editors spend less time telling the reader what the law is, where it is going and what the ramifications of the current or proposed approaches will be. Casebooks represent a shortcut to the case method of education. Because they involve less spoon-feeding of information, they do a better job than textbooks do in developing students' independent legal judgment and ability to read cases and statutes. However, casebooks can frustrate people who would prefer just to be told what the law is rather than try to figure out the relationship between the cases themselves.

Legal articles may be excerpted in casebooks but generally appear in scholarly journals and are aimed at academics and, in some cases, practitioners in the field. Although these works can be a bit dense at times, they are often more up to date than textbooks or casebooks, since journals are published more often than textbooks or casebooks. Therefore, your lecturers or tutors may suggest you read several articles to round off your learning in a new area of law. Articles will also be tightly focused on a single subject, giving you depth, rather than breadth, of insight. Those articles with a historical bent can provide useful analyses about how and why a line of cases developed as it did. Articles may also suggest how the law might evolve in the future and can therefore be helpful to students who need to answer questions about potential reforms in the law. Some legal journals also publish casenotes, in which an academic briefly summarises and critiques a recent judicial opinion or piece of legislation. Casenotes can provide an illuminating look at how experienced lawyers read cases and statutes.

Reading legal articles may be slightly more problematic for two reasons. First, scholarly articles are written for an academic audience and therefore assume the reader has a level of knowledge beyond that of the average student. Therefore, you may find it hard going at first, though you should persevere. Some authors are easier to follow than others and, in any event, you gain a facility with the materials with time and practice.

The second reason that articles cause students difficulty is because articles relate only to very narrow topics which may or may not relate to the issues arising in your syllabus. If the article falls on your reading list, you can be sure that it contains some relevance to your course, but you may need to parse out the pertinent points from a sea of detail. To ease your understanding, focus on the introductory and concluding paragraphs of the article and of each internal sub-section. If the writer is any good, those paragraphs should give you some idea of the basic argument. Only delve into the internal text if the introductory bits suggest that there's worthwhile material in those sections. While it may be interesting to know everything there is about some small facet of the law – and you shouldn't avoid following up on points that interest you, since the process will help you understand and appreciate legal argument – you need to keep some perspective about what will be most useful to you in terms of your overall learning. Tutors and lecturers can sometimes forget that students in beginning courses don't have the time or interest in learning about some arcane exception to the general legal rule. Learn to use your judgment about how much detail to go into in reading articles.

Treatises are books or series of books that, like journals, are aimed at the academic and practitioner market rather than at the student reader and therefore contain a high degree of detail and technical language. Treatises pre-suppose a certain level of familiarity with the subject and are therefore inappropriate introductory reading. However, if you have a question on a certain point that is not well discussed in your lectures or other materials, you should feel free to go to a treatise for that information. Many treatises are exceedingly well written, once you have a basic knowledge of the issues. Your librarian should be able to guide you to the appropriate sourcebook in your field.

Reading non-binding materials like casebooks and treatises takes no special knack, since you have lots of experience reading textbooks and the like by the time you get to university. Your revision methods may be affected, somewhat, by both the amount of reading you have to do as a law student and by the fact that you can either purchase or photocopy most of the materials. Because law students have so much reading to get through in a week, they often rely on marking up their books and photocopies with highlighters, rather than taking notes and making outlines. While marking up the text is a useful shortcut, don't fall into the trap of thinking that just because you have scribbled in a book or on a photocopy, you actually understand and will remember the points.

EXAM TIP

Highlighting your textbook is not the same as creating an outline.

Try summarising your reading as you go, such as by identifying the three major points of an article or outlining the basic structure of a textbook chapter (based, perhaps, on the book's table of contents, as discussed above) as soon as you're done reading that chapter. By forcing yourself to undertake some independent thought immediately after you've read the material, you solidify your learning.

You now have a basic understanding of how to read, understand and summarise the materials used in legal study. These skills will give you a suitable foundation from which to build your essays and examinations. Having set the stage, we can now move to the first step in the CLEO method, namely the claim.

Step one in the CLEO method: the claim

Although the previous chapter's suggestions on how to read, understand and summarise legal materials might help you adjust to the study of law, you should not feel that you must follow any particular approach to note-taking and revision. Instead, you should figure out what is best for you. Rather than completely discarding familiar revision techniques, supplement them with new skills that are uniquely suited to the study of law. Whatever you decide to do, however, realise that the marks you receive on your essays and examinations are directly linked to the effectiveness of your note-taking and revision skills. No matter how well you understand and apply the CLEO method of essay writing, you cannot earn top marks if you haven't absorbed the substantive legal principles first.

Many A-level students are put off by the thought of studying law because they think the subject is too hard. In fact, there is nothing conceptually difficult about law as an academic programme. The hardest thing about the subject is learning how to read statutes and cases and finding a way to organise the materials into a workable form. The previous chapter discussed those points in general outline. The second hardest thing about studying law is learning how to present the material in essays and examinations. That issue is the focus of this and the following chapters.

WRITING TIP

Because law essays do not involve a single answer that is objectively 'right' (as is the case in science or mathematics), to win top marks you must learn how to present and structure your argument effectively. CLEO will help you organise your thoughts and your supporting materials so that you can demonstrate the type of sophisticated legal judgment that examiners want to see.

Much of your thinking and writing time will be spent on the second step of the CLEO method, which involves the law that you will present as part of your answer. Techniques and tips for identifying and discussing the law will be presented in the next chapter. Before you can discuss the law, however, you must know what points you need to make to answer the question. To do so, you must identify what the CLEO method calls the 'claim'. If you follow the suggestions contained in this chapter, you will not only learn how to identify what question the examiners want you to answer, but you will learn how to write a two to three sentence opening paragraph that will take approximately one minute to write. This first paragraph is supposed to be short because the majority of your time should be spent on the second portion of your essay: the law. However, by setting forth the claim quickly and succinctly, you set yourself up to write an equally concise and relevant essay. You also give the reader the impression that you are in full command of the subject matter and the shape of your essay. First (and last) impressions are very important if you wish to receive a top mark on your paper. However, if you do not identify the appropriate claim or claims, it becomes nearly impossible to introduce all the relevant law. Do not short-change the importance of the 'C' step in your analysis.

In order to apply the CLEO system effectively, you need to understand its relationship to the practice of law, a subject which is introduced in the first section of this chapter. Once you have grasped that point, this chapter will discuss:

(1) what a 'claim' is according to the CLEO methodology;

(2) why it is important to identify the claim explicitly in an essay or examination;

(3) how to spot the various claims that arise out of a problem question; and

(4) examples of claim spotting.

WRITING TIP

First impressions matter. Use a short but strong introductory paragraph.

NOTE

Although CLEO relates most directly and obviously to problem questions, it can easily be adapted to 'discuss' questions. See chapter seven for further information on this point.

3.1 Relationship of the CLEO method to legal practice

Although CLEO is expressly meant for use in academic or vocational law courses, the method has its roots in the style and form of argument that is used by legal practitioners, particularly litigators. If, every time you are faced with a problem question, you think, 'how would a barrister respond to this question?' you will be well on your way to winning first-class marks. It is not necessary that you intend to become a barrister to use this system of essay-writing; it is enough that you learn how to think like one. Indeed, the type of logical analysis and presentation that is at the heart of the CLEO method will benefit you no matter what career path you follow. Good writing skills are a benefit in every profession.

How, then, does CLEO relate to legal practice? Simply put, CLEO is based on a litigation model that requires essay and examination answers to follow the same pattern that is used by litigators in their written and oral arguments. When a practitioner presents a case to the court, he or she must identify:

(1) the cause of action that is being alleged (the 'claim' in CLEO);

(2) each of the elements that must be proven in order to prevail on the cause of action (the first, more general, aspect of the 'law' in CLEO);

(3) any particularly contentious areas of law relating to the elements that must be proven as part of the claimant's *prima facie* case (the second, more specific, aspect of the 'law' in CLEO)

(4) how the facts in his or her case fulfil the *prima facie* case (the 'evaluation' of CLEO); and

(5) the suggested resolution of the case (the 'outcome' of CLEO).

This model is appropriate even in an academic or vocational course because the study of law – its problems, methods and issues – is rooted in legal practice. Just as student chemists must learn and be examined on the tools of their trade – ie the practical experiments of the laboratory – and just as student mathematicians must learn and be examined on the construction of a mathematical proof, so, too, must students learning the law learn and be examined on the tools of their trade, namely the construction of a legal argument. This is not to say that adopting the CLEO method will make undergraduate law courses more vocational, something that many academics fear. CLEO does not attempt to replicate the precise form of legal arguments and pleadings, nor does it focus students on practical, as opposed to theoretical, aspects of law any more than university or vocational courses currently do. Instead, CLEO merely uses a practice-based approach to essays in response to practice-based (ie problem) questions. 'Discuss' questions require a slightly different approach, but build on a similar analytical technique.

Having thus set the stage, it is time to consider the first step in the CLEO method, identifying the claim.

3.2 Defining the claim in a legal essay or examination

When initiating a civil lawsuit in England and Wales, lawyers bring what is known as a cause of action, which claims that certain wrongs have been done and certain remedies should be forthcoming.

Therefore, in many subject areas, a claim in CLEO can be equated with a cause of action. For example, a claim in the area of tort would be the same as the various tort causes of action: negligence, breach of statutory duty, trespass to goods, etc. Contract law would give rise to claims (or again, to use the language of litigation, causes of action) for breach of contract, say, or rescission of a contract. Criminal law, which has its own distinctive terminology and procedure, refers to an indictment rather than a cause of action, but the effect is the same: prosecutors are still claiming that a particular crime (be it assault, theft, manslaughter, whatever) has occurred and therefore must prove all the constituent elements in order to make out their *prima facie* case. Constitutional law also has its own special language, in that individuals can apply for judicial review relating to a particular action. Scots law has its own distinctive terminology for many of these procedures. Rather than attempt to replicate the language of the courts with respect to each of the various areas of laws, we will use the term 'claim' to refer to each of these types of actions.

However, when you think about what the claim is in any particular essay or examination, think in terms of the types of actions that you could bring. It is important to frame the initial claim (when at all possible) in terms of legal actions for the following reasons:

(1) framing the claim in terms of a cause of action gives the reader the proper context for the following discussion (this is particularly important when you have multiple claims or multiple parties);

(2) framing the claim in terms of a cause of action leads you directly to the elements that must be proven as part of the claimant's (or prosecutor's) *prima facie* case, which will help you identify all of the potential points of discussion; and

(3) framing the claim in terms of a cause of action gives you a quick and effective introductory paragraph when it comes time to write your essay.

It will be helpful to address each of these points briefly.

3.2.1 Setting the context

If you take the time to identify the claim in terms of a cause of action, you are putting your essay into its proper context. This may not seem important at first, since, as a student, you expect the reader of your essay to know more than you do about what the 'right' answer to any written question is; but, in fact, an examiner has no idea what to expect from any particular essay. After reading dozens, or perhaps hundreds, of essays, the examiner knows the wide variation of possible answers. For example, what appears to the examiners to be a simple question about the availability of rescission of a contract following a misrepresentation can be construed by students as a question about breach of contract, consideration or even intent to create legal relations. To be fair, this sort of variation is not always due to students misreading the question; some questions are just badly written. However, after reading all of these different essays, the examiner becomes sceptical. He or she does not know how you are going to answer the question. Therefore, it is your responsibility, as the author, to put your answer into its proper context and tell your reader precisely what aspects of the question you are going to address.

This technique is even more important when you have multiple claims arising out of the same set of facts or multiple parties. It's perhaps easiest to see the possibility of multiple claims in criminal law, since we're all used to hearing reports of defendants who are charged with multiple crimes arising out of a single event. For example, someone might be charged with both kidnapping and rape or both theft and manslaughter. However, civil cases can also involve either multiple causes of actions or multiple theories of liability. An example of the first possibility is most easily seen in tort, where, for example, the escape of water from a commercial site could result in an action for negligence, nuisance and *Rylands v Fletcher* liability.[1] A claimant need not choose one type of action over another – he or she can assert anything that is legitimately supported by the facts. This ability to pursue various actions becomes even more apparent when one recalls that different types of remedies attach to different types of actions: for example, one type of tort may only offer damages to an injured party whereas a different type of tort will offer injunctive relief as well.

However, it is also true that a litigant can offer alternate theories of liability or non-liability. For example, a defendant in a contract case could argue that no liability exists because the claimant repudiated the contract, which the defendant accepted before the act that the claimant says constituted a breach. Alternatively, the defendant could argue that no contract ever existed due to vagueness of terms or the lack of consideration. Because the rules of civil procedure in England and Wales

> **NOTE**
>
> Problem questions can be quite complex. You may have multiple claimant–defendant party pairings or multiple claims (ie causes of action or theories of liability).

---

[1] For example, see *Cambridge Water Co Ltd v Eastern Counties Leather plc* [1994] 2 AC 264.

allow parties to proceed in the alternative and essentially say 'I think that I should win because of X, but if I'm wrong, then I should win because of Y', students can – and should – do the same in their essays and examinations. However, in order to avoid confusing yourself and the person reading your paper, you need to be clear what it is that you are doing.

You also should break apart the different claims that arise between different parties. In an essay or examination scenario, no two parties will be situated in precisely the same manner. Sometimes the parties will be asserting different claims. In those situations where two parties have identical claims, the sub-issues (as discussed below) will vary slightly. You won't need to duplicate all of your earlier discussion, since you can incorporate prior points by reference (as explained further in chapter four), but you do need to set forth the different claims and sub-issues for the different parties. That way your reader knows that you will be addressing each party and each claim in turn.

3.2.2 Leading the reader through the elements of the claim

The second benefit to framing your claim as a crime or civil cause of action is that, by doing so, you will be required to recall and list each of the elements that must be established as part of the *prima facie* case. For example, when you decide that a party can make a claim of negligence, you will list the elements of negligence, first to yourself, then explicitly in your essay. When you do this, you will be forced to consider each of the constituent elements and whether you can or should enter into a detailed discussion of any of them.

For example, you may read a question and immediately think that you can and should talk about the extent to which a local authority owes a duty to school children playing on property owned by the city council. If you were not using the CLEO system, you might start writing your essay immediately on the existence and breach of duty, without telling your reader that you were talking about negligence (as opposed to, say, breach of statutory duty). Not only could the reader be confused (and a confused reader is a reader who cannot award a first-class mark), but you might miss the fact that you could also talk about causation, another of the necessary elements for the tort of negligence. The facts might also support a discussion of other torts, such as breach of statutory duty or occupiers' liability. If you don't take the time to consider all of your various options, you could either miss potentially fruitful areas of discussion or spend too much time on a relatively minor point. The first area of discussion that you identify may not be the best area of discussion, in that it may not address the most pressing legal issue or offer you sufficient scope to demonstrate your sophisticated reasoning skills. Slow down and consider all the potential issues before starting to write your essay.

WRITING TIP

A confused reader cannot give you first-class marks. Be crystal clear about the claims you will be addressing.

3.2.3 Creating an easy introductory paragraph

The third advantage in identifying the claim is that it allows you to create a simple introductory paragraph. As will be discussed later in this chapter, you should run through each of the CLEO steps before you put pen to paper, since that will help you formulate a strong writing plan and thus a concise and effective essay. However, many students find that once it comes time to start writing, they struggle to find a way to ease themselves into their argument. Many essays begin with one, two or even three superfluous paragraphs that either fail to introduce or fail to advance the points that the writer wishes to make. Some essays spend so much time setting the scene that they don't start properly until the second page. Valuable time is lost as a result, and the reader begins to wonder whether the writer really knows what he or she wants to say. Presentation is an important part of legal argument, and you need to learn how to make your points quickly, logically and effectively. By forcing students to start their essays by identifying the claim, the CLEO method provides an easy route into the substantive discussion.

3.3 Identifying sub-issues within the claim

Once you equate the claim with a cause of action or crime, you will generate a list of elements that must be proven before the claimant can establish a *prima facie* case. For example, to establish the tort of negligence, you must prove existence of a legal duty, breach of that duty, causation and damages. If you were to discuss each of these elements in detail, you would run out of time. You would also fail to show your judgment in discerning what is important and what is not. What you leave out is as important as what you put in. While it is important to introduce each of the elements that must be proven and provide some general legal authority to support that assertion (a point that will be discussed in more detail in the next chapter, which deals with the 'law' portion of CLEO), you need to identify those sub-issues – ie those legal elements – that are most difficult to establish as a matter of law, since those are the points that you will focus on in your discussion. Remember, you are working from a litigation model. Judges don't want to hear a treatise on basic legal premises that are not in dispute, and neither does your examiner. Under the rules of civil procedure currently in effect in England and Wales, parties (meaning their counsel) must identify all points of fact and law upon which there is no reasonable dispute. Courts will not hear argument on these points, since to do so would waste time and resources. You must learn to do the same thing in your essays and examinations – focus on the points in dispute and

WRITING TIP

Treat your reader as you would a judge.

not on those areas of law upon which there can be no disagreement between the parties. Similarly, for reasons discussed more fully in the next chapter, you should not spend your time on issues of fact.

Identifying the sub-issues that are in contention is a learned skill. To some extent, you can see the issues arising on the face of the question, just as you will see the basic claims arising out of the facts presented. Sometimes you will see the sub-issue before you see the claim and must therefore work backwards to identify the claim. For example, a question in contract law may present you with a rogue purchaser of goods who presented him or herself as a famous celebrity. Your first thought is to discuss the issue of mistake, from which you build backwards to identify a claim that no contract exists because of mistake. As will be made clear in the discussion below, the claim is not one of mistake, since no one walks into a court and says, without more, 'M'lord, my client is alleging a mistake.' That statement gives no context and identifies no possible remedy. Instead, a lawyer would say, 'M'lord, my client alleges that no liability exists in this instance because no contract was formed [ie the claim] due to the existence of a mistake as to identity [ie the sub-issue].'

3.4 Spotting claims

When you are first presented with a fact pattern question, you should proceed line by line, looking for both claims and sub-issues within those claims. Read the question two to three times to be sure that you've spotted everything. Operate under the assumption that each sentence will give you a different topic for discussion or will further define the scope of discussion for a previously identified topic. This is not always the case, but if you use that assumption as your baseline, you will be less likely to miss potentially fruitful topics. Some examiners may throw a red herring into the question, but that is unusual, since a badly written question yields badly written answers. Since it is more difficult to wade through a badly written answer than through a well-written answer, most examiners try to set questions that will allow students to show themselves off to their best advantage.

Nevertheless, questions must contain some twists to separate first-class papers from less meritorious responses. Therefore, to the extent that a question contains a red herring, it will usually take the form of seeming to point down an easy (but ultimately incorrect) analytical route. Second-class students will take the bait and give a simple answer, based often on one case that appears to control.

First-class students see through the deception and use the opportunity to discuss why the simple analysis is inappropriate and why the issue is either (1) a non-starter or (2) better resolved in a more complex manner. Remember always to explain your thinking, even if you are deciding to set aside a point.[2] This will show the examiner that you are not only clever enough to see the potential relevance of the point, but you are so clever that you know enough to set it aside on further analysis.

As you work through your question, you will need to differentiate between questions of law and questions of fact. As discussed further in the next chapter, your job, as a law student, is to argue the law, not the facts. Arguing the facts is something that practitioners do and involves poking holes in the evidence, noting what could have happened and delving into motivation. This technique is irrelevant to your study of the law. When you are looking for possible claims and sub-issues, you should concern yourself solely with legal disputes, since you will be arguing your points based on legal authority. While you will need to evaluate the law in light of the facts – a process that will be discussed in chapter five – that is a different thing than arguing the facts.

There are several ways to identify potential claims and sub-issues. One is to look for similarities to well-known cases. For example, if your tort question involves children playing on council land, you will immediately think of *Jolley v Sutton London Borough Council*,[3] which also involves children on council land. You should also think about any other tort cases that involve children, since those cases may also be pertinent and may give you an idea about potential claims that you can discuss (see chapter four for further discussion of the relevance of factually similar cases). Now you see why chapter two suggested that you spend time during revision cross-referencing your notes. Since cases and statutes involving children may appear at different points during your course, you need to compile one list of those materials so that you can identify them immediately in your essay or examination. You may not refer to all of these cases and statutes when it comes time to start writing – as discussed further in the next chapter – but you should at least consider their potential applicability. Of course, you cannot consider their applicability in the second stage of CLEO if you have not spotted the potential issues in the first stage.

WRITING TIP

Be sure to say why you're doing what you're doing. You don't win points for knowing that some aspect of the question is legally (ir)relevant; you win points for saying that it is legally (ir)relevant and why.

NOTE

Don't argue facts – argue the law. The distinction is discussed more in chapter four.

---

[2] You will, of course, need to use some judgment in this regard. Describing why you have disregarded a point that was obviously irrelevant doesn't make you look clever. On the other hand, describing why you have declined to pursue a potentially relevant line of argument can show a great deal of intelligence.

[3] [2000] 3 All ER 409.

The second way of identifying potential claims and sub-issues is to consider all the different ways someone might sue on a particular set of facts. While it is possible that an essay or examination question might give rise to only one claim, it is at least equally possible that a question will give rise to more than one claim. Because there are times when a single set of facts can give rise to multiple causes of action – for example, a tort question could allow you to discuss claims in nuisance, negligence and *Rylands v Fletcher*[4] – you must be ready to assert any and all claims that are relevant. Again, this is why you have taken the trouble to cross-reference your notes during your revision period – you want to know immediately what kinds of claims can arise together and, significantly, how they differ so that you can discuss those differences cogently. If you decide that one of these related claims does not apply, you can and should devote one or two sentences to saying why that claim cannot prevail. Again, this is a matter of judgment – the length of the discussion (and, indeed, its appearance in the essay in the first place) will depend upon how meritorious a claim it is. Don't include ludicrous claims only to say they don't apply – 'straw man' arguments (easily created, easily knocked down) don't demonstrate great legal judgment. Instead, they suggest that you have nothing more interesting to discuss. Don't waste your time on minor points when you are operating in a format that often provides more meritorious claims and sub-issues than you have time to discuss fully. Just because you can write on a subject doesn't mean you should.

WRITING TIP

Don't construct 'straw man' arguments..

Remember also to consider each of the possible claimant–defendant pairings and how each party is situated differently. No two people will be placed in exactly similar situations; find what makes them different. Doubtless that small variation will yield fruitful discussion. Also be sure to look for potential parties who are not named but who may have a claim to assert or to defend. For example, a question on defamation may involve a series of named individuals but may also refer to an unnamed print shop where the libellous material was photocopied prior to distribution. Take the time to say that, because it was involved in the publication of the material, the print shop would be a potential defendant in a defamation action if the Defamation Act 1996 didn't contain an exemption from liability for those who are involved in the unknowing and merely mechanical reproduction of the material.[5] Note that you are not hypothesising about or adding new facts to the question, nor are you constructing an elaborate argument

NOTE

Not all potential parties will be identified by name. Some will be identified by category. However, don't hypothesise completely about potential parties.

---

[4] For example, see *Cambridge Water Co Ltd v Eastern Counties Leather plc* [1994] 2 AC 264.

[5] See section 1(3) of the Defamation Act 1996.

about the liability of the copy shop under common law rules, only to knock it down by reference to the 1996 Act. Instead, you are identifying a legitimate potential claim and quickly (but explicitly) dismissing it so that you can demonstrate your ability to think creatively and comprehensively. One sentence – that's all you need.

Be sure to read the question before starting to frame your answer. Sometimes students become so excited about all the potential claims and parties that they forget that the question focuses specifically on one aspect of the fact pattern. For example, a question may give rise to the following claims: A v B, A v C, B v C and B v an unnamed party, such as the photocopy shop in the defamation example discussed above. In an open-ended question (for example, one that just says 'discuss'), you can and should bring up each of the four claimant–defendant pairings.

Other questions will not allow you to be so broad in your response, however, and will limit you, for example, only to those claims that A can assert. In that case, you would only discuss A v B and A v C. It might be that part of B's defence is that C is entirely or partly to blame for B's conduct, in which case you can bring up those aspects of B v C that relate to B's or C's defence (for example, contribution under the Civil Liability (Contribution) Act 1978 or whether B's act constituted a sufficiently superseding act so as to foreclose any liability to A on behalf of C). You would not, however, discuss B v C directly, nor would you bring up B v the unnamed party, since those points fall outside the question set by the examiner. It is not that you wouldn't be correct, as a matter of law, to consider those claims; it's just that they are irrelevant to the question asked. Think about it: a barrister hired to represent A in court wouldn't suddenly start discussing the liability of C or some other third party to B. The barrister would only be concerned with arguments for and against B and C's liability to A. Other arguments would be left for another day and another trial.

Therefore, do as practising lawyers do and answer only the question asked. There are times (usually in the pre-action stage, when a party is considering whether to bring on a lawsuit) when barristers and solicitors must look at the potential liability of all parties. In those situations, a broad answer is appropriate, as in the 'discuss' questions. There are other times (such as during trial) when the focus is on one party only. In those situations, a narrow answer is appropriate, no matter how much you could say about another party's liability. Limit yourself to what is relevant in this particular circumstance. If you have prepared yourself properly during the term and during your revision period and if you apply CLEO correctly, you will not need to digress into forbidden territory, no matter how tempting it may be.

SUMMARY

Identify potential claims and contentious sub-issues by:

- going line by line through the question, looking for items to discuss;
- noting similarities to existing cases and identifying any lines of related cases;
- considering all the different ways someone could sue on the facts given to you;
- considering differences between different party pairings, including those concerning 'invisible' parties; and
- re-reading the question to make sure that you answer the proper question.

Having set forth the basic parameters of identifying claims and sub-issues, we can turn our attention to specific examples.

3.5 Writing the 'C' portion of your essay

The CLEO method provides you with a four-step analytical framework for your law essays. The goal is to produce a simple (but not simplistic), well-focused essay that answers the question asked with brevity, precision and power. Because each of the four steps build off one another, you will need to plan out all four steps, at least in rough form, before you start writing. It is perfectly acceptable to go back and make insertions into earlier paragraphs by using arrows or asterisks, although you should, of course, try to minimise the number of such insertions. Also, it's easier to insert one or two additional cases than it is to completely revise your argument when you suddenly remember the key case. Therefore, take your time in the planning stages. With CLEO, the writing stage takes far less time than you are used to, since the information and analysis speak for themselves once they are compiled.

WRITING TIP

Feel free to scribble down notes to yourself on your scratch paper as you write the essay. There is nothing more frustrating than remembering the killer case and then forgetting it again before you have finished the paragraph (or sentence) you are currently writing.

When you plan out each step, you don't need to use a complex or wordy outline that will take as much time to draft as the essay itself. What you do need to do is walk through each of the four steps, think about what you will say in each step, and write down some notes so that you don't have to carry that information in your head as you write. It is most important to write notes for the C and L portions of your essay, since they are the ones that tax your memory and analytical skills the most. The E and O portions of the essay merely require logic which results from proper application of the first two steps. The notes can be in any form you wish – cryptic abbreviations of legal authority, lists of party pairings and potential claims, mnemonics that you have devised to help you remember the elements of each claim – whatever works best for you. The point is to be creative and broad in your initial thinking; you can narrow the field down later, after you've covered everything. Once you have made a note of something potentially relevant, you can move past the fear that you will forget it and can focus on ascertaining whether the point is important enough to be put into your essay or whether it is too tangential.

When you have finished that process, stop. Do not start writing. Instead, re-read the question. Make sure you will be answering the question as asked. Look for more claims and contentious sub-issues. Think again about whether you can supplement your legal authority. Only when you are sure you have considered everything and have prioritised your points should you start writing. Because CLEO gives you a straightforward approach to structuring your essay and eliminates the need for flowery rhetoric, you will not need to spend as much time writing as you usually do. Spend that time in thought – it will be well worth it. Most errors are made in the 'C' stage of a CLEO essay. Students either fail to spot relevant claims or phrase claims in an unhelpful manner.

Having gone through all these steps, you can now put pen to paper. There is no need to introduce your essay with a complex or thought-provoking paragraph that takes you forever to write. Instead, simply state the claim and the sub-issues in contention.

WRITING TIP

When you think you're ready to start writing, stop and think again. Have you identified all possible claims?

EXAMPLE

'According to these facts, Anton (A)[6] can sue Bob (B) for the tort of defamation. To establish defamation, A must prove [here you would set forth, in one sentence, the basic legal standard for establishing defamation, as discussed in chapter four]. Of these elements, the only issue that can seriously be disputed is [identify which aspect or aspects you wish to discuss]. I will begin by setting forth the law concerning [that sub-issue].'

You then move on to your second paragraph, which sets forth the legal standard concerning the areas of dispute. The law falls under the second step of CLEO and is discussed in the next chapter. However, you now see how quickly you can identify (1) the claim and (2) the sub-issues you will discuss.

There is no need to ease your way into your essay with a discussion of the history of the tort of defamation (or whatever your claim may be) or a recitation of the facts of the case. No barrister would

WRITING TIP

There's no need to 'ease' your way into your argument. The best essays open with simple, direct statements.

---

[6] It's fine to abbreviate the names of the parties, as long as you define the terms you're going to use at the outset.

walk up to a judge and start giving a mini-treatise on the evolution of the tort of defamation or the crime of manslaughter – he or she would be immediately asked by the court to focus on the case at hand. While a barrister may sometimes begin with a summary of the facts for the court or the jury, there is no need to do so in an essay or examination scenario, since the examiner is familiar with the facts. You are under time pressure and operating in an academic environment, so not everything must conform to professional legal practice. Still, you can imagine a barrister standing up and saying, 'M'lord, this case involves the tort of defamation. To establish that tort, the claimant must prove X, Y and Z. I propose to focus on Z, since the parties agree that there is no dispute about the existence of points X and Y.' The barrister will then proceed to argue about whether the standard in Z has been met. That is what you are doing in your essay: you are arguing about the contentious sub-issue in a particular tort, crime or other cause of action, otherwise known as a claim in the CLEO system.

Those who are being very creative and open-minded about potential sub-issues may come up with as many as seven or eight possible discussion points. While this demonstrates an admirable level of ingenuity, you should try to limit your discussion of sub-issues to two or three major points. This doesn't necessarily mean that you should discard your other ideas. Instead, you should try to group your sub-issues together under a larger heading. For example, you may have a question in contract that involves sub-issues including sufficiency of consideration, promissory estoppel and modification of a contract. You could group these all as relating to consideration: sufficiency as a necessary element under formal rules regarding consideration, promissory estoppel as a stand-in for consideration (although promissory estoppel could also stand on its own as a non-contractual basis for a remedy) and the need for consideration when modifying a contract. By combining these points under a single heading, you are not eliminating any potential areas of discussion. Instead, you are presenting a more cohesive argument about how the sub-issues relate to one another. In an academic essay, you don't have a lot of time or space to make your points, and it is better to focus on a few very strong arguments rather than dispersing your time and energy among many weak ones.

Why should you aim for two or three major points? Research into communications theory suggests that people grasp information better when it is arranged in groups of three. While you need not adhere to this rule slavishly, a three-tiered argument gives the appearance of balance

WRITING TIP

Aim for three major points, which each may include several sub-points.

and strength.[7] In addition, it is unlikely that all seven or eight points will really stand alone; no fact pattern is that complex. It is much more likely that some of those points can be combined in some way and those that cannot are either mere spectres or too minor to merit a mention.

Don't worry if you don't come up with that many sub-issues. It may just be that you are thinking in larger conceptual terms than your colleagues. What they may consider a sub-issue you may think is a sub-sub-issue falling under a larger heading. Neither style of analysis is inherently better – there are benefits and dangers in both approaches. For example, someone who only comes up with one or two sub-issues may be in danger of missing something of importance. If you are the type who only sees one or two points to discuss, take an extra moment to re-read the question and see if you've missed anything. Don't think of this extra step as 'wasting' time – your colleagues will be spending that time compiling their many sub-issues into two or three key points, so you're not losing anything by taking a second look at the question.

Once you have decided which claims and sub-issues you are going to discuss, you should arrange them in the order in which you will discuss them. In most cases, you should start either with the sub-issue which logically comes first as a threshold matter (for example, when you need not address question B until you have answered question A in the affirmative) or the one which yields the longest and most complex legal analysis. How to identify and present the relevant law is discussed in the next chapter, but you see now why you must proceed mentally through the various stages of the CLEO analysis before you put pen to paper. If you don't know which legal points are most important before you start writing, you run the risk of spending too much time on a minor point.

Try to frame the claim in terms of legal actions or legal remedies. If you focus too much on factual issues, your essay will often end up arguing the facts instead of the law (this point will be discussed in greater detail in later chapters). Try to use legal terminology when you identify your claim(s), since that will force you into a legal, as opposed to factual, analysis.

In an examination scenario, it is quite common for people to spend too much time either on the first point in their essay or on the first essay of a multi-essay examination. If all essays are given equal weight,

---

[7] Some of you may have been taught to follow a five-paragraph essay structure in school. A five-paragraph essay consists of an introduction, a conclusion and three main points in the body of the essay. While this approach is too simplistic to be used in response to a complex problem question in law, it demonstrates the symmetry of a well-balanced essay.

it is unwise to give short shrift to the last one, since you are unlikely to win a first-class mark with a sub-standard component, no matter how brilliant the other essays are. Balance your time and effort evenly throughout the individual paper or examination. Often, it is helpful in a timed examination to work out ahead of time how many minutes you have to spend on each question. For example, if you have three hours to write four essays, you might allot yourself 20 minutes for calming down and reading over the examination as a whole to decide which questions you are going to answer, leaving two hours and 40 minutes – or 160 minutes – for the four essays you must write (be sure to check your maths!). You therefore have 40 minutes to plan and write each essay. As soon as you sit at your desk in the examination room, write down your 'changeover' times, then stick to them rigidly (or as rigidly as you can – again, your biggest problem will probably be in wanting to spend too much time on question one). For example, for a 9:00–12:00 examination:

EXAM TIP

Figure out how many minutes you have per question and stick to that schedule.

- 9:00–9:20 plan;
- 9:20–10:00, answer question 1;
- 10:00–10:40, answer question 2;
- 10:40–11:20, answer question 3;
- 11:00–12:00, answer question 4.

Depending on your personal exam style, you may want to leave yourself some free time at the end to check over your answers. If you do so, be sure to adjust your planning and writing time accordingly.

WRITING TIP

First-class essays show the following:

- *bold and direct use of language;*
- *a lead-in sentence that goes straight to the point;*
- *separation of claims according to the pertinent claimant–defendant pairings;*
- *precise identification of the claim(s) relevant to the question;*
- *compilation of the sub-issues into two to three discrete points; and*
- *use of legal terms and concepts when framing the claim(s).*

3.6 Worked example

Now that you have the principles and rationales in mind, it is time to see how the first step of the CLEO method is put into practice. We will use the same sample question through each of the following three chapters so that you can see how to build an essay. Additional examples appear in chapter ten.

Assume this question appears on an examination in tort.

QUESTION

Jack, a Formula One race car driver, was driving his standard issue estate car home from his daughter's school, where he had just dropped her off for the day. On the way, he was involved in a road accident. Had he used his expert skill in braking, he could have avoided the accident, although an ordinary driver could not have done so. Is Jack liable for the injuries to the other party?

3.6.1 Identifying the claim and sub-issues

The first thing you have to do is identify the claim and the various sub-issues in contention. As discussed above, you should work through the question, sentence by sentence, trying to spot as many potential claims and sub-issues as possible. Later you can cull through your list and cut those claims that are of minor importance.

3.6.2 Breaking down the question

SENTENCE ONE: 'Jack, a Formula One race car driver, was driving his standard issue estate car home from his daughter's school, where he had just dropped her off for the day.'

ANALYSIS:

(1) Jack is an expert driver. In the law of negligence, questions involving expert skills relate to the standard of care owed from the defendant to the claimant. If we recall that the tort of negligence requires the claimant to establish the existence of a duty of care, breach of that duty, causation (both legal and factual) and damages, then this potential issue (standard of care) relates to whether there exists a duty of care. Therefore, we have a potential claim relating to the tort of negligence and a potential sub-issue relating to the breach of a duty (with the sub-sub-issue specifically relating to the standard of care).

(2) Jack was not driving a Formula One race car, but was instead at the wheel of an average family vehicle. Can he be held to a higher standard relating to his expert skill if he is in a vehicle that cannot (presumably) take advantage of those higher skills? The claim and sub-issue/sub-sub-issue are the same as in point one, although this fact gives us another potential area of discussion.

(3) Jack was driving home from his daughter's school. Obviously he was not employed as a race car driver at the time of the accident. This point can relate to the claim and issues discussed in point one, since it is questionable whether people can be held to a higher standard of care when they are not holding themselves out as having that expert skill.

(4) However, this particular fact could bring up another point as well. Questions regarding employment can relate to the tort of vicarious liability. Potential sub-issues regarding employment would relate to (1) whether Jack was an employee or an independent contractor and (2) whether Jack was acting in the course of his employment at the time of the accident.

(5) The fact pattern does not say whether the school was independent or operated by the state, but when you see a school, you might want to consider whether the question will invoke issues involving public liability. The rest of the question should give you more of an idea, so you should move on to the next sentence.

SENTENCE TWO: 'On the way, he was involved in a road accident.'

ANALYSIS:

(6) The term 'accident' suggests lack of intent, therefore you can probably discount any of the intentional torts (assault, battery, etc). However, it does suggest that negligence might exist, thus giving rise to a claim in negligence. Whereas the previous sentence gave rise to concerns about the existence of a duty of care, this sentence suggests that there has been a breach of whatever duty exists. Nothing has been said yet to raise the level of culpability from negligence (if, indeed, that can even be proven) to recklessness, but you will keep the recklessness question in mind as you carry on through the problem.

SENTENCE THREE: 'Had he used his expert skill in braking, he could have avoided the accident, although an ordinary driver could not have done so.'

ANALYSIS:

(7) Here we see that Jack's expert skills are very much at issue, even more so than the question about the ability of the car to perform at a higher standard, as raised as a potential issue in point (2) above. The negligence claim and related issues, as noted in point (3), remain relevant, since the question of whether expert skill exists outside the realm where the skill is normally exercised is quite interesting, from a legal point of view. However, the vicarious liability claim raised in point (4) appears to be

irrelevant, since there is nothing further about Jack's employer or employment. The same is true of the public body liability question considered in point (5); since nothing more is said about what type of school the daughter attended (and we will not assume, without more, that it was a state school) and nothing is said about whether the school or its employers played a role in the accident, we will conclude that public body liability is not an issue in this question.

SENTENCE FOUR: 'Is Jack liable for the injuries to the other party?'

ANALYSIS:

(8) The question here focuses you on Jack's liability, rather than on the liability of any other parties. The fact that the other party to the accident is not named suggests that he or she is not contributorily negligent in any way, but just because a party is not named does not mean you should always ignore any potential claims or defences. In this case, however, no facts are given as to the relative negligence between the parties, so you should not assume the other party's (or any third party's) negligence is at issue. Don't hypothesise about possibilities that did not arise under the facts.

3.6.3 Discarding extraneous parties, claims and issues

Based on the analysis in point (8), we will focus on one claimant – defendant pairing, namely unnamed claimant v Jack. For the reasons discussed in point (7), we will discard claims of vicarious liability and liability for public bodies. We will therefore proceed with one claim for the tort of negligence, with sub-issues relating to the existence of a duty of care and the breach of the duty of care (and within the sub-issue of breach of duty, focusing on the standard of care for people with expert skill).

3.6.4 Writing your response

DRAFT ANSWER (first paragraph)

The question at issue is whether Jack is liable to the claimant for the tort of negligence. To establish a claim in negligence, the claimant must prove the existence of a duty, breach of that duty, causation (including both legal foreseeability and 'but for' causation) and damages (*Clerk & Lindsell on Torts*, s 7-04). Of those four elements, the claimant in our question will have the most trouble establishing that there was an existing duty and a breach of that duty, with the particular emphasis on what the appropriate standard of care is.

This is the 'claim', identified in one simple sentence.

These are the general elements of negligence. For a further discussion of how and why to set forth the general legal standard for the claim, see chapter four.

This sentence introduces the contentious sub-issues, which arise out of the claimant's *prima facie* case.

In three simple – but not simplistic – sentences, we have set up the framework of our written response. The reader knows precisely which points will be made and why. We have not wasted time constructing unnecessary rhetorical flourishes or repeating the facts of the question. While the language may not seem as elegant as that of a literature or history essay, it is effective, powerful and clear. Having introduced our discussion succinctly and precisely, we are now ready to begin discussing the most important part of your essay: the law.

You now have a basic understanding of how to approach the first step in the CLEO method. For a further discussion of how to handle this step in 'discuss' type questions, see chapter seven. The claims in those kinds of questions cannot be equated with legal causes of action, since 'discuss' questions are not comparable to litigation-style disputes, but the analysis is similar in many ways. For more worked examples of both problem questions and 'discuss' questions, see chapter ten. We will now move to the second step in the CLEO method, namely the analysis and presentation of the relevant law.

CHAPTER 4

Step two in the CLEO method: the law

The preceding chapter discussed how to identify the claim in the CLEO method of legal essay writing. In many problem questions, the claim will be the same as the cause of action that would be brought in court if the situation came up in real life. 'Discuss' type questions use a slightly different analysis initially, but follow the same general model.

Identifying the claim is not enough, of course. Certain sub-issues will be more difficult to establish than others as a matter of law, and these are the elements that are important to you as a student. Practitioners need to concern themselves with issues that are difficult to establish as a matter of fact as well as those that are difficult to establish as a matter of law, but the former group of issues are evidentiary matters that are beyond the scope of this book. As students, you focus on questions of law, not questions of fact. The difference between the two will be discussed in this chapter and the next.

If you follow the essay-writing suggestions in chapter three, you will have a two- to three-sentence opening paragraph that will take approximately one minute to write. This first paragraph is supposed to be short because the majority of your time should be spent on the second portion of your essay: the law. However, if you spend the proper amount of time in analysis and thought, you will find that the 'L' section of your essay writes itself as easily as the 'C' portion does.

To write a first-class essay in law, you must understand:

(1) the purpose of supporting authority ('law') in legal writing; and

(2) what constitutes supporting authority in legal writing.

Once you have grasped those points, you must learn how to:

(3) compile the relevant supporting authority; and

(4) communicate the relevant supporting authority in your essay.

Each of these points will be discussed in turn.

4.1 The purpose of supporting authority in legal writing

Law is unlike other subjects you have studied at school because it has both practical and academic applications. Indeed, that's what's so interesting about it. However, the practical aspect of law means that the purpose of supporting authority in legal writing differs from that in other subjects you have studied. Still, some analogies can be drawn to your school subjects to help you understand how to structure your legal writing. The skills that you already have can be adapted for use in your law course.

4.1.1 Supporting authority in other disciplines

Those who studied the humanities at school (literature, history, politics and the like) typically use supporting texts to illustrate the theories they create in response to a question. Crafting an argument in the humanities often involves finding as much support as possible for the position stated. While contrary arguments can be brought forward, the emphasis is on identifying a position and providing logical support.

Those of you who have studied the humanities know that sometimes it is easy to incorporate the primary texts into your essays. For example, the question 'analyse the character of Mr Rochester in *Jane Eyre*' requires you to refer to the plot and dialogue of the novel. You can refer to secondary texts (such as articles written by scholars in the field) to support your argument as and when you like.

WRITING TIP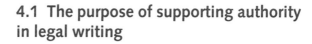

Refer to the primary text (statutes and cases) in the same way that you would in a literature essay.

However, there isn't always such a ready route into the primary texts. Some questions are more general. For example, a question about the causes of the Crusades allows you to refer to the commentary of esteemed historians but does not require you to do so. You will earn higher marks by quoting other people, but you must also construct an independent theory out of facts that you have gleaned from various sources. While those sources can be named, they need not be, since the year that Constantinople fell exists objectively, regardless of who reports that fact. You can obtain a very good mark even though you refer to only one or two authoritative sources, since your creative analysis of the problem is as important as, if not more important than, your ability to reproduce facts and commentary. Lawyers also need to use creative thinking in their arguments. To win top marks, a student must be able to argue by analogy, drawing fine points from seemingly disparate sources.

Those who have studied the sciences at school understand the concept of supporting authority slightly differently. Scientists cannot analyse a problem in chemistry or calculus without providing the underlying scientific principles. One cannot prove an algebraic equation without proceeding step by step through different mathematical principles in a logical manner. The source of the information is of minimal importance. For example, in a physics question, it is more important to know that $E = mc^2$ than to report that Albert Einstein said it or that it appears in your textbook on physics. Of course, you must know and state the significance of the equation $E = mc^2$ in your answer. You must also make sure that the equation is relevant to the question asked. Producing that particular equation in response to a question about organic chemistry will not win you any marks, even if the equation itself is correct, since the information you produce in your answer must pertain to the question asked. The same is true in law. You must produce correct and relevant statements of law to prove your point. You must also introduce those statements in a logical order to persuade your reader that your conclusions are correct.

WRITING TIP

Explicitly describe your legal argument step by step, just as you would in do with a proof in maths.

EXAM TIP

Including irrelevant legal principles in a law essay is as useful as saying that $E = mc^2$ in a chemistry exam. The proposition stated may be correct, but it won't win you any points.

4.1.2 Supporting authority in professional practice

Next, you need to compare how A-level students think about supporting authority with how practising lawyers think about supporting authority. Although not everyone who studies law goes on to become a lawyer, the study of law is influenced by the demands of legal practice. You see this influence clearly in the use and purpose of supporting authority in legal essays. If you understand how legal authority is used in the practice of law, you will better understand how to use supporting authority in your legal essays.

Early on in your law course, you will learn about the ancient concept of *nulla poena sine lege*: no punishment without a law. It means that the state cannot punish someone unless it can prove that the defendant violated an established legal principle. The legal principle in question had to (1) exist prior to the taking place of the act and (2) be well known enough so that the defendant could be said to be on notice that a penalty would occur if he or she acted in that way. The idea was that it was unfair to punish someone for doing something that wasn't outlawed at the time.

The concept of *nulla poena sine lege* can apply to areas other than the criminal law. For example, the law of contract describes the circumstances in which people will be required to live up to their agreements. If an agreement doesn't fall into the recognised pattern, courts – ie the law – will not hold the parties responsible for their actions, since it's unfair to force people to do something that they didn't think they would be required to do at the outset.

NOTE

Your job is to show what the state of known law was at the time the legally relevant act took place. Liability will be measured against that known standard, following the concept of *nulla poena sine lege*.

In deciding what is best in a particular situation, courts do not look to logic or common sense alone. Courts must look to the established law at the time of the event in question to see what should occur. If common sense dictates one course of action, but there is insufficient support in existing law to justify that action, the court cannot follow common sense. Courts must follow legal precedent. Instead of following its own inclinations, the court may suggest that a change in the law would be preferable but that Parliament must take such an action. Courts do not change the law retroactively, since to do so would violate the concept of *nulla poena sine lege*.

4.1.3 Legal authority in university and vocational coursework

How does all of this apply to writing law essays and examinations at university and in vocational schools? It shows that the state – ie a court – will not act unless it is convinced that there is an established legal principle justifying its action. To act without proper legal support would violate the concept of *nulla poena sine lege* (broadly defined).

Therefore, you, as a student, must respect the concept of *nulla poena sine lege* in your essays and examinations by indicating what the state of the law is at the time your particular question arises. There may be good reason to change the law – and, like the courts, you may wish to recommend legislative reform – but your final conclusion must be based on pre-established legal principles, not on common sense or even on logic.

EXAMPLE

See *Airedale NHS Trust v Bland* [1993] AC 789 (per Lords Browne-Wilkinson and Mustill) for an example of how a court might suggest legislative reform.

What constitutes 'the law' is discussed in more detail in the section below. A distinction is made between binding legal authority and persuasive legal authority. Both will be important to you as a law student, just as both are important to practitioners.

How does the study of law relate to the study of other subjects? Law is similar to the hard sciences in that it is important to demonstrate what principles have been proven and accepted by the scientific community as reflecting the true state of scientific discovery at the time of your discussion. Both lawyers and scientists must cite these pre-existing principles (be they theorems, axioms, statutes or judicial opinions) in an orderly fashion to demonstrate that their conclusions are correct. Both lawyers and scientists must also guard against the introduction of irrelevant information – such as $E = mc^2$ into an organic chemistry problem – since such information is extraneous to the problem at hand.

Law is dissimilar to the hard sciences in that there is seldom (if ever) one correct answer or one correct statement of the law. As will be discussed in the next section, law is a matter of nuance and persuasion, and you must look at all the evidence – even conflicting evidence – before you can come to a reasoned conclusion.

Those who have studied the humanities will appreciate the way that the law exists in shades of grey, rather than in black and white. Historians, for example, will know that while one person may argue that the Crusades were caused by X, another person may argue equally persuasively that the Crusades were caused by Y. A first-class historian will explicitly consider all possible theories before discussing why one particular approach should prevail. A second-class historian will construct a plausible theory which contains sufficient supporting authority but which ignores any conflicting evidence. The same is true in the study of law. First-class students explicitly consider all possible arguments before weighing them up. Second-class students focus on only one way of reading the supporting authorities.

The study of law differs from the study of history quite radically in one respect. As mentioned above, historians can refer quite easily to objective facts (such as dates) that do not require citation to underlying sources. As is discussed in the next section, lawyers do not have this luxury. They must indicate the source of the 'law' they cite, since a principle alone does not constitute 'law'. The persuasiveness of a legal proposition depends on who said it. That is why you must identify your source material.

> **✳ NOTE**
>
> The law does not exist in black and white. There is seldom a single, indisputable, 'right' answer, unlike in science.

4.2 What constitutes supporting authority in legal writing

Chapter two introduced the concept of supporting legal authority in its discussion of how to analyse statutory law, case law and legal commentary. As mentioned earlier, these are the most important sources of authority for law students and legal practitioners. However, a few additional words may be helpful before we consider how to use this authority in legal writing. For ease of comprehension, we will break legal authority into two types: binding authority, meaning those sources that must be followed when they are found to be relevant, and persuasive authority, meaning those sources whose principles may guide, but do not control, courts and lawmakers.

4.2.1 Binding authorities

Common law jurisdictions recognise two sources of binding legal authority: statutory law and case law. 'Statutory law' may also include directly applicable European legislation or international treaties. 'Case law' may also include relevant European cases. The essence of legal argument involves identifying what the various statutes and cases require in your particular situation and whether those statutes and cases even apply to the situation at hand.

As your study of law progresses, it will become rapidly apparent to you that the law is seldom clear. The essence of the laws of science is that they hold true in all circumstances, but the law that you are studying does not reach anywhere near that degree of certainty. There are even instances where two sources of binding law appear to contradict each other. For example, you may have a case that says a person will be held liable in negligence if he or she does X, while another case says that a person will not be held liable in negligence if he or she does X.[1] These types of conflicts very often show up in examinations, since an unwary student may know one case but not the other, or may not know how to reconcile the conflict.

Direct conflicts in binding law do not occur very often, however. It is more likely that a broad, general principle – for example, people may not kill others – will be subject to various conditions and exceptions – people may not kill others unless in self-defence or unless the death was a pure and unforeseeable accident. You will need to know and be able to refer to both the general principles and the exceptions.

Chapter two introduced the idea of distinguishing and harmonising cases. As you recall, when two cases both seem to apply to a question but require different outcomes, they must be 'distinguished' from one another, meaning that you must find a way to describe how the cases are dissimilar from your scenario and each other on either the facts or the law (the 'ratio'). If you are trying to show how a line of cases works together, you are harmonising those cases. Distinguishing and harmonising different cases requires the type of sophisticated analysis that separates first-class marks from second-class marks. Practising lawyers are not permitted to forget or ignore inconvenient law; indeed, they are obliged by the rules of professional conduct to refer the court to relevant cases that go against their own arguments. Practitioners thus must be able to distinguish away unhelpful case law. Students must learn and display the same skill by discussing cases that are difficult to reconcile in the 'L' section of their essays.

Although, as was said in chapter two, statutory law is the first place you go to find the relevant law, it is never the last. Statutes cannot, and are not intended to, cover every possible situation. Instead, they are often

EXAM TIP

Examiners often test in areas where there are direct conflicts in binding authority.

---

[1] One of the most famous inconsistencies arises between *The Wagon Mound* (holding that negligence did not exist because the damage that occurred was held not to be reasonably foreseeable) and *The Wagon Mound (No 2)* (holding that negligence did exist because the same damage was held to be reasonably foreseeable). See *Overseas Tankship (UK) Ltd v Morts and Dock & Engineering Co Ltd, The Wagon Mound* [1961] AC 388; *Overseas Tankship (UK) Ltd v Miller Steamship Co Pty, The Wagon Mound (No 2)* [1967] 1 AC 617.

supplemented by case law that describes how the statute is to be applied in particular circumstances. You must know and describe pertinent clarifying cases whenever you think the statute is relevant to your problem.

Sometimes statutes do not cover the entirety of a certain area of the law. Instead, they address certain aspects of a field of law while retaining common law definitions or principles in other regards. If a practising lawyer were to discuss the statute without the accompanying case law or the case law without the accompanying statutory language, he or she would give a court an incomplete description of the law. Therefore, the practising lawyer and the law student must cite both types of law to give an accurate representation of the full status of the law.

In a common law jurisdiction, there will be instances where no statute applies. Instead, the law is embodied in all of the various cases that have grown up over time. However, because each of these cases is tailored to the particular factual situation out of which it arose, it is unlikely that one of them will be so similar to your essay question that you can refer to only one case. It is far more likely that your essay question will be similar to one case or line of cases in one respect, but to a different case or line of cases in another respect. As you will see in this and the next chapter, you must not only introduce all of these arguably relevant cases but discuss how they apply to your factual situation. What is 'arguably relevant' is a matter of judgment; it is not your task to list every case in that particular area of law. Instead, you must use your discretion to decide which cases to discuss and which cases to discard. More will be said on this point below.

Just because a court has not specifically discussed your fact pattern does not mean that no law exists to cover your point. Instead, general principles of law that exist in similar cases can be extended to cover your point. You should also look at the exceptions that have been made to the general rule and try to understand why those exceptions were made. Your facts may be different, but you may be able to argue that the reasoning behind the exception should apply in your case as well. Legal argument involves showing how – *and why* – your situation resembles or doesn't resemble these pre-existing principles of law.

> **EXAMPLE**
>
> Section 1(2) of the Occupiers' Liability Act 1957 explicitly retains some elements of earlier case law.

> **WRITING TIP**
>
> *More than one case will be relevant to your essay question. You must introduce all arguably relevant cases into your discussion. Use your discretion in deciding what to include and what to discard.*

> **EXAMPLE**
>
> Early contract cases concerning when an offer was made or accepted in writing focused on when the offer or acceptance was put into the post. As technology changed, questions arose involving telexes, telephones, facsimiles and electronic mail. However, new rules of law were not created to address these new innovations; courts merely looked at existing principles of law, evaluated those principles in light of new facts and decided, by analogy, how new cases should be decided. When you approach your essay, you can and must adopt the same technique.

First-class scholars get behind the facts of the cases they are citing to the rationales supporting the judges' conclusions. First-class scholars also make sure that they identify their sources. Remember, you may very properly say that it is illegal to kill someone, but that statement, on its own, carries little or no weight in a courtroom. The law according to Jane Smith is not the same as the law according to Lord Justice So-and-So or the law according to Parliament. Because your statements about the law are not published in the same way that statements made by the legislature or the courts are, your statements about the law do not constitute binding legal authority. That is why you must identify the source of your legal statements, either by name or, if you can't remember the name, by description (for example, 'the snail in the bottle case' for *Donoghue v Stevenson*[2]). If a statement is not contained in a case or statute, it is not binding law. To hold otherwise would violate the principle of *nulla poena sine lege*.

CONCLUSION

In your writing, do as courts do and indicate three things:

(1) what the legal principle is;

(2) why it should apply in the current case; and

(3) what the source of the legal principle is.

4.2.2 Persuasive authorities

The term 'persuasive authority' refers to those sources or principles which may guide, but do not control, courts and lawmakers. Persuasive authority cannot be used to negate relevant binding authority, but it can be used to justify a particular course of action when there is no clear-cut answer contained in the case or statutory law.

There are at least four types of persuasive authority:

(1) public policy arguments;

(2) legal commentary;

(3) legislative documents, such as Green or White Papers or committee reports; and

(4) case or statutory law from other jurisdictions.

---

[2] [1932] AC 562.

a) *Public policy arguments*

A public policy argument is one that arises out of logic and/or morality rather than a particular case or statute. Public policy arguments appeal to common sense, rather than to binding legal authority, and are thus attractive to students who feel their knowledge of case and statutory law is sketchy. Humanities students who are used to being encouraged to offer their own opinions in essays have a particular tendency to over-rely on these types of arguments. Examiners know the ease with which common-sense arguments can be made and therefore do not award high marks for a legal discussion based entirely on general statements of public policy (unless, of course, the question specifically asks you to do so).

Public policy arguments are misleadingly attractive because they often appear in both case law and legal commentary. Having seen both courts and academics argue the relative merits of a particular public policy, the unwary student gives undue weight to such arguments. In fact, public policy is not 'law' in the same way that statutes and court decisions are law. Public policy concerns give reasons why a lawmaker should act in a certain way but do not dictate a specific outcome. In that sense, public policy is persuasive, not binding.

Student lawyers must also realise that every public policy argument that demands one outcome can be countered with a similarly persuasive public policy argument that demands a different outcome. You must be able to argue both sides of a problem. Presenting one perspective alone does not make your discussion stronger and more cohesive; it is simply incomplete. The art of legal argument lies in recognising opposing strands of thought and stating why one position is more convincing than the other. This method of analysis holds true for both binding law (when you are noting which strand of cases and/or statutes is the most applicable to your fact situation) and for persuasive law (when you are noting which public policy rationale is the most convincing).

> **EXAMPLE**
>
> Laws requiring motorists to take out insurance cover are based on the public policy that it is better to force motorists to pay for the costs of accidents or possible accidents than to let the risk of loss fall on the person injured by a motorist.

WRITING TIP

When presenting a public policy argument, remember:

- *public policy is persuasive, not binding, legal authority;*
- *there are two sides to every public policy argument; and*
- *you must define what you mean by 'public policy'.*

A third reason why public policy arguments fail to win students high marks is because many students allude to public policy generally, without stating precisely what they mean. The term 'public policy' can refer to a variety of social interests. It can mean that public bodies should not be subject to individual lawsuits in tort because to do so would detract from public bodies doing their jobs and result in ratepayers' money being used to pay for individual damages rather than for public services. Public policy can explain the existence of compulsory motor insurance, as mentioned above. Public policy lies behind the legislative decision not to hold manufacturers responsible for defects in their products until scientific discovery has advanced far enough along to allow the defect to be detected, since to do otherwise might slow research into socially useful inventions. Students must be careful to define what they mean by public policy before using the term in an essay. The meaning cannot be simply gleaned from the context of the case, since, as stated above, public policy rationales exist on both sides of an argument. For example, some might say that public policy should require manufacturers to be held responsible for all defects in their products, since the public should not have to suffer risks as a result of manufacturers' commercial decisions to rush their products to market. Therefore, in a discussion of section 4(1)(e) of the Consumer Protection Act 1987, you can't allude to 'public policy' without first explaining what you mean by that term.

For these reasons, public policy arguments cannot constitute the entirety of your discussion of 'law'. Instead, public policy can, and in appropriate cases should, be used to supplement your discussion of case and statutory law, because it gives reasons why existing law should or should not be extended to the situation at hand. Public policy arguments can also fill gaps between existing (and possibly conflicting) lines of cases. However, discussions of public policy cannot replace arguments based on existing law.

b) *Legal commentary*

The second type of persuasive legal authority is legal commentary generated by academic lawyers that appears in textbooks, treatises and legal journals. Legal commentary describes the current state of existing law, offers critical analysis of that law and/or provides suggestions on legal reform. Because commentators have spent a significant amount of time researching and reflecting on the problems they discuss, their analyses are valued by courts and legislators who do not have the luxury of spending several months or years working on a particular issue. Referencing legal commentary will round off your essays and will, like arguments based on public policy, give highly persuasive reasons why the question you are answering should be decided in a particular way. Indeed, some commentators are so highly esteemed that courts grant great deference to their opinions. Nevertheless, commentary does not constitute binding law, just as public policy does not.

Of the different types of commentary, articles and treatises are the most persuasive to courts and examiners. Student textbooks are helpful, but generally do not contain the type of detail and sophistication that is necessary to craft a first-class essay. Nevertheless, don't hesitate to refer to a helpful point just because it appears in a textbook.

Whenever you refer to a commentator's ideas, you should provide his or her name. Not only does citation to sources avoid the problem of plagiarism, it gives more persuasive weight to the statements themselves. As you are beginning to realise, the 'L' portion of the CLEO method is all about law and legal authority. While it is important to give your opinion in your essay, that step does not come until later in the process. As clever or as innovative as your ideas may be, they do not rise to the level of legal authority. Therefore, focus at this point on the views and statements of others.

> **NOTE**
>
> Legal commentary is a highly persuasive source of authority in civil law jurisdictions. If you work in a practice that is international in scope, you will need to appreciate the differences between the civil and common law.

> **NOTE**
>
> If you use the exact words of anyone else, be it court or commentator, use quotation marks ('inverted commas') and attribute the quotation. Failing to do so constitutes plagiarism and fails to win you marks for citing supporting legal authority. Quotes are a good thing in law. Use them and acknowledge their presence fully.

c) Legislative papers

Another source of persuasive authority lies in legislative papers. These can include Green and White Papers, committee reports, European legislation that is not directly applicable, etc. These documents are not binding, but they are persuasive in that they suggest where the law might be heading. Courts will take these items into account when they are considering cases arising in front of them, and you should do the same in your essays.

d) Case or statutory law from other jurisdictions

Finally, courts will consider case or statutory law from other jurisdictions when a gap exists in binding legal authority. Because these laws have been promulgated in other states, they cannot be binding here, but courts respect the pronouncements of other lawmakers just as they respect the work of legal commentators. Therefore, courts will consider foreign law as suggestive of how they should decide the case pending in front of them. You, too, can bring up law from other jurisdictions as long as you recognise it to be persuasive, rather than binding. However, you must consider which aspects of European law constitute binding law in the UK, and which are merely persuasive. Just because a judgment is handed down by the European Court of Justice rather than the Court of Appeal doesn't mean you should classify it as foreign law.

> **CONCLUSION**
>
> You can find relevant legal authority in:
>
> - statutory law;
> - case law;
> - public policy;
> - legal commentary;
> - legislative papers; and
> - case or statutory law from other jurisdictions.
>
> Remember to consider each of these areas when planning your essay.

4.2.3 Legal authority in 'discuss' questions

In many ways, it is easier to identify what constitutes proper supporting authority in a problem question because you can analogise the situation to litigation in real life. 'Discuss' questions are slightly more difficult and are handled specifically in chapter seven. However, at this point it is sufficient to say that the same types of authority that are used in problem questions are used in 'discuss' questions. You might be required to rely somewhat more heavily on persuasive sources of law, but you cannot and should not ignore binding sources of legal authority.

4.3 Assembling your legal authority and planning your essay

WRITING TIP

Knowing what to leave out of an essay is as important as knowing what to put in and requires ruthlessness and courage on your part.

Preparing the 'L' section of your essay is a two-step process. First, you must consider the realm of potentially relevant law, both binding and persuasive. This process requires both creativity and knowledge of the law. Second, you must use your judgment to identify which legal authorities you will actually discuss and which you will discard. Most students fail to recognise that examiners are more interested in testing your judgment than they are in testing your memory. Therefore, be sure to complete both steps of your legal analysis. Only after you have completed this two-step process should you begin to write the 'L' section of your essay.

4.3.1 Compiling relevant law

The CLEO system requires you to compile two sorts of relevant law: first, the law supporting the various elements of the claim, as that term is defined in the previous chapter, and second, the law relating to the various sub-issues that you have identified in the 'C' section of your analysis.

a) *Law supporting the elements of the claim*

As was discussed in the last chapter, the 'C' in CLEO stands for 'claim', which is analogous to a cause of action in a court case. The claim can be a tort, a crime, a dispute about the existence or terms of a contract, etc. When it comes time to discuss the law relating to your claim, you must set out each of the elements that must be proven as part of a claimant's *prima facie* case. For example, if you decide that your question involves the tort of negligence, you must state that negligence requires the claimant to prove the existence of a legal duty, the breach of a legal duty, causation (meaning both 'but for' causation and foreseeability) and damages. If any one of those elements is missing, the claimant cannot prevail in a court case. Similarly, if the state wishes to bring a case for theft, it must prove that the defendant 'dishonestly appropriate[d] property belonging to another with the intention of permanently depriving the other of it'.[3]

As will always be the case, you should try to support your statements, even statements as general as these, with binding legal authority. For example, the Theft Act 1968 contains the elements of theft. Cite it by name for full marks. Defamation, on the other hand, is a common law tort, despite the existence of the Defamation Act 1952 and the Defamation Act 1996. Find or create for yourself a brief one-sentence formula that explains the elements, with appropriate support. For example: 'To prove defamation, the claimant must establish that the statement was defamatory (ie that "the words tend to lower the plaintiff in the estimation of right-thinking members of society generally" (*Sim v Stretch*, per Lord Atkin)), that the statement refers to him or her (*Knupffer v London Express Newspaper Ltd*) and that the statement was published (*Pullman v Walter Hill*).' You may know different cases for these propositions, but the method is the same regardless. Alternatively, you could cite to a well-known treatise such as *Clerk & Lindsell on Torts* to establish these basic elements. We will discuss how to go about writing your essay in greater detail below, but this gives you an idea of what you should hope to achieve.

You must take this first step of setting forth the required elements because it requires you to slow down and think about all the different things you can discuss in your essay. As we mentioned in the last chapter, jumping straight to what you think is the most important sub-issue can lead you to miss other potential areas of discussion, thus losing you marks. In addition, you may find yourself in a situation where you have several potential

---

[3] Theft Act 1968, section 1(1).

claims. For example, a tort question might allow you to discuss negligence, nuisance and *Rylands v Fletcher* liability.[4] Although each of these torts has different elements that must be established before a claimant can prevail, some aspects, such as causation, overlap. If you set down the basic elements as the first step in your discussion of each cause of action, you can insert internal cross-references into your essay that will save you time. As we discussed in the previous chapter, problem questions often have multiple claims and multiple parties; CLEO gives you the means to address such complex discussions in a straightforward and logical manner.

Setting forth the elements of the basic claim and the supporting authority is an important planning point but, as discussed below, should comprise one or two sentences of your essay at most. The majority of your time should be spent on identifying the law relevant to the various sub-issues that you have identified in the 'C' step as being in contention.

b) *Law supporting the contentious sub-issues*

As we discussed in the last chapter, a contentious sub-issue is one that is difficult to prove as a matter of law. For example, there might be two lines of cases that point to different outcomes. Similarly, liability might hang on whether some act was 'reasonable', in which case you must discuss previous cases or statutes that define when an act is reasonable.

As mentioned in the previous chapter, when considering what is going to be contentious as a matter of law, you will have to remember the facts of your problem. You won't discuss those facts until you get to the 'E' element of CLEO, but there's no use discussing some aspect of the law that isn't relevant to the question. Examiners often complain that students provide pre-prepared treatises on the law that have little, if any, relevance to the question. Avoid that mistake.

The way to avoid bringing irrelevant bits of law into your essay is to make sure that you have enough relevant law from the very beginning. In this stage of your preparation, your task is to identify as many different sources of authority – both binding and persuasive – as you possibly can. You will discard some of these authorities later, but that's the second step. This first step is all about identifying as many potential discussion points as possible. In doing so, you should consider each of the types of legal authority introduced above:

(1) *statutory law*

Thus, for example, if you have a tort question dealing with land, consider whether any or all of the following statutes apply: the Occupiers' Liability Act 1957, the Occupiers' Liability Act 1984, the Defective Premises Act 1972 and the Unfair Contract Terms Act 1977.

WRITING TIP

Avoid pre-prepared treatises on the law. Tailor your response to the question asked.

WRITING TIP

Be as broad and as creative as possible at this stage of your analysis. You can discard material later.

---

[4] See *Cambridge Water Co Ltd v Eastern Counties Leather plc* [1994] 2 AC 264 for an example of how to pursue alternative claims in tort.

(2) *case law*

When considering what case law to include, think about the following categories of cases:

- cases that construe or supplement the statutes you have considered in the first step of your analysis of the law;
- cases that are factually similar to your problem
  - for example, if you have a question involving a motorist, consider all the motoring cases you know;
- cases that are legally similar to your problem
  - for example, if you have decided that your question involves the standard of care in negligence of a person holding expert skill, consider all the expert skill cases you know (whether or not they are factually similar to your problem).

As you think about each cateogry, write down any potentially applicable case in your notes. Later you will evaluate the relative importance of each item and delete those that are not relevant or useful.

(3) *persuasive authority (public policy, legal commentary, legislative papers and/or case or statutory law from other jurisdictions)*

You should be aware that some types of questions (such as 'discuss' questions or invitations to reform the law) will require more discussion of persuasive authority than pure problem questions. However, one hallmark of a first-class essay is the ability to incorporate short theoretical discussions into problem questions, so don't ignore persuasive authority completely, even if you have lots of binding authority to discuss.

At this point, you are not trying to create an argument for one side or another. Look for cases or statutes supporting both sides. Look also for any possible defences, remembering that some defences stand by themselves (for example, contributory negligence or self-defence), whereas other defences can be seen as a negation of one of the *prima facie* elements of the claimant's case (for example, *volenti non fit injuria* (voluntary assumption of risk) may be seen either as a defence or as a negation of the existence of a duty).

This may sound like a lot of things to remember under time pressure, but in fact you probably know quite a lot of law already. The important thing to do is to start organising your ideas so that you can see how different aspects of the law interact. You also must learn how to think creatively. Chapter two has given you some hints in this regard. Most people will be able to see how cases with factual similarities relate to an essay question, but fewer people are immediately able to see legal similarities between factually diverse cases. Again, chapter two has given you some tips regarding this skill. Remember, it is the

WRITING TIP

Imagine yourself acting as counsel for both the claimant and the defendant.

ability to see legal similarities that will move you into the realm of top marks. You must learn to argue by analogy; if you can make a good, logical argument why a case relates to your problem, an examiner will have to respect it. This is not to say that every case can be made relevant to every problem, only that arguing effectively by analogy shows the kind of legal sophistication that wins top marks. Remember also that this is a learned skill that will take time to develop. Don't be too hard on yourself if you find it difficult at first. However, the more law that you know, the more fun the 'L' step will be.

4.3.2 Discarding irrelevant law

At this point in the process, you have compiled a large amount of potentially relevant law to discuss in your essay. You should have more material than you will ever have time to cover properly. Now you must start to make decisions about what lines of argument you should discard.

WRITING TIP

Aim to have more law listed in your notes than you can possibly discuss in your answer. You want to present your best argument in your essay – not your only argument.

It may seem odd to require you, in the first place, to identify more material than you will be able to use, but there are benefits to this approach. First, forcing you to be creative and come up with all possible arguments stops you from starting to write the minute that you find a halfway decent case or theory. Often the best arguments or authorities are not the ones that you think of first.

Second, you need to give yourself time to think not only of arguments in favour of one position, but also of arguments against that position. Sometimes one position will seem so overwhelmingly right to you that it will take a moment to figure out how it can be attacked. Making a good opposing argument is the difference between a first- and second-class mark.

WRITING TIP

Argue the law, not the facts.

Third, having a large amount of law to discuss means that you will spend more time discussing the legal authorities and less time arguing the facts. Arguing the facts is something that practitioners do and involves poking holes in the evidence, noting what could have happened and delving into motivation. This technique is irrelevant to your study of the law. Argue your points based on legal authority. Arguing the facts is like arguing public policy. Both are based on common sense, and both are given relatively few points as a result. While you will need to evaluate the law in light of the facts, that is a different thing from arguing the facts. We will return to this subject in the next chapter.

Finally, forcing you to create a large stockpile of material means that you will not be (as) tempted to include references that are not really relevant to the problem at hand. Students often worry that they will not know enough law to get a good mark. In fact, most students know more than enough law. They just don't present it well. Instead, they start writing about the first thing that comes to mind, even though that first thing may not be the most important. If you have identified a large amount of material, you will feel confident discarding some of it.

NOTE

CLEO helps you remember law as well as present it.

You will also be past that first flush of enthusiasm that leads you to spend too much time on one case or statute. Because you know you have a lot to write about, you will prioritise your arguments and which aspects of the law you will discuss. Remember, you want to show the examiner how discerning your judgment is.

Eager students often believe that an effective method of examination revision involves preparing large blocks of ready-to-use law that can be dropped into an essay. This approach is, in fact, not helpful at all. Pre-prepared blocks of information demonstrate memory, not critical judgment. While you must know and remember the law before you can produce it in an examination scenario, simply regurgitating information will not win you first-class marks. You must use your judgment to tailor your response to the question asked. Obviously judgment is a more difficult skill to attain than simple memorisation, which is why it is a hallmark of a first-class paper. Because you cannot demonstrate your judgment without having the information to hand, learning the law is the first, necessary step. To get top marks, however, you must learn how to use your knowledge effectively.

How do you know which law should be discarded and which should be retained? That is something that is difficult to describe in the abstract, since it all comes down to judgment. Since, in the 'L' section of your essay, you will present only the law that will support your final arguments, you must determine what those arguments will be. One way to develop your judgment is to read some closely contended appellate cases, not for content, but for style. See how different judges handle the arguments presented to them. Observe the different ways they weigh up legal precedent and arguments based on public policy. Sometimes the reported decisions include counsel's arguments. That's even better for seeing how experienced lawyers use the same body of law to argue in favour of two different outcomes. Notice also how counsel presents only law that relates to the arguments that they are making.

WRITING TIP

To increase your understanding of how to use legal authority, read a complex case (with counsel's arguments, if possible) for style rather than substance. Do this maybe once a month with different cases, since your understanding of legal argument will be increasing all the time.

Developing judgment is a matter of practice, so you should take some chances in your essay writing, particularly early on. Even if you are not fond of public speaking, you should try watching or, better yet, participating in some mooting competitions. Not only will you see how the same body of law can be used to support two different arguments, but you should get an immediate response from the judge as to which arguments carry more weight.

4.4 Writing the 'L' portion of your essay

As was discussed in chapter three, you should plan out the 'C', 'L' and 'E' portions of your essay, at least in rough, before you start writing. It is perfectly acceptable to go back and make insertions into earlier paragraphs, through arrows or asterisks, but of course it will serve you better if you minimise the number of such insertions. Also, it's easier to insert one or two additional cases than it is completely to revise your argument when you suddenly remember the key case. Therefore, take your time in the planning stages. With CLEO, the writing stage takes far less time than you are used to, since the information and analysis speak for themselves once they are compiled.

NOTE

A CLEO essay takes comparably little time to write.

You will put down your legal authority in two steps. First, you will give support for the various elements that a claimant would have to prove as part of his or her *prima facie* case if the claim were a real cause of action. This should take one or two sentences at most.

Second, you will give support for the contentious sub-issues you have identified in the 'C' portion of your essay. This will form the bulk of your writing. It is best to cover each contentious sub-issue separately, beginning with general legal principles (ie it is unlawful to kill someone) before moving on to more specific exceptions and condi-tions to that rule (ie it is not unlawful to kill someone in self-defence – and you will then need to define self-defence). Each statement of law should come from either a statute or a case and be followed by a refer-ence to that source. Be sure to include law that supports your desired or anticipated outcome as well as law that opposes it.

If the law is not clear or if the outcome required under the law seems unjust, you may want to introduce persuasive authority. Remember, you cannot overcome bad precedent with persuasive authority, but if there is a gap in the law or a need to extend the law to a novel situa-tion, then persuasive authority will be useful.

As you begin to put down your legal authority, remember the fol-lowing points. First, general statements of legal principle will ensure that you pass, but they will not get you top marks. You must demon-strate detailed knowledge and in-depth analysis of the law to do well.

Second, use precise language – for example, the exact formula for *res ipsa loquitur* or the negligence carve-out in the Unfair Contract Terms Act 1977[5] – and legal terms of art. Your essays will be tighter and more

---

[5] See Unfair Contract Terms Act 1977, section 2. This suggestion about precise language assumes that you are not permitted to have a statute book with you in the examination. You win no marks for copying out large sections of the statute if they are readily available to all. However, short quotations are acceptable and sometimes necessary to your discussion.

sophisticated if you can use phrases such as subrogation, servitude or trespass *ab initio* correctly. Many students find it useful to start a vocabulary list for each of their subjects, both to help them understand the cases that they read and to help them during their revision.

Third, specific statements of law, without attribution to the source, will raise your marks but will not put you into the top level because you are forgetting the first principle of legal analysis: that legal controversies are decided on the basis of existing law (the *nulla poena sine lege* idea). If you are going to take the trouble to learn what the specif ic principle of law is, put the source down and get full credit for it. The statement carries much more weight if someone else said it. The time for your opinion is in the 'E' section of CLEO.

Fourth, be sure to include enough information to demonstrate, even in the 'L' section, why you are citing a case. A list of cases or statutes, without more, is not legal argument. Some sources may be useful for several propositions,[6] and you need to indicate why you are including the reference. It's also true that some cases are important for their outcome whereas others are important for their analysis (ie why they come out the way they do). You do not always need to include a recitation of the facts of the cases you are citing – indeed, you should not do so – but you need to convey the reason why the case is important to your discussion.

> **NOTE**
>
> Start a vocabulary list for each of your subjects.

WRITING TIP

If you can't remember the name of the source, put down enough details to indicate where it can be found: for example, 'the snail in the bottle case' (Donoghue v Stevenson) or 'the first Occupiers' Liability Act'.

TIP

You must indicate why you are citing a case. Remember, you're trying to persuade your reader. Lists are not persuasive.

CONCLUSION

First-class essays show the following:

- detailed knowledge
  - you must be able to reference specific sections of statutory law as well as highly relevant cases (not just the big leading cases);

- precise use of terms
  - you must use specific language from cases and statutes where necessary;

- creative and sophisticated analysis
  - you must be able to craft arguments for and against your final position, using your knowledge of binding legal authority and, if possible and appropriate, persuasive legal authority;

- judgment
  - you must know which arguments and bits of law to retain and which to discard.

---

[6] For example, *Caparo Industries plc v Dickman* [1990] 2 AC 605 is important both for establishing the incremental approach to novel categories of negligence liability and for establishing the parameters for liability for economic loss associated with negligently given advice. You must identify which proposition is at issue in your essay.

4.5 Worked example

Now that you have the principles and rationales in mind, it is time to see how the second step of the CLEO method is put into practice. We will use the same sample question that appeared in chapter three, since you now know the claims and sub-issues in contention.

> **QUESTION**
>
> Jack, a Formula One race car driver, was driving his run-of-the-mill estate car home from his daughter's school, where he had just dropped her off for the day. On the way, he was involved in a road accident. Had he used his expert skill in braking, he could have avoided the accident, although an ordinary driver could not have done so. Is Jack liable for the injuries to the other party?

4.5.1 Identifying the claim and sub-issues

NOTE

We are building on the example begun in chapter three.

The first thing you will have to do is identify the claim and the various sub-issues in contention. That process has been discussed in chapter three, where we concluded that the claim involved the tort of negligence. The sub-issues involve the existence and breach of the duty of care and what the standard of care is for people with expert skill.

4.5.2 Compiling legal authority

WRITING TIP

Creating a long list of potentially relevant legal authority is easier than you may think.

The second thing you will have to do is identify a list of potentially relevant legal authority, starting with statutes. While there may be some statutes which discuss motoring accidents of this nature, those statutes are not usually included in the first-year tort curriculum. Therefore, we will conclude there are no relevant statutes on motoring. Whenever you are faced with a negligence question, however, you should consider the potential relevance of the Law Reform (Contributory Negligence) Act 1945 and the Civil Liability (Contribution) Act 1978. Remember that contributory negligence relates to negligence attributable to the claimant and contribution relates to negligence attributable among several defendants.

There are, of course, relevant cases. We will need to consider factually relevant cases and legally relevant cases for both the claim and the sub-issues. We will also need to be sure to look for cases that favour liability and those that oppose liability.

To establish liability in negligence, a claimant must prove the existence of a duty of care, the breach of that duty, causation and damages. These elements are found in virtually every case and treatise on tort, so you can provide support for this proposition by citing to *Clerk & Lindsell on Torts*, for example, or a seminal case on each point (for example, *The Wagon Mound (No 2)*[7] for causation).

The notes you make regarding the cases you will initially consider will be quite brief. No one will see them but you, so use your own shorthand. The list below assumes that you have some familiarity with the cases. The purpose here is not to teach you the law of negligence (or indeed the law of any substantive subject), but to show you how to manipulate the information that you have learned from other sources.

Factually relevant cases include any motoring case that you know:

- *Froom v Butcher*[8] – contributory negligence for not wearing a seatbelt
- *Daly v Liverpool Corp*[9] – 67-year-old victim, dealt with contributory negligence
- *Roberts v Ramsbottom*[10] – defendant had stroke at wheel, held negligent
- *Mansfield v Weetabix Ltd*[11] – hypoglycaemic at wheel, held not negligent
- *Nettleship v Weston*[12] – learner driver held to standard of reasonable person

Legally relevant cases include:

(1) cases establishing the general standard for duty of care (the reasonable person):

- *Glasgow Corp v Muir*[13] – the standard of care is that of the reasonable person in the circumstances
- *Parkinson v Liverpool Corp*[14] – standard of care during an emergency

---

[7] *Overseas Tankship (UK) Ltd v Miller Steamship Co Pty, The Wagon Mound (No 2)* [1967] 1 AC 617.

[8] [1976] QB 286. References to the reported decisions are included in this section in case you want to look up the cases as you review the worked example. You would not need to include a full citation in your essay or examination. The case name above would be enough, supplemented by the year of the decision, if relevant.

[9] [1939] 2 All ER 142.   [10] [1980] 1 All ER 7.   [11] [1998] 1 WLR 1263.
[12] [1971] 2 AC 691.   [13] [1943] AC 448.   [14] [1950] 1 All ER 367.

(2) cases involving special skill

- *Philips v William Whiteley Ltd*[15] – jeweller doing ear-piercing work
- *Wells v Cooper*[16] – DIY carpenter in home

(3) cases involving professional negligence

- *Bolam v Friern Hospital Management Committee*[17] – professional standard of care need only be in conformity with a responsible body of opinion
- *Bolitho v City and Hackney Health Authority*[18] – professionals must act in accord with a body of opinion that has a logical basis

All of these cases were culled from a well-known student textbook on tort law. Your textbook might not include all these cases or might include other, equally helpful cases. You may also glean additional cases from your lectures. The above list is merely indicative of a 'first cut' of cases you might want to discuss.

Persuasive authority on the duty and standard of care might be found in Atiyah and Cane, *Accidents, Compensation and the Law*.

4.5.3 Discarding legal authority

TIP

Prioritizing your legal authorities and eliminating those that are unnecessary is a high-level legal skill that is deeply satisfying.

The third step involves the culling out of extraneous cases, keeping in mind the facts of your problem question. This section describes what criteria you can and should use to prioritise the legal authorities you have identified in step two of the 'L' analysis.

First, consider the two statutes you have listed as potentially relevant. Although the fact pattern does not discuss negligence on behalf of the other party, you might want to allude – briefly and in passing – to the possibility that contributory negligence under the Law Reform (Contributory Negligence) Act 1945 exists, since that might be a possible defence to a negligence action. As a rule, you do not want to add additional facts to your question or speculate about 'what if' situations, but a line here about contributory negligence might be appropriate because it is a common defence. Remember, though, it is a low-priority remark because the problem does not raise the negligence of the victim. Since there is only one tortfeasor here, it would be inappropriate to introduce the idea of contribution. Therefore, you will not refer to the Civil Liability (Contribution) Act 1978.

---

[15] [1938] 1 All ER 566.   [16] [1958] 2 QB 265.   [17] [1957] 2 All ER 118.
[18] [1998] AC 232.

Next, consider the cases you have listed. Among the motoring cases, you could refer to *Froom* in passing if you make the contributory negligence point referred to above, but it's really not necessary, since the statute will control and this is not a seatbelt case. *Froom*, therefore, will be low on our list of priorities. *Daly* seems like a possibility at first, since it involves someone with special characteristics, and Jack, our defendant, also has special characteristics. On reflection, though, *Daly* might not be a good case to cite, since there the person with special characteristics was the claimant, not the defendant. *Daly* also relates to a pedestrian, rather than another driver. Our question does not classify the injured party one way or another, and it may very well be that the question of whether the injured party was a driver or a pedestrian is immaterial. Nevertheless, the fact that *Daly* involved a claimant with special characteristics rather than a defendant with special characteristics means that the case, though apparently factually relevant (in that it is a motoring case), is not all that relevant legally and should therefore be discarded in favour of more meritorious cases.

The final motoring cases all involve special characteristics of the defendant and are therefore similar to our question. The conflict between *Roberts* and *Mansfield* might give you an opportunity to demonstrate your ability to distinguish between conflicting cases. However, you must note that all three of these cases involve defendants who had dropped below the 'reasonable person' standard, whereas Jack is a person with special characteristics that exceed the 'reasonable person' standard. We will bear this in mind, but these three cases look like they might be appropriate for discussion, bearing in mind that some similarities to our question exist.

The two cases concerning the general legal standard should both be mentioned in your essay. *Glasgow* sets forth the general standard which must be established before you go on to consider special cases and exceptions to the rule, so it (or something like it) must be included. *Parkinson* recognises the special facts of our case – that there is an emergency situation – and so constitutes one of the broad exceptions to the general rule.

There are many other potential cases involving special skill and professional standards, but the four listed here will give you an opportunity to show off your creative legal skills. The *Philips* case and the *Wells* case both discuss whether someone will be held to a higher standard of care than that of the reasonable person. Although neither case involves someone with special skills – in fact, both cases involve defendants with ordinary skills – they are relevant because they discuss whether someone has held himself or herself out as having extraordinary skills. That will become relevant as we consider whether Jack has held himself out as being a driver of particular skill and thus should be held to that standard. *Bolam* and *Bolitho* are good cases for discussion because they both involve defendants with greater than ordinary skill. The cases are not precisely on point because they have to do with what was a reasonable professional act in the context of conflicting professional opinion. However, the question will arise whether Jack – like the defendants in those two cases – was operating as a professional at the time of the accident. This will go back to the 'holding oneself out as a person of exceptional skill' point in *Philips* and *Wells*, as well as to the context of the discussion in *Bolam* and *Bolitho*.

If we consider the final list of law that we are going to discuss, we come up with, in order of priority:

- *Glasgow* and *Parkinson*; reference to *Clerk & Lindsell*
- *Philips*, *Wells*, *Bolam* and *Bolitho*
- *Roberts*, *Mansfield* and *Nettleship*
- Law Reform (Contributory Negligence) Act 1945 and *Froom*

We could discuss the cases in slightly different order than they are presented here – for example, the motoring cases might be introduced before the expert and professional skill cases – but we should remember that the motoring cases do not have as many discussion points as the expert and professional skill cases. Therefore, even if we discuss the motoring cases first, we will not spend much time on them.

You will also see that out of this simple question, given early on in the course syllabus, we have come up with ten cases, a treatise reference and a statute to discuss. This number of citations is about right, even for a timed essay. As you will see, several of the references are made only in passing. The bulk of the discussion will focus on four to six cases. None of the cases is especially arcane, and several appear in different parts of the tort syllabus, so your learning will be reinforced by constant cross-referencing. Remember, doing well in law essays and examinations is not about knowing more law than everyone else: it is about how you present and argue the sources that you have.

It is important to remember that there is no 'magic number' of authorities that you should discuss in the 'L' step. Some examiners may prefer more authorities (if the examiner places a high premium on issue-spotting) and some may prefer less (if the examiner constructs his or her questions to focus tightly on one particular case). However, four to six authorities would appear to be a good starting point for a solid, meaty discussion.

EXAM TIP

Ask your examiners whether they prefer you to focus your discussion narrowly on fewer cases or give a more expansive answer, covering more issues. Be prepared for an evasive answer – examiners may not know how to describe what they want. Also be prepared for different examiners to have different preferences.

4.5.4 Writing your response

DRAFT ANSWER (first paragraph)

The question at issue is whether Jack is liable to the claimant for the tort of negligence. To establish a claim in negligence, the claimant must prove the existence of a duty, breach of that duty, causation (including both legal foreseeability and 'but for' causation) and damages (*Clerk & Lindsell on Torts*, s 7-04). Of those four elements, the claimant in our question will have the most trouble establishing that there was an existing breach and a breach of that duty, with the particular emphasis on what the appropriate standard of care is.

> *This is the 'claim', as defined in chapter three.*

> *These are the general elements of negligence.*

> *This sentence introduces the contentious sub-issues, which arise out of the claimant's prima facie case.*

We have now set up the framework of our response quickly and concisely. We have wasted no time and no words on rhetorical flourishes or repetition of the facts. While the language may not seem as elegant as that of a literature or history student, it is effective, powerful and clear. After three sentences and two minutes of writing, you are now ready to begin discussing the most important part of your essay: the law concerning the contentious sub-issues.

> *Note that you have already introduced the general elements of negligence, so you can start with the sub-issues.*

DRAFT ANSWER ('L' section)

According to *Glasgow Corp v Muir*, the legal standard relating to duty of care is that of the reasonable man (person), taking into account the circumstances of the case. *Parkinson v Liverpool Corp* stated that people should not be held to the same standard of behaviour in an emergency as in ordinary circumstances.

What constitutes a 'reasonable person' may depend on whether the defendant has any expert skill and whether that person holds him or herself out as having that expert skill. *Philips v William Whiteley Ltd* involved a jeweller who was doing ear-piercing work who was not held to the same standard as a doctor, since the jeweller did not advertise himself as a doctor. *Wells v Cooper* involved a DIYer who was not held to the standard of care of a professional carpenter, but merely to that of a reasonably competent person doing that sort of domestic job. Notably, both these cases involve the question of whether to hold a defendant with ordinary skill to a higher standard rather than the other way around.

> *Use gender-neutral language when you can.*

continues

The author thought of this idea after beginning to write the essay. You could include citations for this sentence, if you wish and if you remember them.

DRAFT ANSWER ('L' section) continued

These cases may be compared to other cases where the defendant had a higher degree of skill than the ordinary person. *Bolam v Friern Hospital Management Committee* states that doctors need only act in conformity with a responsible body of opinion. The *Bolam* test for professional conduct has been extended to other professionals, such as accountants or solicitors. *Bolitho v City and Hackney Health Authority* states that professionals are not permitted to act in any way they wish: instead, the court will intervene if the body of opinion relied on by the defendant as justifying his or her action has no logical basis whatsoever.

Depending on how fast you write, you may decide to stop here. You have included legal support for your major points and could go on to evaluate the law (the 'E' in CLEO) in light of the facts of your case if you wanted. The next chapter will discuss how to apply the law to the facts of your question. As you will see, certain 'legal' statements can be made in that section as well. If you write quickly, though, you could go on to introduce a few more of your less-important cases.

DRAFT ANSWER ('L' section – optional)

Drivers are held to the same 'reasonable person' standard as workers and professionals. *Nettleship v Weston* involved a learner driver who was still held to the standard of a reasonably competent driver, despite the fact that the claimant in that case (her instructor) knew that she was only learning. *Roberts v Ramsbottom* is another motoring case which involved a defendant who had a stroke while driving. He was held to be negligent, although the defendant in *Mansfield v Weetabix Ltd* (whose hypoglycaemia also caused an accident) was held not negligent. These somewhat contradictory outcomes can be explained by reference to the latter decision (*Mansfield*), which suggested it was inappropriate to hold a defendant liable for an essentially involuntary act. Victims of tortious negligence may sometimes find their damages award reduced if they were contributorily negligent in some way (Contributory Negligence (Law Reform) Act 1945; *Froom v Butcher*).

There are lots of cases on contributory negligence. What is good about citing Froom *here is that it is a motoring case. These are certain legal principles that can be supported by numerous cases. Try to find the best case and use it.*

The best case will either be:

- *the leading case (first precedent or highest court);*
- *the most specific case (meaning it has the most precise and complete legal language); or*
- *the most factually similar case.*

Notice how the discussion sometimes includes brief reference to the facts of the case cited and sometimes states nothing more than the legal rationale. A slightly higher number of facts may be necessary when, as with the expert and professional skill cases, you will be discussing whether or not conflicting cases apply to your problem question. Pure statements of law are more appropriate to instances where there is no dispute about the applicability or boundaries of the law (for example, the reasonable person standard or the statements regarding contributory negligence).

Notice also how the essay relies on succinct statements of the law and does not make judgments about the state of the law or discuss the facts of the question. Those discussions are more appropriate in the third step of the CLEO method, which will be discussed in the next chapter.

The organisational style is simple. Begin with the general rule associated with the claim, then move to the general rule associated with the sub-issues. Here we had only one real sub-issue, but if you look at the worked examples in chapter ten, you will see how to handle multiple sub-issues. Next, set up your specific exceptions to the rule and any cases you need to distinguish. You can categorise your case law by facts or by areas of law, as we have here. Possible defences usually come at the end of your discussion. If you are discussing a line of cases, try to relate your later, more specific cases to your more general standard. That makes your discussion look more cohesive and less like a list of cases and holdings.

WRITING TIP

When discussing the law, begin with the most general point and become increasingly more specific.

EXAM TIP

Don't forget to include a discussion of exceptions and defences to the general rule.

You now have a basic understanding of how to approach the 'L' step in the CLEO method. For a further discussion of how to handle this step in 'discuss' type questions, see chapter seven. In those instances, you may rely more heavily on persuasive sources of law, since you may be discussing the theoretical propriety of a certain reform movement or contextualising a certain public policy position, but you will still need to refer to binding sources of law and prioritise your arguments, as we have here. For more worked examples of both problem questions and 'discuss' questions, see chapter ten. We will now move to the third step in the CLEO method, namely the evaluation of law in light of the facts.

CHAPTER 5

Step three in the CLEO method: the evaluation

The preceding chapter discussed how to identify the law in the CLEO method of legal essay writing and how to present it in a concise and logical manner. Thus far, you have not made explicit reference to the facts of the case but have instead focused on stating the claim and the relevant sub-issues and setting forth the applicable legal authorities. Now, in the third part of your essay, you can begin to bring the specific facts of your question into your essay. This is also the section where you can demonstrate some originality in your thinking and writing style, since this is where you attempt to persuade the reader of your argument. Although the 'L' portion of the essay is, in many ways, the most important, in that it demonstrates your knowledge of the materials presented during your course, the 'E' portion comes a close second, since a properly written evaluation of the facts in light of the law demonstrates your legal judgment. Remember, in a problem question you are being asked to think about the question as if you were a barrister, and a barrister would not be giving proper legal advice if he or she merely identified the leading cases and statutes for a client and left it at that. The client would not know how to interpret that information and how it would apply in his or her case. A barrister's job is not only to find the relevant information but to explain how it relates to the problem affecting the client. Explaining the importance of each of the legal authorities is particularly necessary since many of the same materials will be used by the barrister's opponent to argue precisely the opposite outcome.

> **NOTE**
>
> To excel on a law exam or essay one must show both knowledge (ie recollection of the law) and judgment (ie the ability to apply and analyse the law).

Therefore, practising lawyers must evaluate the facts in light of the relevant law if they are to carry out their duties to their clients properly. The same is true in an academic course. To carry out your 'duty', for lack of a better word, to your reader properly, you must indicate both what law applies to the question and how it applies. Both elements – law and evaluation – are necessary if you wish to earn top marks.

To implement the third step of CLEO properly, you must understand:

(1) what 'evaluation' means under the CLEO system;

(2) the need for evaluation in legal writing;

(3) how to distinguish 'evaluation' from the 'law' in the CLEO system; and

(4) various stylistic and practical issues concerning the evaluation of the facts in light of the law.

Each of these points will be discussed in turn.

5.1 What constitutes 'evaluation' under the CLEO method

The third step of your CLEO analysis requires you to apply the law to the facts of your case, although you could think of it, conversely, as applying the facts to the law. Either way, you must demonstrate the connection between the law you have presented and the facts in the question. In the 'L' step of the CLEO analysis, you set forth the general legal standard that exists outside any particular fact scenario. Although you were not writing a mini-treatise on the law, in the sense that you were not merely listing the legal principles that exist in a certain area without any regard to how those principles would eventually apply to your case, you were providing an objective analysis of the standards that apply to all persons and situations. However, you were careful to tailor your analysis to your particular fact scenario by introducing only those cases and statutes that were relevant to the question you were answering. As you progressed through your discussion, you weighed up any competing authorities and came to some sort of conclusion about how a court would decide any particular issue, as a matter of law. Of course, you could not come to any final conclusions about the outcome of your particular problem, since you had not yet introduced any facts particular to your question. The factual analysis relates to the third step of the essay framework. However, because you went through all four steps of the CLEO analysis in the planning stages, you knew, in your mind, why you were introducing each case and statute.

It is in the 'E' step of your essay that you make your thoughts about the relevance of your legal sources explicitly known. Remember, examiners cannot award you marks for your thinking unless you put your thoughts down on paper; examiners do not have access into your inner mind. Many students are convinced, at the time of writing, that their arguments are clear and easy to follow. Very often, they are not. Walk your reader through each step of your

WRITING TIP

Although the 'L' step of your CLEO essay is objective in tone and content, you still need to (1) weigh up any conflicting precedents as you go and (2) anticipate what you will say in the 'E' step of the essay.

WRITING TIP

You cannot go wrong by being too clear in your writing.

analysis. You may feel as if you are being incredibly obvious, but it is virtually impossible to be too clear.

What connections must you draw between the facts and the law when you undertake an evaluation in the CLEO system? Essentially, you must explain how your facts do or do not live up to the objective standard identified in the 'L' step. The evaluation stage is where you use logic and common sense to argue your position. As you recall, arguing on the basis of logic and common sense was discouraged in chapter four, primarily because logic and common sense do not constitute binding principles under the law. Legal precedent, in either case law or statutory form, is what is important when you are defining the legal standard. Now, however, you have an objective basis upon which to build your arguments regarding how these particular parties are situated under the law.

For example, in the 'L' stage of an essay on defamation, you would have stated that publication of the allegedly defamatory material must be proven as part of the claimant's *prima facie* case. You would have gone on to define, with appropriate references to relevant legal materials, what constitutes publication under the law. You then would have moved on to introduce the next issue, sub-issue or claim. Now, in the 'E' stage of the essay, you are in a position to state how and why the defendant's actions constitute publication. In some cases, the analysis is simple: for example, if the defendant, Jim, wrote 'Felix embezzles the company's money' on a piece of paper and stood on the street, handing photocopies to passers-by, you would have few problems proving publication. When it comes time to evaluate this particular aspect of the defamation claim, you would simply need to note how the act falls under the definition of 'publication' and move on.

The facts can be slightly more problematic. Suppose, for example, that Jim is in the middle of photocopying the defamatory statement when a fire alarm goes off. What if he runs out of the building, leaving the copy in the machine? You would have noted in the 'L' portion of your essay that publication exists in the eyes of the law if it ought to have been foreseen. Is publication here foreseeable? Possibly. You can argue it either way. What if Jim had an inordinate, unusual and unreasonable fear of fires which caused him not only to run out of the building in a panic as soon as he heard the alarm but to his refusing to re-enter the premises, even after the fire marshals gave the all clear? Would that constitute 'negligent publication'? What if the paper jammed in the machine just as the fire alarm went off and he was pulled out of the building by a colleague as he tried to clear the jam? You see how the facts may vary, but the legal standard of negligence remains the same. You may or may not have cases that help describe what constitutes negligence, but at a certain point you will have to decide

> **✳ NOTE**
>
> Do NOT introduce these types of hypothetical events into your answer in an attempt to demonstrate your legal judgment. Work only with the facts you have been given.

whether a particular fact falls under the legal definition of negligence or not. Although this series of bizarre fact scenarios may look odd out of context, examiners do their best to concoct something unusual so that you can discuss how and why Jim's acts do or do not constitute publication. While the examiners are testing your ability to identify the relevant legal standard when they set you a question, they are also testing your ability to judge whether the facts fall within that standard. These are two separate skills in the examiners' minds, which provides yet another reason why you should break your discussion into two separate sections dealing with the law and the evaluation. It also explains why you must be explicit about your evaluation of the question: it is the only way you can demonstrate the legal judgment that the examiners want to see.

Despite these admonitions, you still have a great deal of freedom in how you construct your argument. As will be discussed further in the next chapter, your final decision about the outcome is, in most cases, nowhere near as important as how you arrived at that answer. Students who are trained in the sciences will appreciate this notion, since they are used to receiving marks for the manner in which their responses are constructed, even if the final answer is incorrect as a matter of simple arithmetic (due to simple errors such as forgetting to carry the one, for example) or other minor technical mistakes. The same idea applies in law: what is important is how you arrived at your answer, not what the final answer itself is.[1] If the study of law simply involved the determination of a single, objectively correct answer, then there would be no need for essays: a single sentence ('Jim is liable') would be sufficient. However, you know that if you submitted a single sentence like that in an exam scenario, not only would you fail to win top marks, you would most likely fail to win even a simple pass mark, even if the examiner agreed with your conclusion. Therefore, you must admit that how you arrive at your final answer is as – if not more – important than the final answer itself.

Sometimes the evaluation step involves the straightforward determination of whether a particular act falls within the legal standard established in the second section of the essay, as described in the preceding paragraph. Other times, you may have two conflicting cases

EXAM TIP

A lot of examiners look to real life for inspiration. Keep up to date with current events if you want to do well on an exam.

EXAM TIP

There is typically no simple, single 'right' answer in law. Why you conclude as you do is more important than what you conclude. The 'E' step is the 'why' of your analysis.

---

[1] There are exceptions to this general rule, of course. For example, if your facts gave you a person who drove a motor vehicle to the pub on a dark and stormy night, knowing that the tail-lights were faulty, it would be difficult to argue successfully that the person was not at least negligent when an accident arising out of the faulty tail-lights occurred on the way to the pub.

which you have had to harmonise or distinguish in the 'L' section of your essay. You will have drafted that portion of your discussion with an eye to your facts, anticipating how you were going to handle a fact pattern that either puts you halfway between the two cases or squarely under the less attractive outcome. Sometimes you can weigh up the competing authorities in the 'L' section and indicate which way the court will rule, as a matter of law. Your evaluation will be much easier if you can come to this sort of legal conclusion. However, there may be times where it is impossible to come to a definite conclusion about the state of the law (for example, if the cases are utterly irreconcilable, a situation that occurs far less often in practice than students think). If that happens, you may want to wait to resolve the conflict until the evaluation section. Once you get into the fact discussion, you can argue that your problem is much more similar to one of the two lines of cases and that you anticipate the court will adopt that approach for reasons X, Y and Z. When your facts fall halfway between the two lines of established cases, you must state why your facts are more similar to one of the two conflicting cases. Hopefully, you have also been able to argue in the 'L' section of the essay that the same line of cases is better or more likely to control as a matter of law. However, you must always acknowledge the extent to which your facts resemble the troubling cases or the extent to which your facts fall outside the general standard.

> **NOTE**
>
> You mustn't ignore troubling precedent. Addressing it head-on is your best bet.

Persuasive legal argument is not the same as ignoring difficult precedent; instead, a good argument anticipates rebuttal and proposes a solution that is in keeping with your preferred outcome. If you fail to indicate the merits of an opposing argument, you are throwing away an opportunity to dismantle it.

When your facts place you squarely under a legal precedent that you don't like or don't intuitively feel is correct, you can try to argue for another outcome, based on persuasive law (relying, for example, on a case that has been overruled, but on distinguishable grounds, or referring to a case that has been decided in another jurisdiction), but you must realise that you are arguing for an extension and/or alteration of the law. While this is appropriate at times (without extensions or alterations, the common law would stagnate), it is not the same thing as arguing that a certain set of facts falls under an established legal standard. If you argue for a change in the law, you should show, in the 'L' section of your essay, that such a move would be possible as a matter of law (for example, to fill a gap in existing law) and then argue in the 'E' section that your current fact pattern gives good reason for that extension. 'Good reason', in this context, means persuasive public policies (and, as stated in chapter four, you need to enunciate precisely which public policy is at issue) or cognisable concepts of justice or fairness. Be aware that arguments based on such ideals can become very woolly, so use care and tie your statements to established legal principles as often and as closely as possible. For example, if you are arguing in tort that reasons of fairness and justice should establish a duty of care in a novel situation, be sure to reference *Caparo Industries plc v Dickman*[2] and the principles outlined therein for extending a duty into new areas of law.

WRITING TIP

Sometimes you can't find a conclusive reason to dismiss an opposing argument. In that case, you can say that you simply believe the opposing argument is not as persuasive as your own. Use this device sparingly, though, since you are trusting that your reader's sense of fairness corresponds with your own – something which cannot be guaranteed in all cases.

Even if you take advantage of all of these techniques, there will be times when your analysis leads you to conclusions or outcomes with which you disagree. You may not think it is fair for a particular claimant to lose or a particular defendant to be found liable. Double-check your work, by all means, and make sure that you have identified all the possible legal authorities and made the proper evaluations. Cases often turn out the way we would expect or want them to. However, you need to realise that sometimes a worthy party will not prevail. The law does not remedy all ills. Don't distort the evaluative process just so that you arrive at a conclusion that satisfies you. Use your intuition as a back-up resource, but don't try to follow your instincts in every situation. Examiners commonly set questions that intentionally tug at your heart strings. Don't let yourself fall into those traps.

Chapter four admonished you not to argue the facts but instead to argue the law. Hopefully, you are now beginning to see the difference between the two techniques. When you argue the law and then evaluate the facts in light of the law, you are building your argument on an objective foundation. Although you use logic and common sense to ascertain whether the facts fall under the legal standards, you are not basing your entire argument on those kinds of nebulous concepts: every argument you make has its roots in the legal principles that you set forth in the second step of your essay. You may sometimes have to argue by analogy, particularly when your fact pattern falls into a

> ✳ **NOTE**
>
> Listen to your gut instinct, but don't let it control your legal judgment.

---

[2] [1990] 2 AC 605.

gap between two conflicting lines of cases, but you will still base your position on the legal authority that you have previously identified.

When you argue the facts, you skip the discussion of legal principles and go straight to the facts of the case, often arguing that reasons of justice, fairness, morality or public policy require a certain outcome. Sometimes you are quite clear in your mind about what the law is, which is why you go straight to the facts. Your intention is laudable, since you want to show the examiner how the situation works out in your particular scenario, but in skipping over the detailed discussion of the legal authorities, you miss out the important step of establishing what the law is. It may be that your unspoken position is absolutely correct; however, the examiner can't read your mind and can't know the assumptions on which you are operating. More importantly, the examiner can't award points for something that is not written on the paper. When you jump ahead of yourself and start discussing the facts before discussing the law, you also run the risk that your unspoken understanding of the law is only partially correct, in which case your analysis will be faulty or one-sided. Something about writing down the law, by itself, without any explicit consideration of the facts (though they are always in the back of your mind, since you know better than to introduce cases or statutes that have no bearing on your particular question) gives structure to your thoughts. Jumping straight into the facts often leads to emotive or muddy thinking. The first idea that comes to you might not reflect the best approach to the question. Therefore, the CLEO method suggests that you evaluate the facts after you have presented the law, leaving questions of logic, justice and common sense until late in the day. In so doing, you will find that many questions can be answered satisfactorily without recourse to inherently ambiguous concepts such as morality or public policy. Since questions of law are always a stronger basis for argument than questions of fairness or justice (since law is assumed to be more objective than morality, a statement that is open to dispute), try to frame your response in terms of the law.

5.2 The need for evaluation in legal writing

Once students become accustomed to the CLEO system, they sometimes become enamoured of the 'L' step and begin to short-change the 'E' step. Their philosophy seems to be that the reader knows that the law would not be presented if it did not apply to the question and that, therefore, to analyse the facts in light of the law is repetitive and belabours the point.

While this approach shows an admirable reverence for legal authority, remember that an objective presentation of the law, without more, is nothing but a narrowly focused treatise. While your discussion of the law should make sense on its own and should be placed in the kind of context that suggests how the materials will be used in the evaluation section, a well-written 'L' section does not eliminate the need for a well-written 'E' section. Remember the example of the barrister set out at the beginning of this chapter: a practising lawyer cannot just present his or her client with a list of legal authorities and consider it sufficient legal advice. The barrister must explain how and why those authorities are relevant to the question at hand. You must do the same thing in your essays and examinations. No matter how clear and obvious the link between the law and the facts is in your mind, you must connect the dots for the examiner, for several reasons. First, your 'L' section may not be as clear as you think it is. Often an examiner can see that a student is trying to make a point, but that point is submerged beneath the surface of the essay – a kind of 'submarine' argument. Be explicit. Spell things out. No essay has ever been marked down for being too clear.

Second, you must evaluate the facts in light of the cases and statutes you have presented earlier in your essay, because law can be considered akin to an applied science. Although legal principles can be studied and learned in the abstract, they cannot be divorced from real life. Indeed, problem questions mimic the kind of questions practitioners face on a daily basis. Law becomes relevant only when it is placed in its social context. Therefore, you must make every analysis individual by relating it to the question asked.

Finally, almost any fact pattern can be read in several different lights. What appears obvious to you as requiring one outcome will not seem so to another person. As strange and as wrong-headed as it may seem, people really do take different views of the same set of facts. When you hear two lawyers arguing a point in court or in a mooting competition, it is not just that they are asked to take different sides; they may actually believe in their positions just as much as you believe in yours. Certainly their clients do. Therefore, when answering a question, you cannot assume that others will follow your unspoken train of thought, nor can you assume that others will be persuaded by the same things by which you are persuaded. One of the great misconceptions in life is that everyone thinks as we do. Rather than hope that your reader is one of the few people who shares your beliefs and values, you should rely on citing influential legal authority and crafting detailed, logical arguments to persuade your reader of the wisdom of your perspective.

The evaluation step carries an objective element to it, in that you are discussing how certain aspects of the problem relate to the legal points you have made in the preceding sections of your essay. Your

WRITING TIP

Don't engage in 'submarine' arguments. Bring your thoughts to the surface of your essay.

NOTE

Don't assume that everyone sees the problem in the same light you do. They don't!

goal is to demonstrate either that (1) each element of the claimant's *prima facie* case can be sustained by reference to the fact pattern or (2) some element of the *prima facie* case can be defeated, because it either (a) fails to rise to the legal standard set forth in the 'L' section of the essay or (b) falls victim to a defence asserted by the defendant. Sometimes the question will direct you to take the perspective of one of the parties ('Advise Company A regarding its liability.'). Sometimes you will discuss the case more generally. As stated before, in both situations you must consider both the viability of the claims asserted as well as any defences that can be brought to bear.

Evaluation also carries a certain element of advocacy to it as well. Though you should not identify so closely with your 'client's' case that you ignore arguments and facts that support your opponent's point of view, you can frame the argument in a way that shows your perspective in the best light. Advocacy includes downplaying facts or cases that go against you – downplaying, mind, not ignoring – by minimising their importance or demonstrating how and why they do not apply in your case.

Recall the defamation example from above, where the person was photocopying the defamatory material when the fire alarm went off and was pulled away from the machine. If you decided that liability should result, you would argue that the Defamation Act 1996, while not stating specifically that defamation was a strict liability tort, does take a very strict line against those who are involved in the publication of defamatory material. Cases that allow liability to attach, even when the publication was merely foreseeable, would appear to provide legal support for this line of argument. When it came time for you to evaluate your individual facts, you would emphasise that the defendant intended to publish the material and was taking steps to do so. The fact that the actual publication came earlier than the defendant intended is irrelevant, since the Defamation Act's tough stance on liability suggests that the defendant should run the risk of any negligence once the course of action is begun.

If you thought that the defendant should not be liable, you would present the same statutes and case law, but would, in your legal discussion, emphasise the element of personal culpability in both. Although negligence refers to a very low level of personal fault, there is still some determination that the actor morally 'deserves' to be held liable – ie responsible – as a matter of law. When it came time for you to evaluate your individual facts, you would point to the defendant's attempt to retain the defamatory material and note that it was the act of a third party – the officious colleague – that actually caused the publication, since that person pulled the defendant away from the machine before the paper jam could be cleared. You could refer to the mechanical reproduction exemption in section 1(3) of the 1996 Act to justify your reading of the Act as failing to attach strict liability on an unknowing or unwilling party. Because the defendant did not intend publication at this time (and thus could have changed his mind before publication, even if he had the requisite intent to publish the material when he was pulled away from the photocopier) and took affirmative steps to avoid publication at the time the fire alarm went off (and thus was non-negligent), liability should not attach. The facts are the same in both examples, but it is your construction of their relative importance that makes the difference. Notice that neither example relied on the existence of additional or hypothetical facts; both analyses proceeded on the information contained in the original fact scenario.

5.3 Distinguishing evaluation from the law in the CLEO method

Some people naturally see the difference between law and evaluation, whereas others have difficulty either distinguishing between the two or trusting that an entire section of an essay can be written without reference to the facts. If you remember that the 'L' step of your essay relates to the binding legal standard applicable in the matter at hand, and if you organise the law in a logical manner – beginning with more general statements and then narrowing your focus with greater precision to address the specific area that will be important in your case – then you will have fewer difficulties in leaving consideration of the facts until after you have completed the discussion of the law. In the 'E' step, you build on the information given in the second stage of the essay to explain how those cases and statutes affect the situation at hand. You will need to refer to the materials cited, but without repeating all that you have said before. Similarly, you will need to refer to the facts in the question, but without repeating everything said there. Your goal is to tie the relevant statement of law together with the relevant statement of fact so that you can justify the outcome you will propose in the final step of the CLEO analysis.

To some people, it may seem preferable to introduce the facts at the same time you introduce the law, since that would appear to be more concise and logical. As will be discussed below, separating the 'L' step from the 'E' step can sometimes lead to unnecessary repetition. In the beginning, however, you should try to keep your legal analysis separate from your factual analysis, simply because it is more likely that you, as a student, will short-change your discussion of the law if you don't make a concerted effort to stick only to the law in the second portion of your essay. It is very easy to fall into the trap of arguing the facts,

WRITING TIP

Be rigorous about separating the law and the facts, especially at first. What may seem odd initially quickly becomes second nature.

rather than the law, especially in the early stages of your studies, when you are still learning how to read and analyse the materials. Once you get used to the presentation of the law on its own, the discussion will look less sterile, particularly as you learn how to shape your discussion of the legal principles to foreshadow your discussion of the facts. As discussed in chapter nine, some practising lawyers like to blend their discussion of law and facts, but they are more likely to separate the two sections, as suggested here. Once you get used to the method, you may even start to think that any combination of law and facts in the legal standards section of an essay appears messy and unprofessional.

The key benefit to separating out the facts from the law is that it allows you to parse out the finer nuances of your legal argument. If you mix your discussion of law with your analysis of the facts, you can forget to point out why one line of cases should control as a matter of law in your enthusiasm to show why the facts fall under that line of cases and not under another series of decisions. You could also fail to see a gap in the existing law and, as a result, miss an opportunity to introduce the work of a legal commentator who has written in that area. It's therefore best if you try to separate the two analyses, at least until you are well versed in presenting a full discussion of the relevant legal authorities.

Some students, in an attempt to split the difference, introduce the evaluation step immediately after the law for any particular sub-issue has been introduced, leading to an organisational structure resembling the mnemonic CLELELEO. If well done, that approach can be as effective as a straight CLEO analysis, but can become repetitive if done in a sloppy manner. Of course, if you are not careful, the demon of excess repetition can rear its ugly head no matter what organisational approach you use. Students who use a CLELELEO approach also run the risk of arguing the facts, rather than the law, particularly if they evaluate each case as soon as it is mentioned. Remember, you want to introduce lines of cases rather than individual cases so that you can demonstrate your skills of legal analysis. Try different techniques to find out what works best for you, but do so only after you have given the regular CLEO method a proper chance.

If you are going to discuss several claimant–defendant pairings and/or several different claims, you should separate out the law for each pairing or claim and follow it with its own evaluation. Remember, as stated in chapter four, you can incorporate previous discussions by reference, thus avoiding the need to repeat points of law or relevant facts. The emphasis here is on incorporation by reference – you must refer to the previous discussion explicitly rather than just assume your reader will know that you mean to apply the same principles in your current discussion. You can provide a single joint outcome at the end of the essay or give the outcome following each claim, whichever suits you best.

WRITING TIP

Separate your 'L' and 'E' steps for each party pairing and each claim. Incorporate prior discussions by reference.

5.4 Stylistic and practical concerns regarding the evaluation step

As mentioned above, you can adapt the CLEO system in several different ways, such as by separating out each individual sub-issue and following it with its own evaluation in a type of CLELELEO approach. However, your biggest stylistic concern will likely relate to how strictly you adhere to the separation of law and evaluation. As you will find, there are times when an overly rigid application of the rule leads to confusion. For example, you may undertake a rigorous analysis of two conflicting cases and feel that to add a short reference to a minor case that relates to your facts but in an almost tangential manner would detract from the power or logic of your discussion of the law. In that case, it's perfectly acceptable to pop the reference to the case into the 'E' section of the essay. This is particularly true if the point you are making regarding the legal aspects is very brief and would have to be repeated nearly verbatim when you referenced the case in the evaluation section.

Similarly, there may be times when an excessively abstract discussion of the law could give the impression that the writer did not have the relevant facts in mind. While you should learn the art of structuring your legal analysis so that the links to your problem are apparent – for example, by highlighting the facts or legal issues in your legal sources which most apply to the question you are answering – some times a quick reference to the facts can be helpful. For example, if your facts raised the issue of whether legal relations were intended in an alleged contract between a married couple and you were discussing *Balfour v Balfour*[3] and *Jones v Padavatton*,[4] you could note that '*Balfour* involved a married couple, as in our fact pattern, whereas *Jones* involved the question of legal relations between a mother and daughter'. Although you are mentioning salient facts, you are focusing on the legal analysis, not on the evaluation of the law in light of the facts. Of course, you would not make the mistake of thinking that *Jones* didn't apply just because it involved a minor factual dissimilarity to the fact pattern under discussion.

However, the basic rule is that you should discuss the facts in the 'E' section of your essay. When it comes time to begin writing that section, don't start with a general recitation of the facts. Instead, just start applying the law that you have already introduced in the preceding section to the facts, beginning with the general principles that must be established to satisfy the claimant's *prima facie* case. For

---

[3] [1919] 2 KB 571.   [4] [1969] 1 WLR 328.

WRITING TIP

Remember to reference cases and/or legal standards explicitly as you evaluate your facts. The link to your earlier discussion may be clear to you, but it may not be clear to your reader.

example, in a different sort of negligence problem, you might focus on the calculation or type of damages. There, you would state that 'the existence of a duty can be established by the fact that drivers have a general duty under *Donoghue*'s neighbour principle not to hit pedestrians, a duty that was breached when A's car hit B. Causation is not at issue, since the damage that occurred was a proximate and foreseeable result of A's action. With respect to the damages, however, …' and then you would go on to discuss the more involved question of whether the type of damages that occurred falls under the general rubric of damages in tort and/or how those damages should be calculated.

Note how quickly you have run through the relevant facts and related them to the legal standard briefly outlined in the 'L' section. Granted, the above example relates to issues which are not in contention and which can be dispensed with summarily, but the same principles hold true even for those issues central to your essay. When you evaluate the facts, you are not repeating the law section, though you can and should reference case or statute names as appropriate. You are identifying which aspects of the facts bear a similarity or dissimilarity to the legal standards introduced in the 'L' section.

However, you should also recognise that those brief evaluative statements cannot be made unless you have already laid out the basic legal principles in the preceding section. If you hadn't done so, the reader would be inclined to ask what *Donoghue*'s neighbour principle is and why damage must be proximate and foreseeable. When you leap straight to the legal conclusions and apply them retrospectively to the facts, you lose an opportunity to discuss the law (and remember, the law is what you have come to university to study) as well as an opportunity to persuade. It is true that you are under time pressure and cannot write on everything in great detail; it may very well be that you do not spend much time discussing *Donoghue* and the basic cases on causation if they are not in contention. However, you should also guard against rushing to the 'E' step too quickly and making conclusory statements of law. While it will take some time to master the technique, just as with any new skill, with practice you should learn how to manage your time and the amount of detail you introduce into your essays.

NOTE

Your 'L' section should be longer than your 'E' section.

During the 'E' portion of your essay, you are, in a sense, justifying the inclusion of every legal reference you have made in the 'L' portion of your essay. If you cannot draw a direct link from a fact to any of the cases and statutes you have mentioned, then reconsider whether you should include that fact in your essay. This is what is meant by having the facts in the back of your head as you write (or, even better, as you plan) the law section of your paper. Of course, the reverse is true as well: do not introduce a case or statute unless it relates to a fact you intend to discuss. If you take the time to think about the evaluation step before you begin writing your essay, then you know that you are introducing each of your cases and statutes for a reason. The 'E' step is when you explain that reason.

Once it comes time to discuss the issues that are primarily in dispute, you may not have to note how the facts fall under the general, leading precedent for that area of law. Instead, you will focus on explaining how the facts apply to the more specific cases that flesh out the bare bones of the general precepts of law. Because you have explained in the 'L' section that these cases are merely more specific manifestations of the general standard, you often can get by without evaluating the facts with reference to the general cases. Alternatively, you might find that you can demonstrate how your facts fall under the general rule, but not the more nuanced cases. This means that the claimant fails to meet the required standard for the *prima facie* case. Use your judgment as you balance what needs to be said versus what can be implied. As stated above, it is dangerous to rely implicitly on an examiner's understanding of your mental processes, but there are times when you do not need to spell out everything.

5.5 Worked example

Having discussed the evaluation step in the abstract, it may now be helpful to put that discussion in context by working through the example we have used in previous chapters.

> **QUESTION**
>
> Jack, a Formula One race car driver, was driving his run-of-the estate car home from his daughter's school, where he had just dropped her off for the day. On the way, he was involved in a road accident. Had he used his expert skill in braking, he could have avoided the accident, although an ordinary driver could not have done so. Is Jack liable for the injuries to the other party?

As you recall, the claim in the above example involves the tort of negligence, while the sub-issues involve breach of the duty of care and what the standard of care is for people with expert skill. The relevant legal standard has been set forth in detail in chapter four. Now you need to evaluate the facts in light of the law you have introduced.

> ✳ **NOTE**
>
> We are building on the same worked example that was discussed in chapters three and four.

5.5.1 Considering your facts

Chapter three suggested that you proceed through the question, line by line, to identify potential claims and sub-issues. While you could use the same procedure to identify those facts that you wish to bring to the examiner's attention, you should have already figured out those facts in your analysis of the claim and sub-issues (see the line-by-line worked example in chapter three). What is most useful at this stage is to track your legal analysis, as described in the second part of your essay, and demonstrate how the facts apply to each of those standards. The presumption, of course, is that you have presented your legal materials in a logical fashion and have anticipated which points are most relevant to your question. If you have not planned out your essay ahead of time, you will find it difficult to track your evaluation along the lines of your legal presentation. If, however, you have taken the time to consider what legal points you wish to make and how those points fit in with the fact pattern before you start writing, you will find that the 'E' portion of your essay writes itself.

To walk through the evaluation analysis, we need to recall the law, as it has been presented in the sample essay. Of course, as noted in chapter four, before you decided which law to present, you took the facts into account.

DRAFT ANSWER ('C' section, with general 'L' reference)

The question at issue is whether Jack is liable to the claimant for the tort of negligence. To establish a claim in negligence, the claimant must prove the existence of a duty, breach of that duty, causation (including both legal foreseeability and 'but for' causation) and damages (*Clerk & Lindsell on Torts*, s 7–04). Of those four elements, the claimant in our question will have the most trouble establishing that there was an existing duty and a breach of that duty, with the particular emphasis on what the appropriate standard of care is.

DRAFT ANSWER ('L' section)

According to *Glasgow Corp v Muir*, the legal standard relating to duty of care is that of the reasonable man (person), taking into account the circumstances of the case. *Parkinson v Liverpool Corp* stated that people should not be held to the same standard of behaviour in an emergency as in ordinary circumstances.

What constitutes a 'reasonable person' may depend on whether the defendant has any expert skill and whether that person holds him or herself out as having that expert skill. *Philips v William Whiteley Ltd* involved a jeweller who was

continues

DRAFT ANSWER ('L' section) continued

doing ear-piercing work who was not held to the same standard as a doctor, since the jeweller did not advertise himself as a doctor. *Wells v Cooper* involved a DIYer who was not held to the standard of care of a professional carpenter, but merely to that of a reasonably competent person doing that sort of domestic job. Notably, both these cases involve the question of whether to hold a defendant with ordinary skill to a higher standard rather than the other way around.

These cases may be compared with other cases where the defendant had a higher degree of skill than the ordinary person. *Bolam v Friern Hospital Management Committee* states that doctors need only act in conformity with a responsible body of opinion. The *Bolam* test for professional conduct has been extended to other professionals, such as accountants or solicitors. *Bolitho v City and Hackney Health Authority* states that professionals are not permitted to act in any way they wish: instead, the court will intervene if the body of opinion relied on by the defendant as justifying his or her action has no logical basis whatsoever.

As you recall from chapter four, you could stop at this point if you run out of time. However, because the CLEO method streamlines your analytical and writing process, you may be able to carry on with the following section.

DRAFT ANSWER ('L' section – optional)

Drivers are held to the same 'reasonable person' standard as workers and professionals. *Nettleship v Weston* involved a learner driver who was still held to the standard of a reasonably competent driver, despite the fact that the claimant in that case (her instructor) knew that she was only learning. *Roberts v Ramsbottom* is another motoring case which involved a defendant who had a stroke while driving. He was held to be negligent, although the defendant in *Mansfield v Weetabix Ltd* (whose hypoglycaemia also caused an accident) was held not negligent. These somewhat contradictory outcomes can be explained by reference to the latter decision (*Mansfield*), which suggested it was inappropriate to hold a defendant liable for an essentially involuntary act.

Victims of tortious negligence may sometimes find their damages award reduced if they were contributorily negligent in some way (Contributory Negligence (Law Reform) Act 1945; *Froom v Butcher*).

To identify which facts you need to discuss, start at the beginning of your law section. In our example, the first paragraph of the essay contains the claim as well as the basic elements needed to establish the tort of negligence. Therefore, you should state in your 'E' analysis how your facts demonstrate the non-contentious issues relating to negligence, ie the existence of a duty (to the extent the existence of a duty does not relate to the standard of care), breach of that duty, causation and damages.

Because the *Glasgow Corp* 'reasonable person' standard is further explained and clarified by *Parkinson*, *Philips* and *Wells*, you should consider all of those cases together when deciding what constitutes a reasonable person in this context. The *Bolam* and *Bolitho* cases further describe the extent to which a skill used in a professional capacity carries over outside of employment. The driving cases are less important than the 'reasonable person' cases, so you should leave those until the end. Similarly, the contributory negligence point should be made briefly and in passing.

5.5.2 Writing your response

Following on from the draft response begun above:

Use a brief introductory sentence to take the reader into the next section. Your reader may not be familiar with CLEO, so you have to explain your essay structure.

Run through the facts relating to the general (non-contentious) elements quickly.

This identifies a factual question that could be determinative. However, the author rightly refuses to hypothesise about the matter.

DRAFT ANSWER ('E' section)

Next, we will evaluate the facts of the current case in light of the law discussed above. First, the existence of a duty can be established by the fact that drivers have a general duty under *Donoghue*'s neighbour principle not to hurt others, a duty that was breached when Jack hit the other party. Causation is not at issue, since the damage that occurred was a proximate and foreseeable result of A's action, nor are damages in dispute. The key question is whether the reasonable person standard under *Glasgow* has been met. The extent to which Jack's acts were the result of an emergency situation (*Parkinson*) would need to be determined further as a matter of fact but could lower the standard sufficiently to relieve Jack of liability.

Jack was not holding himself out as an expert driver at the time of the accident, so, according to *Philips* and *Wells*, should be held to the regular 'reasonable person' standard rather than that of an expert driver. Though *Bolam* and *Bolitho* could seem to go in the opposite direction, since both involved people with expert skill (as opposed to reduced skill, as in *Philips* and *Wells*), both cases involved doctors acting in their professional capacity. Jack here was not acting as a professional driver; therefore, he should not be held to the higher standard of care, since he did not take that duty upon himself or cause others to rely upon it.

It is also questionable whether courts would view Jack as a 'professional' in the same sense as a doctor, lawyer or accountant. A driver might be seen as more of a technician than a professional, and it can therefore be argued

continues

DRAFT ANSWER ('E' section) continued

that *Bolam* and *Bolitho* should not apply and that Jack should be held to the reasonable person standard under *Philips* and *Wells*. In addition, *Bolitho* involved the weighing of a professional body of opinion versus the court's independent evaluation of the propriety of the action. The court's view was held to be controlling if the professional body's opinion was based on unreasonable evidence. It is likely that both the court and any professional drivers' body would, after taking full account of the circumstances of this case (see *Glasgow Corp*), conclude that Jack acted reasonably in the circumstances.

This conclusion is supported by reference to the three motoring cases cited. In those cases, the driver was held to the standard of a reasonable driver, unless the act causing the accident was so completely involuntary as to take it out of the realm of volition (*Mansfield*). In a way, *Mansfield* negated the move towards the type of semi-strict liability demonstrated in *Roberts*. If *Roberts* had been left unchallenged, one might argue that Jack should be held to the higher standard of care as a type of strict liability (ie holding people to the highest standard they had attained as a matter of fact), but that approach is less likely in light of *Mansfield*.

Although the fact pattern does not explicitly raise the question of contributory negligence, Jack will of course argue as part of his defence that any liability that may be established against him should be reduced in accordance with the 1945 Act and *Froom*.

Again, the author avoids hypothesising about contributory or comparative negligence, since the facts don't really support a discussion of such issues. However, it is appropriate to mention possible defences briefly, even if they don't apply, so long as they are not entirely outside the facts. Thus, a brief mention of contributory negligence in the context of a road accident is appropriate, but raising the possibility of self-defence (ie that Jack was fending off some intentional act by the other driver) would not.

You now have a basic understanding of how to approach the 'E' step in the CLEO method. For a further discussion of how to handle this step in 'discuss' type questions, see chapter seven. 'Discuss' questions do not have the same sort of facts that a problem question does, but still require you to pay attention to the particular context of the question and answer it as asked. For more worked examples of both problem and 'discuss' questions, see chapter ten. We will now move to the fourth and final step in the CLEO method, namely the discussion of the outcome of the case.

Step four in the CLEO method: the outcome

The first three steps of the CLEO system are, in many ways, the most important. If you do not properly identify the claim, you cannot present the relevant law, nor can you construct a persuasive argument once it comes time to evaluate the facts in light of the law. The fourth step, which relates to the outcome of your analysis, is the least important element of the essay.

Nevertheless, an essay that fails to provide a conclusion about the arguments made by the parties is incomplete and cannot be given the highest marks. Again, drawing on the litigation analogy, a barrister who discusses the applicable legal authorities and states how those authorities apply to a client's situation, but fails to tell the client how the case is likely to be resolved, cannot be said to have given proper legal advice. Just as a practising lawyer must come to some sort of conclusion about the outcome of the dispute, so too must you.

To implement the fourth step of CLEO properly, you must understand:

(1) what 'outcome' means under the CLEO system; and

(2) the need for an outcome in legal writing.

Both of these points will be discussed in turn.

> ✳ **NOTE**
>
> How you ultimately decide the legal issues in your exam or essay is far less important than how you arrived at your decision.

6.1 What constitutes the 'outcome' in the CLEO method

In the outcome, you indicate how you believe the question would be decided by a court. All legal advice – whether it is given in the context of a contentious matter or a non-contentious matter – revolves around how a court would resolve the issue, since courts are the ultimate arbiters of legal disputes in the UK. While it is true that courts take their lead from Parliament, when two individuals (or an individual and the state) disagree about a particular course of action, it is the courts, rather than the legislature, that decide who is right and who is wrong. Therefore, when you are faced with a problem question, you must anticipate how a court will act in response to that question. Part of the question may ask you how you might reform the law, in which case you can consider the issue from the point of view of Parliament. For the most part, however, you should look at the outcome as if you were a judge.

What constitutes the outcome in a CLEO essay depends to some extent on what you have said in your earlier discussion. Parts one, two and three of your essay required you to consider all of the relevant law and facts. Because you have already explicitly discussed both the facts and the law, you do not need to summarise either in the 'O' step of your essay. What you do need to do is tie up loose ends and come to a final determination about which part of the preceding argument controls the disposition of the case, to the extent you have not already done so. For example, during the 'L' and 'E' portions of your discussion, you indicated how much weight you would give to each aspect of your argument and whether the individual facts fulfilled the requirements needed to establish the claimant's *prima facie* case. In that sense, you have already carried out the necessary analysis for determining the outcome. Further discussion is unnecessary except to make the final determination absolutely clear.

Therefore, the 'O' step in a CLEO essay is very different than a conclusion in an A-level essay. In other academic subjects, you use a concluding paragraph to tie the threads of your argument together and put the argument into context, perhaps by repeating your main themes or indicating why one particular piece of evidence should be determinative. A CLEO outcome, on the other hand, simply clarifies which party has ultimately prevailed. That result should be apparent from your earlier discussions, since your essay should have been tightly constructed. However, it is good practice for you to get into the habit of concluding your essay with a single sentence stating the resolution of the dispute, for two reasons. First, examiners want to see a clear conclusion at the end of an essay. The outcome may be implicit in your earlier discussion – or indeed even explicit at some point – but it will not hurt to add the words 'On these facts, the claimant will prevail and will receive damages in X amount' at the end of your essay. Second, your 'L' and 'E' discussions may not make the outcome as clear as you think it is. In the heat of the moment, it is very easy to think that you have said something when in fact you have only thought of saying it. Take the time to make your essay completely circular by indicating who will win.

Your description of the outcome can and should be quite brief. As will be discussed in chapter nine, which deals with legal writing

> **NOTE**
> You must decide the issue presented, one way or another. Waffling is not 'being lawyerly'.

> **NOTE**
> A CLEO conclusion is much shorter than a conclusion in an A-level essay.

in professional practice, some practitioners set forth their legal arguments in great detail and then conclude their court submissions with the simple phrase, 'For the aforementioned reasons, [my client] should prevail.' That is the type of brevity to which you should aspire. As demonstrated in the worked example below, you can, in many cases, conclude your CLEO essay with a one-sentence paragraph stating which party prevails. Why that party prevails has already been demonstrated in the 'L' and, to an even greater extent, the 'E' portions of your discussion. Therefore, you need not repeat those reasons in the 'O' step.

The one exception to the rule of brevity is if your 'L' and 'E' steps contain a lot of sophisticated and complex arguments that make it difficult (as a matter of substance or style) for you to weigh up the opposing strands in that portion of the essay. In that case, the essay might be better served by discussing or recapping the weight of the various points in the final paragraph. For example, if you have a checklist of six attributes that define whether a particular act is 'fair and reasonable', and your evaluation of the facts demonstrates that two attributes exist and four do not, you may want to note in your final paragraph that because Judge So-and-So required all six elements to exist prior to a determination that the defendant was liable, and only two elements (ie X and Y) could be proven, the defendant could not therefore be held liable for the damages claimed. If Judge So-and-So did not require all six elements to exist, but merely stated that a court should consider those elements in considering whether a defendant could be found liable, then you could spend slightly more time and indicate why X and Y either should or should not outweigh the four elements that were not proven. In both cases, the closing paragraph will be slightly longer than a single sentence but will still not attempt to summarise (in the sense of repeating) the preceding paragraphs. Nevertheless, you should try to keep your discussion quite brief, since the bulk of your analysis will already exist in the 'L' and 'E' sections of your essay.

Another example of when you need to write a longer concluding paragraph is when your 'E' step suggests that there is not enough factual information to come to a reasoned conclusion or when your 'L' step suggests that the state of the law is either too close to call or not determinative of the particular question. Both circumstances are extremely – repeat, extremely – rare. In the first place, an examiner will seldom create a fact pattern question that does not contain all the necessary information. An incomplete question yields problematic answers, and an examiner wants to give students every opportunity to show off their learning. In the second place, an examiner will seldom create a fact pattern question that cannot be resolved as a matter of

WRITING TIP

Most outcomes can be summed up in a single sentence. Only a few cannot.

law, first because it is impossible to create a problem that is so evenly balanced and second because every legal dispute must be decided one way or another. Litigation is a zero-sum game: it does not allow for ties. Scottish courts allow for criminal verdicts of 'not proven', but even those decisions grant victory, of a sort, to the defendant.

If you come to the conclusion that you do not have sufficient facts or the law is too evenly balanced to suggest an outcome, check your analysis again. You may be missing something or you may not be weighing up the evidence or the legal authorities as well as you first imagined. Nevertheless, if you do conclude that a straightforward outcome is impossible, say that the case cannot be decided without additional facts (which you should identify generally) or that the legal position is too complex or too much in a state of flux for you to suggest an outcome. Do not hesitate to make a decision just because you think it is wrong or unpopular. The examiner will prefer you to make some sort of decision, even if it is different from the decision he or she would make. Being a lawyer is all about using your best professional judgment. Even experienced lawyers can end up being wrong, in the sense that the court may disagree with their analyses, but clients still need to know what their lawyers think the outcome will be. Similarly, a trial judge cannot throw up his or her hands and say the matter is too close to call; a decision must be made once a dispute makes it into court.[1] It may be that the trial judgment will be overturned on appeal, but the court of first instance must come to a reasoned decision. You are in the same position. Make the best judgment you can, if at all possible.

As has been mentioned before, your actual decision about the outcome of the dispute is not as important as how you get there. As you recall from your A-level and GCSE studies, student mathematicians get credit for how they work out a problem, even if they produce the wrong number in the end because of an arithmetical error. The same is true for student lawyers; you will still get credit for how you analyse the problem, even if you reach a different outcome than the examiner would. The exception, of course, is if you attempt to rewrite the law with no legitimate basis for doing so, such as by claiming that a trial court need not adhere to principles set down by the Supreme Court (formerly the House of Lords), since the concept of *stare decisis* is nonsensical and outmoded. Since you will not be making these sorts of

EXAM TIP

Make every effort to come to some conclusion about the outcome of your dispute. Examiners don't create unanswerable problem questions.

---

[1] For an example of a case in which the court did not want to come to a decision, see the opinion of Robert Walker LJ in the case of the conjoined twins: *Re A (children) (conjoined twins: surgical separation)* [2000] 4 All ER 961 at 1069 (stating 'as the matter has been referred to the court the court cannot escape the responsibility of deciding the matter to the best of its judgment').

outrageous claims, you should do your best to indicate what the outcome of the dispute will be and, if you have not already done so, why.

Some of you may be nervous about coming to a conclusion in case you have missed or misread a key case or statute. Of course you will lose points as a result of the omission, but you will not remedy that error by failing to come to a conclusion. Do the best you can with what you have. A well-written and well-reasoned essay can still win a very good mark, even if you have had a lapse of memory or understanding.

6.2 The need for an outcome in legal writing

As suggested in the preceding section, practising lawyers are required, either by the demands of their client or the court, to come to a conclusion when dispensing legal advice or arguing a case. Sometimes the conclusion is not the one the client wants to hear. As a matter of good professional ethics, you should not say that a case can be won just because that is what your client wants to hear. You must identify the likely outcome based on the law and the facts in front of you. It is better for a client to know bad news early on, when settlement is possible and less expensive, than to go to court not knowing that failure is likely.

WRITING TIP

Don't try to force the outcome in one direction or another. Your essay won't be as good.

Although law students are obviously under no professional or ethical obligations to speak the truth, you should still give your honest opinion about the dispute rather than trying to force the decision one way or another, since your answer will undoubtedly read better.[2] Just because the question directs you to advise one party does not mean that you should try to persuade the reader that that party should or will prevail. As the preceding chapters have indicated, you should present a balanced analysis of the dispute. If your designated client is likely to lose, say so. You may be able to identify and exploit certain weaknesses in the other side's case, but don't overestimate your client's chances of success. Many practitioners purposefully take a conservative approach to legal advice so that their clients do not get their hopes up too high. While you need not adopt a particularly conservative approach to your academic essays and examinations, do be realistic.

Very few of you will have seen a professional legal opinion, so it may be difficult for you to model your essays on legal advice. Suffice it to say that professional opinions look very much like CLEO essays. They identify the relevant law, evaluate it in light of the particular facts and offer advice on the probable outcome of the matter. Abstract

---

[2] The exception to this rule, of course, is when the question directs you to make the best possible case for a particular party. Examiners seldom ask students to adopt this approach, however.

discussions of the law and hypothetical assumptions about the facts do not advance the goal of providing legal advice and therefore have no place in a professional opinion. While practitioners may identify further questions that need to be answered (a technique discussed further in chapter nine, which deals with adapting the CLEO method to professional practice), lawyers focus on giving advice about how the law influences the problem in front of them.

No one expects you, as a student lawyer, to have flawless legal judgment. However, you'll never have a better opportunity to learn these skills than in a university or professional school setting. There are no financial or legal implications if you get the answer wrong; your client will not lose money and you will not be subject to malpractice suits if your conclusion is radically different from that of a court or other legal authority. You will not prejudice your career, which is what some junior lawyers fear will happen if they make the wrong recommendation to their supervisors. Now is the time to make mistakes. If you play it too safe, you are robbing your tutors of the opportunity to give you their advice and suggestions.

WRITING TIP

Don't be afraid to take a risk. Now is the best time for you to learn.

Although it is most helpful to you to test your legal judgment in situations where you will be given detailed feedback, it is equally important that you exercise your judgment in examination situations. Part of the task which you have been set in a legal examination involves the question of judgment and discretion: how do you weigh up the conflicting legal authorities and how do you prioritise the facts given to you? If you don't offer an opinion on the outcome of the dispute, the examiner cannot evaluate your judgment. You may be absolutely correct about how you think the case will play out, but the examiner can't get inside your head to access that information. It has to come out on the page. You may think that the outcome is obvious from your discussion of the law and your evaluation of the facts, but don't take the risk of offering an incomplete analysis. Take the time to write one sentence stating your conclusion.

NOTE

Law exams test your judgment and discretion as well as your knowledge of the law.

If you don't put down an explicit conclusion about the outcome, the examiner may think that you are unable to do so, ie that you lack legal judgment. The examiner may also think that you lack the kind of forthright, decision-making capacity that is necessary in a legal career. Alternatively, the examiner may think that you do not know how to construct a proper response to a legal question, ie one that includes a determination about outcome. The conclusion (or outcome, in CLEO parlance) is the last thing your examiner will read: make sure it counts in your favour.

WRITING TIP

End on a strong note. First and last impressions matter.

Therefore, there is no downside to making an educated guess and stating your outcome. Give it your best effort and don't worry about finding the single right answer; remember, law is more about persuasion and argument than it is about finding an objectively identifiable, universally accepted right answer.

6.3 Writing the 'O' portion of your essay

As you recall, CLEO involves two stages: the planning stage, in which you work your way through the potential claims, legal authorities and factual analyses; and the writing stage, in which you present your best arguments after discarding the more tangential or minor points. In your planning stage, you come to a preliminary decision about who will win the case. You then shape your legal and factual discussions with this outcome in mind so that you can have as brief a concluding paragraph as possible (optimally one line long).

However, it is altogether possible that you will think of additional arguments as you write your essay, or you will become convinced that what seemed to be a straightforward win for one side is closer than you thought. By the time you're done with the essay, you could have an entirely different opinion as to the outcome of the case.

If this happens, don't worry. While your goal is to be as organised as you can be before you start writing, the process of writing often clarifies your points for you in an entirely new way. Your shift in perspective will probably be visible in your writing, which is objective (ie non-biased) but which still takes a view as to the weight of the opposing arguments. However, since you have begun your essay with a discussion of the basic principles of law that are applicable to the situation, you should be able to make a mid-course correction without too many problems. In any event, there is no shame and no detriment to changing your mind. If you suddenly recall a new case or realise that you misread the question, it is better to say so than to hold firm to an indefensible point out of a misplaced sense of pride or the fear that any sort of waffling will undermine your argument. This is particularly true in timed essays. Readers know that you're under time pressure and don't have time to go back and refine your arguments. When you realise you want to change directions, you have two choices: either go back and amend your preceding language through inserts or scratch-outs or change your analysis going forward, indicating how your thinking has changed as a result of X case or Y fact. Examiners are used to seeing both techniques, so do whichever makes the most sense and is the most time-efficient in the circumstances. While changing your mind mid-way through your essay is not recommended (and you can generally avoid it in a non-timed essay), it does happen and you should do whatever it takes to make your point in an exam scenario.

EXAM TIP

Readers know when you're under time pressure and will evaluate your submission accordingly. Just do the best you can.

TIP

Don't create your own time pressures by waiting until the last minute to draft your weekly essays or take-home examinations. The conventional wisdom that people work better under pressure is actually incorrect; the best writers draft early, let the piece sit for a time, then revisit their submission later with a fresh and critical eye. Good writers are really good editors.

Once you get to the writing stage, the recommended approach is to use one sentence that identifies the legal outcome of the dispute. For example, in a tort case, you might write, 'For the reasons mentioned above, Joe will fail in his claim of negligence but will prevail on his claim of nuisance, and will receive compensatory damages equal to the cost of his damaged rhododendrons.' One sentence should do it. In the beginning, it may feel somewhat abrupt to end that way, just as it feels abrupt to start the essay with a sentence identifying the claim, but soon you will see the strength of ending an essay on a concise note.

A second exception to the rule of brevity occurs when you want to include a short discussion about potential reform or the direction in which the law is moving. This is when you exceed the expectations of the examiner and go beyond the question to demonstrate your understanding of legal theory or legal history. As you recall from chapter one, one of the things that distinguishes a first-class essay from a second-class essay is a strong understanding of the theoretical issues associated with the area of law under discussion. Because you have so much information to cover in a response to a problem question, it can be hard to find the opportunity to include some comments on legal theory. Such information can also seem out of place in what is primarily a pragmatic response to a real-life legal dispute.

Nevertheless, if you want to earn top marks, you should try to find a way to contextualise your discussion into the larger debate in that field of law. Sometimes your comments can be incorporated into the 'L' or 'E' steps, but you might want to be cautious about spending too much time on 'extra credit' material in the early stages of your essay, in case you run out of time. A discussion about reform may also seem out of place in the body of a tightly written CLEO essay. Another alternative is to save your more theoretical points until the end of your essay and place them in a short paragraph following your stated outcome. Remember, the important part of writing an answer to a problem question is to answer the problem. Including theoretical discussions shows good versatility and a wide understanding of the subject, but is like icing on a cake: nice, but not necessary.

EXAM TIP

If you have time, exceed the examiner's expectations by discussing some aspect of legal theory.

6.4 Worked example

Having discussed the outcome step in the abstract, we may now put that discussion in context by working through the example we have used in previous chapters.

QUESTION

Jack, a Formula One race car driver, was driving his standard issue estate car home from his daughter's school, where he had just dropped her off for the day. On the way, he was involved in a road accident. Had he used his expert skill in braking, he could have avoided the accident, although an ordinary driver could not have done so. Is Jack liable for the injuries to the other party?

NOTE

Here we are returning to the same essay that has been developed in chapters three, four and five.

As you recall, the claim in the above example involves the tort of negligence, while the sub-issues involve breach of the duty of care and what the standard of care is for people with expert skill. The relevant legal standard has been set forth in detail in chapter four and the relevant facts have been evaluated in chapter five. The final thing to do is to identify the outcome of the question.

6.4.1 Writing your response

First, we identified the claim, adding in the general legal standard as part of the introductory paragraph.

DRAFT ANSWER ('C', section with general 'L' reference)

The question at issue is whether Jack is liable to the claimant for the tort of negligence. To establish a claim in negligence, the claimant must prove the existence of a duty, breach of that duty, causation (including both legal foreseeability and 'but for' causation) and damages (*Clerk & Lindsell on Torts*, s 7-04). Of those four elements, the claimant in our question will have the most trouble establishing that there was an existing duty and a breach of that duty, with the particular emphasis on what the appropriate standard of care is.

Next, we introduced the most important legal authorities.

DRAFT ANSWER ('L' section)

According to *Glasgow Corp v Muir*, the legal standard relating to duty of care is that of the reasonable man (person), taking into account the circumstances of the case. *Parkinson v Liverpool Corp* stated that people should not be held to the same standard of behaviour in an emergency as in ordinary circumstances.

What constitutes a 'reasonable person' may depend on whether the defendant has any expert skill and whether that person holds him or herself out as having that expert skill. *Philips v William Whiteley Ltd* involved a jeweller who was doing ear-piercing work who was not held to the same standard as a doctor, since the jeweller did not advertise himself as a doctor. *Wells v Cooper* involved a DIYer who was not held to the standard of care of a professional carpenter, but merely to that of a reasonably competent person doing that sort of domestic job. Notably, both these cases involve the question of whether to hold a defendant with ordinary skill to a higher standard rather than the other way around.

These cases may be compared to other cases where the defendant had a higher degree of skill than the ordinary person. *Bolam v Friern Hospital Management Committee* states that doctors need only act in conformity with a responsible body of opinion. The *Bolam* test for professional conduct has been extended to other professionals, such as accountants or solicitors. *Bolitho v City and Hackney Health Authority* states that professionals are not permitted to act in any way they wish: instead, the court will intervene if the body of opinion relied on by the defendant as justifying his or her action has no logical basis whatsoever.

Because we had sufficient time left over, we introduced those legal principles that were of secondary importance.

DRAFT ANSWER ('L' section – optional)

Drivers are held to the same 'reasonable person' standard as workers and professionals. *Nettleship v Weston* involved a learner driver who was still held to the standard of a reasonably competent driver, despite the fact that the claimant in that case (her instructor) knew that she was only learning. *Roberts v Ramsbottom* is another motoring case which involved a defendant who had a stroke while driving. He was held to be negligent, although the defendant in *Mansfield v Weetabix Ltd* (whose hypoglycaemia also caused an accident) was held not negligent. These somewhat contradictory outcomes can be explained by reference to the latter decision (*Mansfield*), which suggested it was inappropriate to hold a defendant liable for an essentially involuntary act.

Victims of tortious negligence may sometimes find their damages award reduced if they were contributorily negligent in some way (Contributory Negligence (Law Reform) Act 1945; *Froom v Butcher*).

The third step required us to evaluate the facts in light of the law. That step tracked the legal principles that had already been introduced in the essay. See how you have already begun to suggest to your reader what the outcome will be.

DRAFT ANSWER ('E' section)

Next, we will evaluate the facts of the current case in light of the law discussed above. First, the existence of a duty can be established by the fact that drivers have a general duty under *Donoghue*'s neighbour principle not to hurt others, a duty that was breached when Jack hit the other party. Causation is not at issue, since the damage that occurred was a proximate and foreseeable result of A's action, nor are damages in dispute. The question is whether the reasonable person standard under *Glasgow* has been met. The extent to which Jack's acts were the result of an emergency situation (*Parkinson*) would need to be determined further as a matter of fact but could lower the standard sufficiently to relieve Jack of liability.

> These lines suggest that you will conclude Jack will not be liable.

Jack was not holding himself out as an expert driver at the time of the accident, so, according to *Philips* and *Wells*, should be held to the regular 'reasonable person' standard rather than an expert driver. Though *Bolam* and *Bolitho* could seem to go in the opposite direction, since both involved people with expert skill (as opposed to reduced skill, as in *Philips* and *Wells*), both cases involved doctors acting in their professional capacity. Jack here was not acting as a professional driver; therefore, he should not be held to the higher standard of care, since he did not take that duty upon himself or cause others to rely upon it.

> Again, here you are hinting that Jack should not be liable.

It is also questionable whether courts would view Jack as a 'professional' in the same sense as a doctor, lawyer or accountant. A driver might be seen as more of a technician than a professional, and it can therefore be argued that *Bolam* and *Bolitho* should not apply and that Jack should be held to the reasonable person standard under *Philips* and *Wells*. In addition, *Bolitho* involved the weighing of a professional body of opinion versus the court's independent evaluation of the propriety of the action. The court's view was held to be controlling if the professional body's opinion was based on unreasonable evidence. It is likely that both the court and any professional drivers' body would, after taking full account of the circumstances of this case (see *Glasgow Corp*), conclude that Jack acted reasonably in the circumstances.

This conclusion is supported by reference to the three motoring cases cited. In those cases, the driver was held to the standard of a reasonable driver, unless the act causing the accident was so completely involuntary as to take it out of the realm of volition (*Mansfield*).

continues

DRAFT ANSWER ('E' section) continued

In a way, *Mansfield* negated the move towards the type of semi-strict liability demonstrated in *Roberts*. If *Roberts* had been left unchallenged, one might argue that Jack should be held to the higher standard of care as a type of strict liability (ie holding people to the highest standard they had attained as a matter of fact), but that approach is less likely in light of *Mansfield*.

Although the fact pattern does not explicitly raise the question of contributory negligence, Jack will of course argue as part of his defence that any liability that may be established against him should be reduced in accordance with the 1945 Act and *Froom*.

Now we must explicitly identify the outcome, even though it is implicit in the draft text. Because we have weighed up the legal authorities as we progressed through the evaluation step, the final, concluding paragraph is quite simple, along the lines of a practitioner's 'for the abovementioned reasons, my client should prevail'.

DRAFT ANSWER ('O' section)

Because Jack was not acting in a professional capacity, nor was he holding himself out as an expert driver at the time of the accident, he should not be held to a higher standard of care. Therefore, he should escape liability for injuries to the other party, since a reasonable driver, acting in the circumstances, could not have avoided the accident.

WRITING TIP

Be sure you answer the question asked: here, whether Jack is liable to the other party.

You could try to identify some sort of theoretical or legal reform issue to discuss, but this question does not raise any truly debatable points, so it is better not to push the matter. Inserting extraneous information just to show off often backfires. If you have something worthwhile to say, include it by all means, but make sure it suits the question. You don't want to leave your examiner with an unfortunate last impression. In this case, the sample essay already contains lots of information and critical analysis, and thus will receive strong marks even without any additional theoretical discussion.

You now have a basic understanding of how to handle each of the four steps in the CLEO method of essay writing. For a further discussion of how to handle 'discuss' type questions, see chapter seven. As you will see, a conclusion is just as important in those essays, though it may not be as brief as an outcome in a problem question. For more worked examples of both 'discuss' and problem questions, see chapter ten.

Using the CLEO method will help you write powerful essays, but there is more you need to do to win top marks. While structure and content are doubtless the most important elements of a legal argument, style plays a role, too. Though they may seem trivial, spelling or grammatical errors can detract from an otherwise persuasive essay and pull you down from a first-class mark to a good 2:1. By the time you move into the working world, you are expected to have mastered the art of writing. Although you can always ask the advice of your supervisors, your peers and your assistants, you cannot expect them to proofread every piece of writing you produce. You are responsible for your work and must know the basic rules of grammar, punctuation and spelling. While there are entire books devoted to this subject, chapter eight will give you some tips in these areas. Before moving to that discussion, however, we will address the second type of law essay: the response to the 'discuss' question.

CHAPTER 7

Adapting CLEO to 'discuss' questions

Although the CLEO system of essay-writing is particularly helpful in answering problem questions, it can easily be adapted for use with 'discuss' questions. The preceding chapters have already provided you with some tips on how you can use CLEO principles in answering 'discuss' questions. This chapter will discuss, in more detail, the following topics:

(1) what a 'discuss' question is asking you to do;

(2) structuring your 'discuss' essay; and

(3) how to adapt each of the four CLEO steps to 'discuss' questions.

Sample 'discuss' questions and answers can be found in chapter ten.

7.1 What a 'discuss' question is asking you to do

Problem questions are designed to probe your ability to analyse a fact pattern and identify the relevant legal issues, discuss the pertinent legal authorities, evaluate the facts in light of the law and come to a reasoned decision about the outcome of the dispute. 'Discuss' questions have similar aims but place a slightly different emphasis on each of the elements. Instead of analysing a fact pattern, you are asked to analyse a quotation or controversial statement. You will still need to identify the relevant legal issues, but they will not be as numerous or as diverse. It is likely that the issues will appear on the face of the question, which means that you do not have to worry about red herrings. In fact, many students have gone astray by trying to get too tricky with a 'discuss' question.

When answering a 'discuss' question, you will need to introduce relevant legal authority, just as in problem questions, but the type of authority used may be slightly different. To do well, you may need

> *** NOTE**
>
> A 'discuss' question is not just asking your opinion. You must offer legal authority to support your analysis, just as you do in 'fact' questions (also known as 'problem' questions).

to discuss the relationship between ideas from different parts of the syllabus,[1] which will require a different sort of evaluative or critical skill than that used in problem questions. Finally, you will need to come to some sort of conclusion about your analysis, although it will probably not be a yes/no or win/lose outcome, as is the case with problem questions. Many people think of 'discuss' essays as objective analyses, but, as shall be discussed further below, you still need to provide some sort of argument which reaches a conclusion.

The major purpose of a 'discuss' question is to give you an opportunity to discuss legal theory, legal reform and legal history. You will still need and be able to cite cases and statutes in a 'discuss' question, but you will often use the materials to support theoretical, rather than practical, arguments. The skills that you need to do well on a 'discuss' question are inherently different from the type of practical analysis that problem questions require. A fact pattern question simulates real life; a 'discuss' question is more academic in nature and resembles the types of essays that you did during your A-level examinations.

As mentioned above, 'discuss' questions tend to focus on three basic areas of inquiry: legal theory, legal reform and legal history. The following discussion will set forth the basic skills that examiners are hoping you will demonstrate with respect to each type of 'discuss' question.

7.1.1 Legal theory

Legal theory evaluates why the law is the way that it is. You can often spot a legal theory question by the way it asks you whether a certain course of action is wise or just or fair. Alternatively, the question may ask you to identify what rights or interests are at stake and to weigh them up. The key is that the question will, most likely, be asking you to evaluate some statement, event or course of action. To answer the question, you must ascertain what was done, why it was done and whether the result is worthwhile.

Many students equate legal theory with jurisprudence, which is a separate course in the law curriculum. Don't be fooled: jurisprudence does deal with legal theory but at the philosophical, rather than practical, level. Jurisprudence answers questions such as 'what is law' (also known as normative jurisprudence) and whether a particular law is just (also known as critical jurisprudence). While some jurisprudential notions can be applied to other substantive areas of law – for example, one can ask whether a particular constitutional norm is 'just' – for the most part you will not need to have studied jurisprudence to answer a legal theory

WRITING TIP

'Discuss' questions focus on legal theory, legal reform and/or legal history.

✳ NOTE

You can answer a legal theory 'discuss' question without having taken a course in jurisprudence.

---

[1] Remember, you have prepared yourself to answer this type of question by cross-referencing different parts of your syllabus during your revision sessions.

in one of your substantive law courses. Legal theory in substantive law (such as tort or contract) often tends to be more practical than the type of 'pure' legal theory one sees in jurisprudence. As a rule, the mode of analysis in jurisprudence is more similar to philosophy than law.

The type of legal theory that you will need to introduce and evaluate in a 'discuss' question has to do with why the court or legislature acted as it did. The ideas will be contained in judicial opinions and legislative documents (White Papers, parliamentary debates, committee reports, etc) and in academic books and articles. Legal academics may sometimes resort to jurisprudential ideas in these works,[2] but they need not do so, nor should you feel that you have to do so in your 'discuss' essays. Instead, legal academics working in legal theory relating to substantive areas of law will argue about competing policy interests (for example, how to allocate the risk of loss or the need to encourage potential tortfeasors or victims to take out insurance) or attack the empirical assumptions underlying the policy arguments. When you answer a 'discuss' question, you should do the same. You do not need to have taken jurisprudence as an academic subject to do well on 'discuss' questions. You do, however, need to have read more than a textbook or casebook, since those books' references to legal theory will be cursory at best.

Legal theory is all about weighing up competing interests. Chapter four noted that you should never introduce a policy argument in a response to a problem question without identifying the opposing policy; if an issue was so clear-cut as to have no competing policy arguments, it would not be in dispute. 'Discuss' questions operate on the same assumption; never will one theory be so persuasive as to eradicate the need to introduce counter-arguments. You – and the experts you cite – may have very good reasons to believe that your approach is best, but you need to explain why you have arrived at this particular conclusion. As difficult as it may be for you to grasp, other people will not necessarily agree with your analysis and your value system; that is why you must persuade the reader to adopt your way of thinking. 'Discuss' questions are just as much about developing an argument as problem questions are, and you therefore need to walk your reader through the analysis in order to persuade him or her that your conclusions are correct. You need to be objective about the merits of your opponents' position, but you should not think that being completely neutral is somehow more lawyerly than making your beliefs known. Take a position and defend it; that is how one does well in 'discuss' questions.

> **✳ NOTE**
>
> 'Discuss' questions are all about persuasion, just as problem questions are.

While 'discuss' questions are more similar to A-level essays than problem questions are, you still may be unfamiliar with the idea of

---

[2] For example, see P Craig 'Public Law, Political Theory and Legal Theory' [2000] Public Law 211.

introducing theory into your arguments. Not many A-level subjects use theory in the same way that law does, although Politics A-levels perhaps come close. Politics students must use political theory to support their arguments, citing eminent thinkers to explain how certain political structures and movements came about. However, politics students also point to certain historical events to illustrate their own ideas about why a certain political structure or concept is a good idea. As a law student, you should distinguish these types of 'social' examples from 'legal' examples and focus primarily on examples drawn from the law (ie cases, statutes, etc) rather than on current or historical events.[3] The same is true when it comes to legal theory – it is better to rely on theories espoused by jurists than to rely on those based on common sense. You should not discard common sense altogether, nor should you avoid bringing in your own original thought, but you should be aware of how and when to use the different types of argument.

Although most academic and vocational programmes will require you to be aware of legal theory as it is reflected in judicial opinions and legislative papers, the different programmes can vary greatly in the amount of emphasis put on legal theory as reflected in academic books and articles. Some universities are known for focusing on the 'black-letter law' rather than on the theoretical and philosophical foundations of law. At other universities, the reverse is true. Although you will need to be aware of how your particular programme approaches the issue, don't be fooled into thinking that 'practical', or black-letter, law is either superior or inferior to a more theoretical approach. Once you move into professional practice, you will need to be familiar with both methods of analysis. Therefore, it is to your benefit to learn how to utilise both types of materials and incorporate them into your 'discuss' essays, although the extent to which you do so will depend on your programme's approach to the issue.

7.1.2 Legal reform

'Discuss' questions may also ask you to comment on legal reform, with respect either to recent changes in the law or to the propriety of and need for changes in the future. You can identify these questions

---

[3] The one exception to this rule would be constitutional law. Although students often over-cite social examples in constitutional law essays, there are times when one must refer to real-life events to illustrate constitutional principles. Discussions of constitutional conventions, for example, must draw heavily on current or historical events, since there is little (if any) binding law relating to conventions. There are many commentators on constitutional conventions, however, and students therefore do not need to rely wholly on social examples. Student authors would often do better to cite more commentators than they do. However, as usual, it is a balancing act.

easily, since they will often include the word 'reform' or 'change' in the text or will refer to a recent legislative shift. There may be some reference in the question to the interests or rationales supporting (or opposing) the change, which will suggest the need to discuss legal theory, but the focus will be on the state of the law before and after the reform efforts.

Reform questions do not exist in a vacuum. To answer such questions well, you must have some knowledge of legal theory, since the issue of reform presupposes the question 'why the need to change?' However, a legal reform question is slightly different from a question relating strictly to legal theory, since you will need to introduce more black-letter law. If you are answering a question about a recent amendment to the law, for example, you will need to know both what the law was (and why) and how it has changed (and why). You will then need to weigh up the facts and the policy interests to see whether the change was successful. Remember, you are not just recounting what has happened; you need to have an opinion about the events you are recounting. You also need to allow your analysis to be guided by the question itself. Earlier chapters discouraged you from providing a stock answer to problem questions: the same is true here. You must adapt your knowledge to suit the question asked. Questions about past reform can be the most problematic to students, since they may have read numerous articles or heard several lectures about what changes were made and why. An unwary student may eagerly recite this information, thinking that the instructors want to see their own ideas presented back to them. Don't fall into this trap. Law is about analysis, not about memory recall (or, better said, not only about memory recall; you do need to remember the law to do well). Think back to the standards set forth in chapter one describing a first-class essay. According to those guidelines, you must demonstrate some independent thought if you want to do well in an essay or examination. Use the information you have learned as the building blocks for your own unique analysis.

WRITING TIP

Don't just regurgitate information gleaned from books and lectures. Manipulate your knowledge to suit the question rather than trying to do the opposite.

If the question refers to the possibility of future reform, you will need to take into account not just the theoretical or policy reasons why change should occur, but which cases or statutes are currently causing problems as well. This requirement demonstrates why you cannot answer a legal reform question only with legal theory (as you might possibly be able to do on a pure legal theory question). You must know the black-letter law as well.

In a question on legal reform, you will be using the same kinds of analyses and materials that you did in legal theory questions. You can find discussions about the need for and success of legal reform in judicial opinions, legislative papers and academic works. You may cite any and all of these sources to support your arguments. As always, you will need to take a position about the merits of the different viewpoints, identifying the strengths and weaknesses of others' analyses before forming your own conclusions.

While it is possible to answer a question on legal reform without having read any articles specifically discussing the subject, obviously you will do better if you are familiar with others' thinking. You can craft a good argument from a combination of logic and black-letter law, but you will do much better if you have read over the work of someone who has taken weeks, if not months or years, thinking about and researching the subject. Academics' thinking is bound to be more sophisticated than yours, if only because they have more time to consider the subject and access to more materials than you do. However, even if you came up with the same conclusions as an academic lawyer, there is still good reason to read and cite these sources. As noted in earlier chapters, law is not just about logic, although there is a strong element of that in every argument made; law is about precedent. Common sense rationales gain additional weight when they come from recognisable legal authority, be it binding or persuasive. If you are able to base your discussion on these outside sources, you will be arguing like a lawyer (ie not just from logic, but from authority) and will therefore receive better marks on your work.

> ✱ **NOTE**
>
> There are many good reasons to cite legal scholars in response to a 'discuss' question. However, don't forget to bring your own critical judgment to your essay.

7.1.3 Legal history

Legal reform questions generally relate to a sudden change in the direction of the law, usually due to legislative action. There can also be sharp shifts in the law due to judicial decisions, but those are less common. Judicial change is more likely to occur as a result of slow evolution, and this is the kind of change on which a legal history question usually focuses. You will often recognise a legal history question by the way in which it asks you to discuss how a certain area of law has changed over time. A legal history question might also ask whether a certain case can still be said to be good law in light of recent developments. You might also be asked to discuss whether two strands of law are growing closer together or farther apart.[4] The focus in historically orientated questions will be on a line of cases rather than a single event, as is often the case in reform questions.

Obviously, a question about legal history requires a high degree of familiarity with case and statutory law. While you may want to have

---

[4] For example, in the years following *Cambridge Water Co Ltd v Eastern Counties Leather plc* [1994] 2 AC 264, questions often came up as to whether nuisance and *Rylands v Fletcher* liability were evolving into a single head of liability.

recourse to the work of legal commentators, you can answer a legal history question adequately if you know the precedents well. Nevertheless, it is unlikely that a 'discuss' question will be set unless your reading list contains at least one highly relevant article or item of supplemental reading. Additional reading is one of the ways that first-class scholars distinguish themselves from second-class scholars; again, citing additional sources doesn't just improve the quality of your analysis, it also demonstrates that you know that good legal arguments are based on precedent.

Often the most difficult aspect of answering a legal history question is identifying the proper point at which to start the analysis. Scholarly articles provide misleading models, sometimes hailing back to the seventeenth or eighteenth century. Seldom is it necessary for a student essay to go that far back in time, although there may be exceptions. When trying to identify your essay's starting point, you should be guided less by what you know and more by what is relevant to the question. If your main focus is on presenting the complete width and breadth of your knowledge on a particular subject, you run the risk of including lots of factually correct but irrelevant information. Remember, you will know more law and theory than you are able to present. You must pick the best information to include in your essay. What constitutes 'the best information' depends, as always, on the question; while leading cases and statutes will be relevant to any discussion of the subject, other materials may be used or discarded at your discretion.

> **✳ NOTE**
>
> First-class essays identify themselves by the number and quality of references to additional reading. This is especially true with 'discuss' questions.

EXAM TIP

Focus less on what you know and more on what the question wants to know.

7.2 Structuring your 'discuss' essay

Over the course of your education, you have gained numerous essay-writing skills. These skills have obviously contributed to your academic success, and you should continue to use them, particularly in your responses to 'discuss' questions, since the 'discuss' format is most similar to the type of essays you wrote for your A-level examinations. However, you may find a few additional tips helpful.

As has been discussed in earlier chapters, people seem to understand information better when it is grouped in threes. Therefore, a common way of organising an essay is to rely on a five-paragraph structure with an introduction, three substantive paragraphs and a conclusion. This basic format can be translated to CLEO terminology in that the first introductory paragraph can be equated to the claim, the three substantive paragraphs can be equated to the law and evaluation portion of the essay, and the conclusion can be equated to the outcome. The five-paragraph method does not work as well with problem questions, since the claims, sub-issues and claimant–defendant pairings tend to provide the overall structure.

WRITING TIP

If you have problems structuring 'discuss' essays, try using a five-paragraph model.

WRITING TIP

Journalists use the 'inverted triangle' approach to writing. They lead with their broadest, most important point and progress downwards to their least important point (the thin tip of the upside-down triangle). Try doing the same in your essays.

If you aim for a five-paragraph format in a 'discuss' question, however, you will achieve a strong, logical structure, even if you end up with six or seven paragraphs. There is no magic in five paragraphs *per se*, and you should feel free to start a new paragraph to create additional white space[5] or to begin a new thought (for example, you may have one or two more detailed points to make under one or more of your three major headings). The idea is to group your thoughts into three major points, preferably of equal weight. Usually you lead with your strongest argument and progress to your weakest argument, but there may be times when you alter that strategy: for example, if one element needs to be established as a threshold matter before you can proceed to the later elements. Each of your three points must be supported by case law, statutory law or scholarly commentary. You can even try to organise your points into groups of three within each major heading, but don't push the structure for merely mechanical reasons.

Usually the three middle paragraphs are the easiest to write, since they contain the hard information you have learned and allow you to give your views on the question. The first and last paragraphs tend to be more difficult to write, which is why the CLEO system is so helpful in problem questions: there the form of your introduction and conclusion comes automatically. When you are writing 'discuss' questions, you should still focus on clarity, brevity and good organisation rather than on an attempt to be tricky or overly stylish. An introductory paragraph is meant to introduce your discussion. Therefore, the easiest way to proceed is to state what you intend to argue (ie the claim) and how you will organise yourself. You should not need to spend a lot of time setting the stage for your argument or giving background information; all of that data should be contained in your substantive paragraphs. If the information is not critical to your argument and doesn't fall into one of your substantive paragraphs, then consider omitting it as irrelevant to this particular essay. Remember, what you leave out is as important as what you put in.

Many students tend to cram too much into the introduction or spend a lot of time setting the stage for their main arguments, primarily because they fear that they don't have enough to say in their essay or because they don't want to 'waste' any of their hard-won information. Remember the admonitions from earlier chapters: if you plan your essays before you start writing, you will find that you have plenty

---

[5] The term 'white space' refers to indentations and breaks in paragraphs. Readers become daunted by a solid page of prose and are much more likely to pay attention to a text that has lots of breaks in it. Paragraph breaks also demonstrate the author's organisational plan and thus guide the reader.

to say and will not want to waste your time on tangential matters. You may not be able to present all of the information that you know, but if your aim is to achieve high marks, you need to resist the temptation to throw everything into one essay and instead focus on writing a strong and relevant response to the question asked. This is particularly hard to do when you get excited about a certain question. The best thing you can do then is to slow down and make sure that the point you are most enthusiastic about is actually relevant to the question asked. Too many students have started writing in the first blush of excitement, only to find halfway through their essay that they're a bit off track. Remember, your first idea is not always your best idea.

The conclusion is the second most difficult paragraph to write. If you have advanced a complex argument, you can pull the various strings together in the conclusion, using it as a type of summary paragraph. Many essays will not be that complex, however. Some students are taught that it's a good idea to include some new point in their conclusion so that it is more than a mere recitation of information given previously. Be careful. If your new point is highly substantive or involves a reference to a case or statute not discussed in the body of the essay, then it may not be appropriate to mention it only in passing. Consider giving the point its own paragraph. If it doesn't deserve its own paragraph, consider again why you want to include it. Don't just add extra information as a tactical move. Such tricks seldom work.

Nevertheless, there may be times when it is appropriate to introduce 'new' points into a final paragraph. For example, you might make some suggestions for reform (if the question itself was not about reform measures) or provide practical arguments about the likelihood of the suggested action (for instance, the likelihood that political pressure would lead to a certain outcome). This approach would be similar to adding a bit of theory to the final paragraph of an essay answering a problem question: you are showing your knowledge of the related issues, though you are wise enough to remain focused on the main points. It is a fine distinction, but one that you can learn to recognise with practice. In the end, how you conclude your essay is a matter of discretion and an issue which only you can resolve.

> **NOTE**
>
> The burden of relevance falls on you, the writer. Don't make the reader do the work of deciding whether and to what extent something relates to the question asked.

7.3 Claims in 'discuss' questions

The first step in a CLEO essay involves the identification of the claim, which, in a problem question, is analogous to the crime charged or a civil cause of action. A claim in a 'discuss' question is slightly different. You might want to think of the claim as your over-arching theme or the point of your essay. Every law essay, whether it is in response to a problem question or a 'discuss' question, has to build an argument and take a perspective on the issues discussed; it cannot be absolutely indifferent to the merits of the different view-points. You need to be objective in your evaluation of the opposing arguments (meaning that you should base your evaluation on logic and facts rather than on emotion or prejudice), but, at the end of the day, you have to come to some conclusion about which approach should prevail.

Therefore, if your question constitutes a controversial statement, followed by the single word 'discuss', your claim will identify the position you intend to take regarding the statement. Some students are taught in school that they can write a stronger and more memo-rable essay if they attack or disagree with the statement. Be careful. This technique can backfire unless you believe, quite strongly, that the statement is indeed wrong and you can support your position with binding or persuasive legal authority. It is always better, in an academic essay, to base your arguments on your beliefs and on the facts and law as you know them rather than try to be overly clever for the sake of mere tactics. There may come a time in profes-sional practice when you have to find some sort of plausible argu-ment even though you believe your opponents have the better case, but you do not need to take this approach during your academic coursework.

If your claim is your basic, overarching response to the question, then your sub-issues are the three main points you wish to make in support of your claim. You need to think of these sub-issues as sup-port rather than merely as points to be made, since your goal is to build an argument rather than just present objective information in written form. Those of you who have studied literature can analo-gise the construction of a legal argument to the typical plotline of a novel. You open the novel by introducing the characters and scene, build the tension to a climax, resolve the ultimate conflict and end the book. A legal argument opens with some sort of stage-setting device (a claim), builds the tension through point and counter-point argument (the 'L' and 'E' steps in a CLEO essay, whether that essay is in response to a problem question or a 'discuss' question), then reaches its climax and denouement (the outcome plus any addi-tional points to be made in the conclusion). Too many students fail to see the need to build an argument to an inescapable (or hopefully inescapable) conclusion. The plotlines of their essays are virtually flat. While there is a place for strictly expository writing, it is not in a law essay.

TIP

Trying to get too tricky or too tactical usually backfires. The better bet is simply to focus on acquiring the necessary skills and knowledge. That is, after all, the point of taking a degree in law.

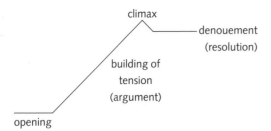

Remember, the study of law is not just about the acquisition of legal facts; it is about applying the facts you have learned to practical problems and using your judgment to come to some conclusion. The organisation of your essay may depend on the information you need to impart – for example, you may have sub-sub-issues to be raised within each of your sub-issues, just as you did with problem questions – but you must structure your essay to build to a logical determination about the outcome of the dispute. The disputes in 'discuss' questions may be slightly more academic or intellectual than the kind of practical disputes you must resolve in problem questions, but there is still a dispute at issue.

To identify your claim and the relevant sub-issues properly, you must read the question carefully, just as you did with problem questions. Use the same techniques that you use with other types of CLEO analyses: proceed through the question slowly, line by line, picking out relevant words and correlating them to areas of law that you know to be contentious. While you will always try to choose a question that relates to a subject about which you feel confident, you should not try to find a question that will suit your pre-conceived notions about how to discuss a particular point. Although it is possible that you will get a question that meshes perfectly with your exam preparation, you must not adjust the question to suit your knowledge. Rather, it's the other way around: you should manipulate your knowledge to suit the question. Be careful.

When you begin your essay and identify your claim, don't be afraid to use the precise words of the question. In fact, you should purposefully do so, even if it feels somewhat mechanistic or trite. For example, if a question asks whether it is 'wise and desirable' to undertake a certain reform measure, use the words 'wise' and 'desirable' in your response and be sure to define what you mean by them. That way, both you and your reader will be sure that you are answering the question as asked. It is also the case that a lot of profitable discussion can come out of defining terms.

WRITING TIP

Be sure to define your terms, even if they are terms which originate in the question.

Once you've identified the key language in the question, figure out what cases, statutes and articles relate to those terms and issues. Then delve into your memory bank and, without reference to the question, recall those issues that arose during your revision as potential discussion points in this area of law. Compare your new ideas with the ideas which arose directly out of the key language of the question. Delete those ideas and source materials that do not correlate specifically to the question as asked and then organise whatever remains into a five-paragraph essay. Again, try to be ruthless, just as you were on problem questions – if there's a small point that doesn't seem to fit in with the rest of the essay, consider whether you need to include it. A strong essay is not littered with minor points of tangential relevance.

WRITING TIP

Your aim is not to put everything you know into an essay. Instead, pick only your best arguments and authorities. Discard everything else.

7.4 Law in 'discuss' questions

There is just as much need to include legal authority in 'discuss' questions as in problem questions, although, as was mentioned earlier, the type of authority that you use may vary slightly according to which type of question you're answering. Problem questions focus primarily on the types of disputes that arise in practice; therefore, the type of source material will resemble that used in practice. Some academic material (treatises, scholarly articles) will be used, just as in professional practice, but it will be used to supplement binding legal authority and fill gaps in the existing law. 'Discuss' questions, on the other hand, are inherently more academic. They deal with critical questions about policy, theory and equity, among other things. Therefore, your source material will resemble the materials used by academics in their work: scholarly monographs and articles (not, typically, textbooks or casebooks, since those are aimed at students rather than at academics, although of course you can refer to those sources if necessary), legislative reports and papers, and, of course, cases and statutes.

NOTE

'Discuss' questions allow you to use a wide variety of legal authorities.

There will be times when you need to refer to binding law in 'discuss' questions, so you should not take the view that you should use only persuasive authority in 'discuss' questions. For example, a legal history question may require you to discuss the evolution of a particular line of cases and/or statutes. Obviously you will have to know what the law is to be able to discuss it intelligently. Similarly, you may be asked to compare and contrast – ie harmonise and distinguish – two competing strands of legal thought. In that situation, you will also need to use particular cases and statutes to illustrate your hypothesis. In fact, those who can use case and statutory law effectively in a 'discuss' question often receive very good marks.

Even when you introduce the ideas of a leading commentator, you may want to illustrate those ideas further through a discussion of the black-letter law. Remember, your job as a law student is not just to repeat the thinking of others without any additional criticism of your own; seldom will you find a journal article or treatise that discusses the question raised so completely and so precisely that you will not need to adapt the commentators' analyses slightly. Even if you did find such an article, you would still need to weigh up the arguments yourself and come to some conclusion about their relative merits (more on this step below). Persuasive legal authority, like binding legal authority, is a building block; it is not the building itself. You need to use the building blocks to create a structure – ie an argument – rather than just tossing the blocks into a cordoned-off area and hoping that the structure will make itself known without any effort on your part.

Problem questions and 'discuss' questions both require you to think independently about the issue at stake. Obviously this is difficult to do in a timed situation, particularly if you have never considered the issue before. If all you do is repeat back the information you have learned over the course of the academic term, you will pass your examination, but you will not do well. To do well, you need to indicate a deep understanding of the issues at stake (and not just the elements of the legal building blocks) and an ability to think critically about those issues. There is no way that you can anticipate any particular question, but, as mentioned in chapter two, you can develop your critical thinking skills by considering these deeper issues during your revision. That way, when you are presented with a novel question in an examination, you know how to go about analysing the question. A good 'discuss' question is designed to test your ability to think independently about the law. Examiners want to see what type of analogies you can draw to different areas of law, what materials you present to support your thinking and how you evaluate those materials. Indeed, the evaluation process constitutes the third step of the CLEO process.

7.5 Evaluation in 'discuss' questions

The evaluation step in problem questions involves the application of the facts of the question to the law introduced in the second stage of the essay. Evaluation, as a critical process, is not as clear-cut in 'discuss' questions, since the type of law that is introduced often consists of scholarly surmises and conjectures. Similarly, a 'discuss' question doesn't give you a set of facts that need to be weighed up and applied to the law that you have presented.

Instead of separating out the two analytical steps and presenting a separate section containing the law and a separate section containing the evaluation, you may want to combine the two steps in a 'discuss' question. Be careful, though: rather than making things easier, the combination of these two analytical steps may make things more difficult for you, since you won't be able to rely on CLEO's easy structural framework quite as much as you do in problem questions. You will have to spend more time in the preparation stage, making sure that you know what legal authority you will present and how you will critically analyse (ie evaluate) it in light of the question asked. The benefit of combining the two steps is that you will avoid repetition. As you know from earlier chapters, you have to use a fair amount of discretion when writing CLEO essays, because a too-rigid application of the steps can lead to repetition of some of the 'L' material in the 'E' section. If you combine the two steps, you avoid repetition. However, you also run the risks mentioned in earlier chapters, such as failing to identify the full scope of legal authority to discuss and tending to argue the facts rather than the law. Therefore, you should use caution if you decide to evaluate your legal authority as you present it.

As mentioned above, it is a good idea to use the precise words of the question as you evaluate the legal authority you have presented. If the question asks you whether a certain course of action is 'fair' or 'efficient', use the words 'fair' and 'efficient' in your response. You may even want to highlight those words by using them in the opening sentence of a paragraph so that your reader knows that you are addressing that portion of the question.

WRITING TIP

In both problem essays and 'discuss' essays, you must answer the question as asked.

Using the precise words of the question will also help ensure that you answer the question as asked. 'Discuss' questions are notoriously confusing, and it can be difficult to know exactly what you are being asked to do. The encouraging thing about 'discuss' questions is that there is usually a wide variety of good responses; if you can argue your point persuasively and retain some connection to the question, you can do well. Problem questions, on the other hand, yield a more narrow band of good answers, which is why students who do not use CLEO hesitate to answer them. Once students know how to structure responses to problem questions, however, they begin to prefer problem questions to 'discuss' questions, since there is less uncertainty involved. That uncertainty constitutes the discouraging thing about 'discuss' questions – although the range of good and acceptable responses is wider than it is with problem questions, you have more scope for going wrong and heading down an unproductive path. However, the more closely you tie your essay to the question, the better off you will be.

Using the same words in your response as were used in the question may seem somewhat mechanistic at times, but it is an effective way to check yourself and keep your focus. It is also a way to make sure that you and your reader are talking about the same thing. For example, you may see no harm in substituting the word 'equitable' for 'fair' in your essay, since you believe the two words are synonymous. Some readers might disagree, however, due to the special legal connotation given to the word 'equitable'. What you believe is a matter of style can become a matter of substance. Avoid those problems by using the words that appear in the question and by defining all necessary terms early in your essay. Often the most important evaluative step you can take is in how you define terms. Don't assume that definitions are clear or that defining terms is a rudimentary task. That mistake could bring your mark down from a first to a good 2:1.

7.6 Outcome in 'discuss' questions

'Discuss' questions need to have a stated outcome, just as problem questions do. However, in 'discuss' questions, you are not giving a succinct opinion on which party will win the dispute. Instead, you are tying together the various strands of your argument to give a final answer to the question. If you have used a five-paragraph essay structure, you will have three substantive paragraphs, each with its own main point and supporting ideas (remember, there is nothing magical about five paragraphs *per se* – you can break one of your substantive paragraphs into two or three parts if it is getting too long). Use the final paragraph to weigh the relative merits of the three substantive discussion points and indicate how the question should be resolved. Remember to walk the reader through your analysis step by step – do not merely state your conclusion. 'Discuss' questions are unlike problem questions in that the essay does not focus on yes or no issues. In a problem question, your analysis proceeds until you hit a yes/no issue: does action X constitute a breach of duty in tort, does action Y constitute an anticipatory repudiation of contract, etc. That is why your final paragraph can be so short in a problem question: you have either proved or disproved the *prima facie* elements of the claim in the body of the essay.

'Discuss' questions, on the other hand, do not contain any intermediate yes/no questions. It all comes down to persuasion, and to persuade, you must illustrate your thinking to your reader. Therefore, your conclusion will be longer than in a problem question, since you must persuade your reader that your thinking is correct.

Some students have been told by their A-level teachers that a good conclusion should contain at least one new point not previously discussed in the essay. This technique can be risky, as mentioned above.

If the new point is relatively minor, then one wonders whether it should be included at all. If the new point is relatively important, then one wonders whether it should be given its own substantive paragraph. As usual, the key is finding a new point that lies somewhere between the two extremes, if you truly believe that you should introduce a new point in the conclusion.

Use your judgment. If you decide not to make a new point in your conclusion, your mark will not drop as a result, although a truly clever twist, popped in at the end of an essay, could show the type of original-ity and individuality that marks a first-class paper. On the other hand, if you refer to something in passing that should have been given more weight, you run the risk of leaving your reader with the impression that you don't understand the material as well as you should. Unfor-tunately, it is almost impossible to say, in the abstract, what types of new thoughts work well in a conclusion. Sometimes a quote from a reputable source gives a slightly different spin on the question or on the issue. Sometimes you can make a point about reform in a ques-tion that is not primarily about reform, or a point about the theory of the law in a question that is not primarily about theory. Sometimes you can demonstrate a bit of legal realism and suggest how the issue would play out in practice. These are just some of the ideas that can work some of the time; they will not work all the time. The best way to develop your judgment in this area is to give yourself permission to make a few mistakes in essays early in the term and to read the work of good writers. Ask your tutor for recommendations on who is a good writer *per se*; in many cases, the best legal thinkers are not the best legal writers. In many cases, the trick is in how the information is introduced rather than in the information itself; that is why it is so hard to discuss this issue in the abstract.

We have now identified ways in which you can adapt the CLEO method for use in 'discuss' questions. Although this should give you some idea of how a 'discuss' question in law differs from a 'discuss' question in other academic subjects, you should not forget the sub-stantive and stylistic techniques that you learned in your A-level studies. Many of them will be helpful to you in your university and vocational courses, since 'discuss' questions in law are very similar to A-level essay questions. Rather than discarding all that you have learned up until this point, focus on adding to the skills that you can bring to bear on your essay writing. If you want to see an example of a 'discuss' essay written in a CLEO style, see chapter ten. As you have learned, presentation and persuasion lie at the centre of good legal writing. No matter how good your ideas, you cannot receive good marks if you do not communicate well. Therefore, the next chapter will discuss the various elements of good writing.

CHAPTER 8

General tips on legal writing

As the previous chapters have discussed, a good, first-class law essay presents clearly identified legal authority through sophisticated and well-organised legal arguments. Although the CLEO method of essay writing does not offer instruction on the content of the law, it provides you with an effective means of conveying your knowledge of the substance of the law and thus constitutes a substantive, rather than merely stylistic, writing tool.

However, as has been mentioned before, law is as much about style as it is about substance. How you say something affects how the reader or listener perceives your argument. People will make judgments about the quality and merit of your legal thinking based on elements that have nothing to do with the content of your writing. If you doubt this is the case, think about your most recent trip to the bookshop or library. When you're browsing for something to read, do you pick up the book that looks crisp and pristine, with clean, white pages and impeccable type, or do you naturally gravitate towards the one with a bent corner, faded printing and crooked lines? When you scan a newspaper rack, looking at headlines, do you trust the truthfulness of the publication that reads, 'Prez Sez, "We Want More!"' more or less than the one that reads, 'Union Leader Seeks Wage Increase'? Chances are, you will find the latter more persuasive and informative (though perhaps less colourful), not only because it uses longer words (more on that later), but because it appears to be more objective and uses proper spelling and grammar. You know that the first paper is misspelling the words 'President' and 'says' on purpose, but doubtless there have been other occasions when you have found errors in newspapers, books, letters or advertising materials. In all honesty, haven't you felt just the slightest bit smug when you discovered another person's mistake? A bit superior perhaps? Maybe a bit disdainful that the other person either didn't know better or didn't care enough to check his or her work?

> **✳ NOTE**
>
> Poor writing can detract from the substance of an essay. The best lawyers and the best law students not only have good content, they have good writing style.

If there is one thing you do not want to do as a lawyer, it is to make the reader of your work feel either superior to or disdainful of you. You want to appear clever, diligent and infallible: certainly not the kind of person who is likely to make a mistake on any level. Someone who is too harried or careless to check his or her spelling and grammar may very well be the kind of person who is too harried or careless to check that a case or statute is still good law. If your reader doesn't trust you, he or she may be more inclined to double-check or argue with points that might otherwise have passed muster. To avoid giving the impression of someone who is inclined to err, you need to make sure that your writing style is crisp and professional and that your use of language is correct at all times.

Unfortunately, many people – students as well as teachers, lawyers and other well-educated professionals – do not know what good writing or good grammar is. In many ways, law students cannot be blamed for not knowing the basic rules of grammar, since it is a common assumption that good writing 'just comes naturally' to some people and cannot be taught. In fact, nothing could be further from the truth. While not everyone can become a Nobel prize-winning author, almost everyone can improve his or her writing style by learning a few simple techniques. Therefore, this chapter will discuss the following points:

(1) why it is important to have a good writing style;

(2) why you need to learn the rules of good writing yourself;

(3) why you should work to develop that style now; and

(4) what constitutes good legal writing.

The chapter will conclude with a series of self-tests and exercises to help you overcome any problem areas.

8.1 The importance of good writing

There are two very good reasons for writing correctly. First, by so doing, you will advance your own career. Think about it. Your written work is aimed toward a very small, very discriminating audience. Almost every time you set pen to paper (or fingers to keyboard), your professional reputation is on the line. For example:

- If you are a student, your work is going directly to tutors or examiners who will (1) write the job references and (2) award you the class markings that will affect your job prospects.

- If you are a solicitor, your work is going directly to a partner, a peer, a client, the court or your opposite number at another law firm.

✳ NOTE

Details matter. In law, matters of form or style can quickly turn into matters of substance.

- If you are a barrister, your work is going directly to the solicitor who hired you, to opposing counsel or to the court.

- If you are in business or working in a corporate legal department, your work is going to your superiors, your peers, other departments, solicitors or barristers you have hired, potential adversaries and possibly even the press.

In none of these cases do you want to look careless. Signing off on a piece of work that contains spelling or grammatical errors makes you look ill-informed at best, sloppy or incompetent at worst. Don't do it.

Good writing often goes unnoticed. It is a quality that is most appreciated in its absence. Seldom does someone say, 'well done, nothing misspelled in that memorandum' or 'fabulous use of commas!' However, fill that same piece of writing with typographical errors, misplaced modifiers and split infinitives, and just watch your reputation plummet.

It may very well be that none of your teachers has ever corrected your grammar, so you may be operating under the assumption that all is well. In fact, few people know what constitutes good writing and even fewer can list the rules of grammar by rote. Your teachers may not have felt qualified to identify misplaced antecedents (meaning the words to which words appearing later in the sentence refer) or give you tips about dependent and independent clauses. This is not to fault your teachers in any way: grammar is simply not taught these days, as you yourself are probably aware. Your teachers may also have been more concerned with the content of your writing than with your style. Again, this is not to fault your teachers but merely to note why you may not have been given the necessary instruction.

Now that you are reading for a degree in law, things have changed. Presentation is as important as substance. Your tutors, employers, opponents and clients may not know why your writing appears awkward or confusing, but they will subconsciously rate someone who has a strong writing style and who avoids errors as a better lawyer. People who are considered better lawyers get better jobs and better work.

The second reason why it is important for you to learn how to write well is so that you can do your job better. Poor writing is not just bad for you personally. It can be bad for your client and for your employer as well. Think of all the contract cases you have read during your years of study. How many of them have turned on the placement of a comma or the existence of a misspelled or misplaced word? You may have thought at the time that the judges were being rather nit-picky, but the English style of contract construction requires that kind of objective, analytical, linguistic analysis. Errors end up in court, and you don't want to be the one explaining to your client or your supervisor how that error passed you by. 'My secretary typed it that way' is not an excuse. You are responsible for your work and for overseeing the product of those whose work you direct. In some instances, you may also be responsible for making sure that your client doesn't write anything that is legally problematic. As the contract cases you have read suggest, the term 'legally problematic' can include errors of style and grammar. You mustn't be afraid to correct your client's or your supervisor's language when necessary. However, to be able to carry out your job properly, you must know what constitutes good writing.

8.2 The need to learn the rules of grammar yourself

Lawyers, particularly those in the big City firms, are spoiled. Not only do they have lots of staff at their disposal – secretaries, word processors, junior solicitors and trainees – they have the most modern computer equipment at their fingertips. Surely, with all this backup, there is no need to learn the rules of grammar oneself?

Not true. First, if you don't know what constitutes good writing, why would you suppose someone junior to you would know any better? In any event, are you sure that those people will feel inclined to tell you of your errors? They might think it is easier or more polite to let the errors go by – after all, it's not their job to correct your writing. On the other hand, you may need to learn the rules of grammar because you will be starting your career at the bottom of the ladder and either need to check your own work yourself or check the work of those who are more senior to you and who allegedly don't have the time to write properly. Whether you're at the top or the bottom of the ladder, you need to know the difference between good and bad writing.

Second, good writing is not something that can be programmed into computer software. For example, a good spell-checking program can correct your spelling of 'there', 'they're' and 'their', but can't tell you whether you've used the right one in the right place. Grammar checkers may indicate when you have a sentence fragment, but that won't help if you don't know what a sentence fragment is and how to correct it. Many grammatical problems or stylistic errors slip past a computerised grammar program altogether. You cannot rely on a computer to pick up every human error (assuming that you have even remembered to run the spell and grammar check features before printing out the final draft of your document).

> **NOTE**
>
> Computer spell-check features cannot replace human proofreaders.

The other problem with relying on others or on computers to check your work is that you often run out of time to do justice to any suggested revisions. Because most people know that an error can creep into their work at any point during the rewriting process, they often don't run the computer checking programs until the very last minute.

Unfortunately, if lots of errors are found, you may not have time to correct them all. If you make fewer errors during the writing process, there will be fewer to correct at the last minute, thus improving the quality of your final product.

Therefore, it is up to you to learn how to write well. You cannot rely on others, nor can you rely on computers to check your work for you. You should seek feedback from other people and run a spell and grammar check on your computer by all means, but you shouldn't expect them to do the hard work for you. The hard work is yours alone.

8.3 The need to develop a good writing style now

You may admit that there are good reasons to develop a good writing style once you enter the professional world, but why work on acquiring it now? Haven't you enough to do, learning the substantive law? Quite simply, there's no time like the present to learn new skills. In fact, university and professional courses are the best time to work on your writing style, since you are not under the same kind of pressure that you will be under in professional practice. Pupillages and traineeships are notoriously difficult, and you will be constantly scrambling to learn new skills and satisfy the demands of your principals and pupil masters. Feedback on your work is even more rare than it is in the academic context. Time is at even more of a premium. Because it takes time and practice to acquire a good written style, you should start ingraining these habits into your routine now. Students are expected to make errors, since there is no other way to learn; professionals, however, are expected to have mastered these skills already and can damage their careers if they make too many basic mistakes.

> **✳ NOTE**
>
> There is never a better time than now to begin to improve your writing skills.

As you consider how to prepare for life after university, consider this: for the most part, trainee solicitors and pupil barristers are considered to be professionals rather than students, despite the legal profession's claim that traineeships and pupillages are an extension of the learning process. Many trainees and pupils feel constantly under scrutiny, as if they are on a one- or two-year interview. Although one would hope that you would find your pupillage or traineeship educational, you will be highly focused on learning vocational skills rather than on the basics of legal writing. Those skills you should know already.

For those of you who are more mercenary, remember that people who have a good writing style get good marks on their university and vocational courses, and people who get good marks get good jobs. Law is about persuasion as much as it is about content. The art of persuasion involves getting the reader on your side and demonstrating the ease and logic of your position. If you confuse the reader in any way or make it difficult for the reader to follow your thoughts, either through the introduction of difficult concepts, illogical structure or awkward language, you cannot communicate, let alone persuade.

8.4 The elements of a good legal writing style

Good writing consists of two basic elements. First, there are the mandatory elements of style: grammar, punctuation, spelling. You cannot consistently break mandatory rules and hope to be considered a good writer. Second, there are the discretionary elements of style: organisational structure, word choice, pacing. While there is a significant amount of variation in how one approaches discretionary aspects of style, deviating too far from the norm can be distracting and therefore undesirable. This is particularly true in legal writing, which is highly conventional. We will begin with a discussion of the mandatory elements of style before turning to the discretionary ones.

8.4.1 Mandatory elements of style

Good grammar is the key to good communication. While not everyone can enunciate the rules of grammar, people become confused when the rules are not followed. Grammar is often absorbed subliminally rather than taught formally, at least in the UK. Other nations take a more rigid approach to the acquisition of language and teach the rules of grammar from an early age. However, just because British schools don't focus on grammar doesn't mean that those rules don't exist or that they do not facilitate understanding.

Consider the following text, for example.

EXAMPLE

Ethan borrowed Andrew's coat and scarf one winter day, but didn't return it. He became quite angry when the holidays were coming and everyone left university to go home. He rang Ethan, but he had already gone, along with his things.

This example does not illustrate all possible grammatical errors, but it demonstrates how improper use of language both grates on one's nerves and leads to confusion. In the first sentence, you immediately see that 'it' is incorrect. If the writer means both the coat and scarf, the word 'them' should be used. If the writer means either the coat or the scarf, then the item should be clearly identified by using the noun.

The second sentence contains a lack of clarity regarding what is meant by 'he'. Because Ethan was the subject in the first sentence, one might think that 'he' means Ethan. However, 'he' might also refer to Andrew, who is the last person mentioned in the preceding sentence. From the context of the second and third sentences, it becomes apparent that 'he' is Andrew. The use of 'his' in the third sentence is equally confusing – it could mean that Ethan has left with Andrew's things (meaning the coat and scarf, presumably) or that Ethan has left with Ethan's things.

As this example shows, major misunderstandings can occur as a result of minor errors. Although most law students have a relatively strong intuitive grasp of the rules of grammar, many people can use a few tips regarding common problem areas. This chapter, therefore, will focus on those basic areas of concern. However, the following discussion is by no means comprehensive, and if you want more detailed instruction in English grammar, you can refer to one of the many books dedicated to that subject. Time spent studying the art of writing is never wasted.

We will now consider several basic problem areas concerning the following:

- parts of a sentence;
- constructing a sentence;
- subject-verb agreement;
- verbs and verb phrases; and
- punctuation.

a) The building blocks: parts of a sentence

To discuss the rules of grammar, we need a common vocabulary. Here are a few terms that you may know as well as a few that you may not.

Noun A person, place or thing

    Proper Noun The actual name of the person, place or thing

    Pronoun A reference to a proper or common noun, ie, 'he', 'she' or 'it'

Adjective A word modifying (describing) a noun

Verb A word showing action

Adverb A word modifying (describing) a verb (an adverb usually ends in '-ly' – for example, 'slowly' or 'coldly')

Gerund A verb form ending in '-ing' that stands in for a noun – for example, 'my understanding of the situation' contains a gerund

---

* NOTE

This problem involves an improper antecedent, which happens when a pronoun ('he', 'she', 'it', 'that' or something similar) refers to the wrong noun. To be correct, the pronoun should refer only to the immediately preceding noun or clause. Fixing the problem will require you either to repeat the relevant noun or change the sentence structure altogether.

Preposition A word that shows a relationship between a verb to a noun – for example, you walk *through* a door or *by* a door but generally not *under* or *into* a door

Conjunction A word that connects nouns – for example, 'and', 'or', 'but' and 'since'

Clause A group of words acting together[1]
> **Independent clause** A group of words that can stand alone as a sentence
> **Dependent clause** A group of words that cannot stand alone as a sentence

These phrases will be supplemented and described in more detail as we progress through this chapter, but this provides a sufficient basis from which to start.

b) Constructing a sentence

Simple sentences require a noun acting as a subject and a verb.

> *John ran.*
>
> (noun as subject) (verb)

Many sentences have a subject, a verb and an object, which is the thing the verb is acting upon.

> *John threw the ball.*
>
> (noun as subject) (verb) (noun as object)

WRITING TIP

Good writers vary the length and complexity of their sentences for effect.

As a lawyer, you will sometimes use these kinds of simple sentences – since they are very good for effect – but will often use more complex sentences. For example, you might write a sentence that has a dependent clause describing the way in which something is done (an adverbial clause) or describing one of the nouns in the sentence (an adjectival clause).

> *Flicking his hair out of his eyes, John threw the ball.*
>
> (adjectival clause describing subject), (subject) (verb) (object)

> *John threw the ball, which was coming apart at the seams.*
>
> (subject) (verb) (object), (adjectival clause describing object)

WRITING TIP

Put modifiers as close to the modified word or phrase as possible.

Notice how these adjectival clauses appear next to the nouns which they describe and are offset by commas. A descriptive, dependent word or phrase should be placed as close as possible to the word it modifies, as a general rule. The rule about commas is slightly more confusing and will be discussed in more detail below. Generally, however, you use

---

[1] Some grammarians distinguish between phrases and clauses, but there is no need to do so for our purposes.

commas when the clause describes an aspect of the noun rather than helps to identify the noun. For example, when you say, 'John threw the ball, which was coming apart at the seams', you are describing the ball's qualities. There is no question about which ball is under discussion, and you could delete the phrase without confusing the reader as to which ball was thrown. If you say, 'John threw the ball which was coming apart at the seams', however, you are not just describing the ball's qualities. Instead, you are identifying the ball that John threw as compared to other possible balls (for example, if he had a selection of three and he threw the one coming apart at the seams, as opposed to the two new ones). Commas will be discussed at more length below, but you need to know the difference in the types of clauses.

> **RULE**
>
> Use two commas when a clause describes an object or action. Do not use commas when the clause identifies the object or action.

Sometimes you can have two verbs both relating to the same subject. For example:

John threw the ball and dodged the tackle.

(subject) (verb) (object) (conjunction) (verb) (object)

Notice how this sentence is different from the following, which has two verbs and two subjects.

John threw the ball, and Bob dodged the tackle.

(subject) (verb) (object), (conjunction)[2] (subject) (verb) (object)

There is a comma between the two clauses in the second example because each clause can stand alone as its own sentence. The first example contained no comma, since that would improperly separate the subject of the sentence (John) from the second of the two verbs. In that sentence, the phrase 'dodged the tackle' cannot stand on its own apart from the subject, 'John'.[3]

Sometimes people realise that two clauses are independent and therefore can stand alone. Thinking they don't need an 'and', they simply slip in a comma as follows:

John threw the ball, Bob dodged the tackle.

---

[2] Some students use commas correctly with the word 'and' but not with the word 'but'. The rules are the same for both words. If you want the subject to apply to both verbs (the one preceding and the one following the conjunction), then do not use a comma. If you do not want or need the subject to apply to both verbs (ie when both clauses can stand independently on their own as sentences), you can split the sentence with a comma.

[3] There is one exception to the general rule that you should not separate a verb from its subject. If a comma is necessary to make the meaning clear, then you can insert one. For example, the comma in the sentence, 'The contract allowed the defendant to deliver apples or oranges, and therefore was not breached upon delivery of oranges', is technically incorrect. However, because the comma groups the term 'apples or oranges' visually, it helps the reader understand the meaning of the sentence and is therefore an exception to the general rule. Usually the 'extra' comma occurs (properly so) in sentences that have multiple conjunctions and need clarification.

This technique[4] leads to a *run-on sentence* – in other words, a sentence which continues on after its logical end. It would be better to use the 'and' that was used in the first example or simply use a full stop and start a new sentence.

John threw the ball. Bob dodged the tackle.

While the meaning in this example is relatively clear either way, due to the extreme simplicity of the sentence, think about a more complex example using legal terms:

The contract between the parties does not provide for a modification in terms except by written agreement between the parties, no such written agreement exists here.

Everything is correct except for the misuse of the comma. Replace it with a full stop or semicolon and all will be fine.

Sometimes you will experience the reverse problem – creating a sentence that is incomplete. Such partial sentences are called *sentence fragments* and lack a necessary element such as a subject, a verb or an object. For example, the following phrase lacks a subject:

Threw the ball.

(verb) (object)

While some types of sentences can have an implied subject (for example, the imperative tense, which commands an implied subject to do something – 'Throw the ball!'), most sentences require a subject. Other errors occur when you use a verb that requires an object to make sense. For example, the following sentence is incomplete:

Susan met.

(subject) (verb)

The verb 'to meet' requires an object to make sense – you must meet someone. Technically, this is the difference between a transitive verb (which is a verb which transfers its action to an object) and an intransitive verb (which can stand on its own). Some verbs can be both transitive and intransitive, depending on the circumstances. Check a dictionary if you're unsure whether the verb you're using requires an object or not.

Sentence fragments can be quite long and can thus look like proper sentences. However, a fragment is often introduced by a word, such as 'which' or 'that', which is normally used to introduce a descriptive clause. For example, the second sentence in the following excerpt is a fragment:

---

[4] You could classify this example as either a run-on sentence or a comma splice, which is discussed below.

Numerous errors exist in this contract, stemming from an improper application of the Sales of Goods Act. That resulted when the parties attempted to anticipate every possible circumstance. Instead, they should rely more on the Act.

It looks as if all the elements of a sentence exist – subject (parties), verb (anticipate), object (the rest of the sentence). However, the phrase cannot stand alone – in this case, the word 'that' is describing the improper application of the Act, rather than the numerous errors in the contract. To correct the error, the author needs to make that connection explicit, either by amending the fragment so that it can stand by itself (for example, saying, 'The improper application occurred when …') or tacking it on to the previous sentence (for example, saying, '… Goods Act that resulted when the parties …'). As it stands, the phrase is improper.

Of course, there are instances where you can begin a sentence with 'that' – for example, when 'that' refers to a noun or concept described in the previous sentence.

Capital punishment is morally wrong. That has been accepted by jurists in many nations.

'That' may also describe a noun acting as a subject.

That party was dull.

You may also begin a sentence with 'that', 'which' or a similar word if you then follow that dependent clause with the noun that it modifies or if the clause itself stands as a noun. For example:

That reform is necessary is an idea whose time has come.

Notice, however, that such phrases are awkward and wordy. You can write much more clearly and powerfully if you cut straight to the important point: 'reform is necessary' or 'reform is an idea whose time has come'.

WRITING TIP

Be particularly careful when you begin a sentence with 'which' or 'that'.

c) Subject-verb agreement

Everyone knows how to conjugate a verb. For example, the verb 'to be' is conjugated 'I am', 'you are', 'he is', 'we are', 'they are'. In the abstract, you would never try to say 'I are' or 'we am'. You know that when you have two subjects, you use a plural verb: for example, 'Joanna and Andy are outside'. When writing, however, you can sometimes become confused about how many subjects relate to the verb.

Often, the problem occurs when you have a descriptive phrase that ends in a noun with a different number than the noun which relates to the verb. Because the last noun is closest to the verb, you think that you should conjugate the verb according to what would be called for by the last noun. For example, you might want to write:

A group of birds fly over the lake.

Here you are conjugating 'fly' to correspond to the plural 'birds'. In fact, you should write:

A group of birds flies over the lake.

The noun 'group' is the subject of the sentence. You could take 'of birds' out of the sentence completely and say, 'A group flies over the lake.' You cannot say, 'A group fly over the lake.' 'Group' is a singular noun, 'fly' is a plural form of a verb. Of course, you could avoid the potential for confusion by saying, 'Birds fly over the lake'. What you cannot do is use the first example, since it violates the rule that the verb should match the subject in number.

Lots of confusion exists concerning collective nouns. For example, the words 'audience', 'team', 'staff' and 'council' describe groups but are themselves singular. You will therefore need to use a singular verb, no matter how many objects exist in any descriptive phrase that follows. Sometimes the convention as to whether a noun is singular or plural will depend on whether the speaker is using American or British English. If in doubt, change the sentence structure to avoid the problem. You may consider it a minor matter, but you don't want to run the risk of violating the one linguistic rule that your reader holds dear to his or her heart.

Another area of confusion involves sentences that use 'either/or' constructions or pronouns that appear to be of one number, but are classified as another. Just remember:

Either X or Y[5]	Requires singular verb
Neither A nor B[6]	Requires singular verb
Everyone	Requires singular verb
Anyone	Requires singular verb
No one (or none)	Requires singular verb

The rise in the use of gender-neutral language can also lead to problems relating to subject-verb agreements. As you may know, the Lord Chancellor has supported the use of gender-neutral language in legal writing. This means avoiding 'he'[7] as a generic pronoun and finding

WRITING TIP

Often the easiest and best solution to a grammatical problem is simply to change the sentence structure.

WRITING TIP

Gender-neutral language is here to stay. Get used to using it correctly.

---

[5] Where X and Y are both singular nouns. If one noun is singular and one is plural, conjugate the verb to correspond with the noun which appears closest to the verb.

[6] Again, where A and B are both singular nouns. If one noun is singular and one is plural, conjugate the verb to correspond with the noun which appears closest to the verb.

[7] Also avoid 'man' as a so-called genderless noun.

some other substitute – 'he or she', 'she', 'one' or using a plural. Problems arise when people try to use 'they' without making the rest of the sentence plural. For example, at one time, one would have written:

A criminal is innocent until he is proven guilty.

Modern versions might include 'A criminal is innocent until she is proven guilty', 'A criminal is innocent until he or she is proven guilty', or, avoiding the pronoun altogether, 'A criminal is innocent until proven guilty.' You might change the first noun to a plural form, thus requiring a change in the verb but allowing the neutral 'they' to be used: 'Criminals are innocent until they are proven guilty.' What you cannot say is: 'A criminal is innocent until they are proven guilty.' The error is quite obvious in this sentence, but there are other times when the disparity between the number of the first and second nouns is not quite so obvious. Watch out for it.

d) *Verbs and verb phrases*

Most people have no problems conjugating verbs once they get past a few minor subject-verb agreement problems. Sometimes verbs are in the past tense, sometimes they are in the present tense and sometimes they are in the future tense. What is confusing is when they are in the subjunctive. Most problems with the subjunctive arise with if-then constructions. Normally, you use the subjunctive when you have a situation involving an imaginary, doubtful or wished-for outcome. For example, you should write:

If I had more money, I would travel the world.

Normally you would conjugate the verb 'to have' as 'have' with the pronoun 'I'. However, because the speaker here is not rich and is speaking about a hypothetical situation, the subjunctive is used. Compare this sort of situation with the following:

If I have enough money, I will visit you next week.

In this case, there is no doubt, or at least not the same kind of doubt – the visit will take place if and when the money is found. While you can have the subjunctive in sentences that do not use if-then phrases – for example, 'Alex wished he were dead' or 'I wish I were rich' (using the subjective 'were' rather than the indicative 'was' to indicate that he's not, in fact, dead and I am not, in fact, rich) – it is usually the if-then sentences that cause the most trouble, although they are the easiest to resolve once you know the rule.

Another problem associated with verbs involves verb phrases: infinitives, gerunds and participles. Most of you already know that you're not supposed to split an infinitive, which is the basic 'to do something' form of the verb ('to go', 'to sleep', 'to eat'), with another word, usually an adverb. No matter how much you like phrases such as 'to boldly go where no man has gone before' (the famous *Star Trek* introductory narrative), do not use them in legal writing. While the rule regarding split infinitives may be ignored by Americans and journalists, British lawyers must adhere to the traditional form, saying either 'to go boldly' or 'boldly to go'.

The second issue with verb phrases involves gerunds, which are words ending in '-ing'. Although they may appear to be verbs, gerunds act as nouns. Therefore, you can use them as subjects or objects of sentences. For example:

Running is beneficial to your health.

The thing you need to remember with gerunds is that they need a possessive when they are preceded by nouns or pronouns.[8] Therefore, you should write:

Father noted that Quentin's driving skills were not up to par.

Jenny's romantic happiness was furthered by her attending the ball.

Finally, you may have heard the phrase 'dangling participle' at some point during your schooling. 'Participle' refers to the two verb forms known as the present participle (words ending in '-ing', referred to in the discussion on gerunds) and the past participle (words ending in '-ed' or the equivalent irregular form). Sometimes phrases beginning with a participle can be used to modify another word in the sentence. For example:

Enjoying their cud, my sons watched the cows.

Rotten to the core, Eustace smelled the fragrant apples.

In these two examples, the dependent clauses which begin the sentences are misplaced and are called dangling participles. As you recall from the discussion above, you should always put dependent, modifying clauses as close to the words they modify as possible. These two sentences put the phrases containing the participles in the wrong place, thus altering the meaning of the sentences. If we put the participles in their proper place, all becomes clear.

My sons watched the cows enjoying their cud.

Eustace smelled the fragrant apples, rotten to the core.

---

[8] Gerunds also act as a singular noun, not a plural noun. Conjugate your verbs accordingly. For example, 'Driving in cities is frustrating.'

Sometimes you will need to correct a misplaced modifying clause by including additional words or altering the sentence somewhat, but if you keep to the rule of putting modifiers as close as possible to the word which they modify, you will avoid most errors.

e) *Punctuation*

A number of common errors fall under the heading of punctuation. While some of these errors may be more confusing to the reader than are others, all violate the technical rules of grammar.

Capitalisation

Capitalise only those words that appear at the beginning of sentences and proper nouns, ie formal names of people and places. For example, capitalise 'Paris' and 'Oxfordshire' but not 'my neighbourhood'. Similarly, capitalise 'Uncle Joe' or 'Mum', but not 'my mum' or 'my uncle'. A good rule of thumb is that if you have to put a possessive word (my, her, their) in front of a noun, it's not a proper noun.[9]

Titles are another kind of word that are often wrongly capitalised. If a title is used as a common noun describing the position, rather than describing the person, then don't capitalise it. For example:

I interviewed the president of the company.

I interviewed President Smith of Acme Plumbing Company.

Students commonly make similar errors with words like 'court' and 'judge'. If you are identifying a particular court or judge by name, capitalise both words. If you are not naming someone in particular, don't capitalise the term. For example:

Timothy McMurry was a judge in the District Court.
The courts are under-funded, according to prominent judges.
Interestingly, the Court of Appeal is not the highest court in the land.

The point is, do not randomly capitalise nouns. Not only is it annoying and incorrect, it can cause problems in legal practice, where capitalised words are often used as defined terms. Reading a lot of contracts will start to confuse your eye, and you may start to think that terms like 'net profit' and 'managing agent' are always capitalised, just because you see them capitalised in the documents you read in your work. Don't be fooled. Those terms would not be capitalised if they had not been

WRITING TIP

Avoid random capitalisation.

---

[9] You could say 'my Uncle Joe' if you were using 'Uncle Joe' as his name, but you would not say 'my Uncle, Joe Smith, ' where the word 'uncle' described a relationship rather than a name. In that circumstance, you would say, 'my uncle, Joe Smith'.

defined in the contract. If you begin capitalising terms unnecessarily, you may be creating an ambiguity that could lead to litigation.

In the course of your studies, you may find that some law books or journals capitalise words such as 'State' in violation of the rules of grammar. The editors of those publications have made a decision to capitalise some words to indicate that they are being used as legal terms. While such capitalisation is unneccessary and technically incorrect, the convention is accepted by many people in academia. Nevertheless, you should try to avoid purely random capitalisation in your written work, for the reasons stated above.

If, for some reason, you are unclear about whether to capitalise something, do not try to hide your confusion by alternating between capitalising the term and not capitalising it. Be consistent. The only exception is if you are at one point discussing a term that is not being used as a proper noun – president, for example – and then go on to refer to President Smith. In that instance, you capitalise the word in one context but not the other, precisely because it is being used differently.

Apostrophes

Apostrophes either denote a possessive or stand in the place of a missing letter in a contraction. A possessive is a word that shows ownership. Not all possessives use an apostrophe – for example, 'hers', 'his' and 'theirs' do not – but most do. Usually, when you have a noun, such as the name of a person or of a company, you make that noun possessive by adding an apostrophe followed by an 's'.

Irving's car

Bumpstead Council's land

If a noun is plural, in many cases it will already end in 's'. In those cases, retain the 's' of the plural but add an apostrophe after it.

a student's book but *all the students' book* (one book in both cases)

a student's books but *all the students' books* (many books in both cases)

The noun following the plural possessive may be singular or plural depending on the context: for example, if you have several poodles, all of whom shared one leash, you would have 'the poodles' leash'.[10]

---

[10] Single and joint possession of single or joint items can be tricky. For example, 'Hiram and Mary's farms' refers to several farms owned jointly by Hiram and Mary. 'Hiram's and Mary's farms' refers to separately owned farms. Seldom will you have to get into this kind of detail, so don't worry about it too much. Remember, if a phrase sounds confusing or is too difficult to figure out, you can always change the sentence structure to avoid the problem altogether.

Another common mistake concerning possessives involves proper names which end in 's' and which need to be made into a possessive. In this case, you add an apostrophe and an 's', rather than just an apostrophe.[11]

Jones's newspaper

Christopher Columbus's ship

This convention is waning in the popular media, however, and has almost disappeared in the US, so you may not see the 's' apostrophe 's' even though grammarians insist on its correctness. Nevertheless, you should adhere to the traditional approach on the assumption that the law will be among the last fields to embrace linguistic change.

Apostrophes are also used to replace missing letters in contractions. A contraction is a shortened word that takes the place of two words. For example:

do not	becomes	*don't*
he would	becomes	*he'd*
I will	becomes	*I'll*

There are too many possible contractions to list here, but you understand the concept. The one exception to the rule involves the contraction and the possessive of 'it'.

it is	becomes	*it's*
it (possessive)	becomes	*its*

The error is common but quite confusing. Be sure that you do not mistake the two words.

There is also confusion about the contraction and possessive of 'who'. Please note:

who's	contraction – 'who is' or 'who was'
whose	possessive – something owned by 'who'

Finally, there are three words that sound alike but are spelled differently and mean different things.

they're	contraction – 'they are' or 'they were'
their	possessive – something owned by them
there	an adverb as to location or to indicate the general existence of an item ('there is' a thing or 'there are' things)

---

[11] The exception is when the penultimate syllable ends in an 's', in which case use only an apostrophe to form the possessive singular: Jesus' robe, Moses' tablets, Ulysses' journey, Onassis' yacht.

While we're on the subject of misspelled words, you should be aware of another group of words that often leads to confusion:

to	preposition (someone is going to a place) or part of an infinitive verb ('to play' or 'to dance')
too	meaning 'also'
two	a number

These may seem like minor errors to you, but they are technically incorrect. More importantly, such errors will drive certain readers mad and cause those readers to doubt your ability or motivation to avoid errors in the substance of the work.

Commas, full stops, colons and semicolons

The subject of full stops is discussed briefly above, in the section concerning run-on sentences and sentence fragments. Basically, when a thought has been completed, you should use a full stop. To begin a new thought, begin a new sentence. While eighteenth- and nineteenth-century writers (both in and out of the law) used long, complex sentences with multiple phrases and clauses, the modern style favours shorter, crisper sentences. You may certainly use longer sentences for variety or effect, but never underestimate the power of short, simple prose. Your audience will appreciate your ability to communicate your ideas quickly and simply. If you make your readers work too hard, they may give up altogether.

The use of full stops is a mandatory rule of grammar to the extent that you must avoid run-on sentences and sentence fragments. Similarly, there are times when you must use commas to comply with grammatical rules, although there are other times when the use of commas becomes a matter of personal style.

People normally use commas to indicate a pause in the sentence, similar to a breathing space in oral communication. While this can be a good rule of thumb, it can lead you astray. For example, people may attempt to use a comma to join two related but still separate thoughts, leading to a run-on sentence (also called a comma splice). The following example can be described as a run-on sentence or a comma splice, since the comma incorrectly joins two thoughts:

The claimant ran to his car, he was attempting to escape.

You should either replace the comma with a full stop, making two sentences, or add other words to make the second clause dependent in some way. Better sentence constructions would be:

The claimant ran to his car as he attempted to escape.

The claimant, attempting to escape, ran to his car.

The claimant ran to his car in an attempt to escape.

There are several proper uses of commas. When you have a list of things or activities, separate them by commas. For example:

Alice owned a bracelet, two watches[,] and six pairs of earrings.

While you must use commas to identify the different elements, whether you include a comma before the 'and' is purely a matter of style. Most people do not use a comma in that situation, but it is correct to do so. Whichever approach you adopt, be sure to be consistent throughout your document – it is never correct to switch between the two styles.

You can also use commas to separate different activities.

Duncan left his house, ran to the gym, lifted some weights[,] and returned home.

Again, it is your decision as to whether to insert the final comma or not. Notice that each of the groups of words exist in parallel form, meaning that they are all past tense verbs constructed in a similar way.

You would not want to mix different types of word groups or nouns. For example, the following grates on the ear and the eye:

Melanie enjoys skiing, swimming and a good run.

Instead, all the activities should be in a similar form:

Melanie enjoys skiing, swimming and running.

Melanie likes to ski, swim and run.

Any time you have a list or a comparison, be sure to use parallel forms.

Sometimes lawyers will construct long lists of activities or word phrases that contain commas within individual phrases. In those circumstances, you should consider the use of a semicolon, rather than a comma, to separate the different items. For example:

The court requires the claimant to produce the following items: all personnel records, whether printed or electronic, relating to the defendant; all telephone logs mentioning the defendant by name; all daily calendars for the years 1995 to 2002, inclusive; and all reports produced by the defendant during his tenure at the company.

Note that, in this case, you do include a semicolon before the 'and' preceding the final entry in the list. You should also use semicolons when you are listing a complex series of items by number. For example:

> **NOTE**
>
> When listing several items, make sure they are in parallel grammatical form.

> *The court requires the claimant to produce the following items: (i) all personnel records, whether printed or electronic, relating to the defendant; (ii) all telephone logs mentioning the defendant by name; (iii) all daily calendars for the years 1995 to 2002, inclusive; and (iv) all reports produced by the defendant during his tenure at the company.*

Shorter lists may use commas instead, but lawyers still tend to use semicolons.

> *The claimant undertakes not to* (i) *sell,* (ii) *transfer or* (iii) *otherwise encumber the property in question until the lien has been paid.*[12]

When commas are used in this way, the convention about the final sequential comma holds true: use it as your style dictates, but be consistent.

WRITING TIP

Do not look to judicial opinions, particularly older opinions, as a guide to proper punctuation.

You may notice that some older judges and lawyers do not use commas when listing a series of items or activities. This is a holdover from older days, when legal convention forbade the use of many types of internal punctuation. It used to be that courts would use internal punctuation to construe the terms of a document in a specific manner and lawyers attempted to evade that sort of construction by eliminating punctuation altogether. Such conventions have now largely disappeared, and you should follow the rules of grammar unless otherwise instructed by your employer.

Parenthetical information

Parenthetical information is that which can be deleted from the sentence without destroying the sense of the phrase. Be careful, however – parenthetical information requires either two commas, one on either side of the phrase, or none at all. It is improper to use just one comma unless the sentence begins or ends where the second comma would be.

For example:

> *Hugh, a tall, striking man, entered the room.*
>
> *The judge, surprisingly, ruled for the defendant.*
>
> *The company, by and large, complied with the tax laws.*
>
> *Of course, Frederick was busy washing the windows.*
>
> *Law books, which are more expensive than other texts, can break a student's budget.*

---

[12] You can use or not use numbers in a series like this, as you wish.

In each of these examples, the phrase set off by commas can be eliminated without destroying the meaning of the sentence. Remember, however, that there are some phrases that do not merely describe a quality of a noun or verb but instead positively identify it. An identifying phrase should not be set off by commas. To take an earlier example, the following sentence includes a descriptive phrase that can be eliminated without damaging the sense of the sentence and therefore can be set aside by commas:

John threw the ball, which was coming apart at the seams.

If you wish to indicate that John picked one particular ball out of a selection of many, you would delete the comma, writing:

John threw the ball which was coming apart at the seams.

Introducing quotations

Students often have many problems regarding the proper use of commas when introducing quotations and speech. Most people know the rule that commas should be used to introduce direct speech. While this rule is most often exemplified in fiction, it can be used in legal writing as well. For example:

Lord Murray said, 'The duty of care was not established by the claimant.'

Note that there is a comma introducing the sentence and that the quote, which is a sentence unto itself, begins with a capital letter. You could also say:

Lord Murray disagreed with counsel, saying, 'The duty of care was not established by the claimant.'

If you were only quoting part of Lord Murray's statement, you might write:

Lord Murray said [that] the duty of care 'was not established.'

Here the quoted phrase is not a complete sentence and thus cannot support an introductory comma. Note also that the use of 'that' is optional: the sentence makes sense with or without it. Some writers prefer always to use 'that' in these sorts of cases, whereas other people are not so strict. Follow the style that is preferable to you, remembering that clarity is your ultimate aim.

Do not use a comma following 'that', even if the quotation that follows is a complete sentence. For example:

Lord Murray said that 'the duty of care was not established by the claimant.'

The question is whether one should capitalise the first letter of the quoted material, assuming that the first word was capitalised in the original. There is never a need to capitalise the first letter of a quoted phrase following 'that', and generally you should not change any aspect of quoted material, including capitalisation and verb forms, unless you indicate the changes with square brackets. Therefore, if the first letter was capitalised in the original and the tense of the verb was something other than what you wanted, you should write:

> *Lord Murray said that '[t]he duty of care [was] not established by the claimant.'*

WRITING TIP

Make your quotes word perfect. Alter nothing from the original, including the punctuation, without indicating the change.

By using the square brackets, you indicate that you have altered the original. While the changes are largely cosmetic, you must not take liberties with quoted material. Use ellipses (three full stops (...))[13] if you delete any text, even a single word. Be sure not to change the meaning of the quote through your amendments.

You may introduce direct quotations with a colon, although that convention is usually reserved for large blocks of material which are offset by indentations on both the left and right. In such cases, inverted commas are not used, since the colon and indentations signify that a quote follows. For example:

> A long quotation, usually numbering 50 words or more, is offset by indentations on both sides. This is called a 'block quotation'. Often the text is single, rather than double, spaced, and is introduced by a colon. If the quoted material begins in the middle of a sentence, the lead-in phrase may end in the word 'that', followed by a colon, despite the rule that quotations introduced by the word 'that' should not be preceded by a comma. Legal practitioners often italicise block quotations to set it off from the rest of the text. Some practitioners also italicise shorter quotations that appear in the text, although the question then arises whether single quoted words require italicisation or not.

The text that follows a block quotation is either set flush left, if it continues the same thought, or is indented once, if it begins a new sentence.

Sometimes students ask whether to use single or double quotation marks (also called inverted commas). Typically, British usage has been to use single marks, with all punctuation (commas, full stops, question

---

[13] If your sentence ends with an ellipsis, use four full stops (three for the ellipsis and one for the full stop).

marks) showing outside the closing mark, unless that closing mark relates to the quoted material. For example:

John asked, 'How do I get to the music shop?'
Do you think it was appropriate for counsel to say that 'the claimant was the wealthiest woman in Bedfordshire'?

American writers often put punctuation inside the final quotation mark and use double quotation marks. However, some British writers and editors have begun to use double quotation marks where they once would have used single marks, so there may no longer be any national convention on this subject. Furthermore, some lawyers may have been taught to use single inverted commas when quoting from documents and double inverted commas when quoting speech, though this is by no means standard practice. The best solution is to use whichever form appeals most to you and the people reading your work. The key is to be consistent, whichever approach you use. However, you should note that when there is a quotation imbedded inside the material that you are quoting, you should change the number of marks to demonstrate what was said by the person you are quoting and what was said by another person. For example:

Counsel stated that 'the witness heard Mrs Jones shouting, "Stop, thief!" when the defendant ran past the witness's shop carrying a woman's handbag.'

Commas may be used in other circumstances as well as the ones listed above, but these are the three major problem areas. If you want to read more about the proper use of commas, consult one of the many books on grammar.

Students also tend to misuse colons and semicolons, but with less frequency, since both forms of punctuation are somewhat archaic. In addition to the uses noted above, a semicolon can be used to separate two full sentences that are closely linked in subject matter; in such cases, a semicolon falls somewhere between a comma and a full stop. Be sure that a proper sentence exists on either side of the semicolon, however, and do not capitalise the first word following the semicolon.

Colons can be used to separate two proper sentences, but are seldom used in this manner today. The link between the two sentences would be similar to a premise followed by a conclusion. For example:

The claimant stated that there was a simple reason why he did not have the requisite mental state to commit the crime: he had been drugged at the time.

However, such sentences are not often seen these days. Modern use of the colon is generally limited to the introduction of either a quotation (as described above) or a list of items. For example:

The thief took everything of value from the house: the jewellery, the electronic equipment, the antique silver, everything.

Remember, do not capitalise the first word following a colon.

Finally, try not to use dashes in any sort of formal legal writing. For the most part dashes – which can be used to offset parenthetical information as in this example – can and should be replaced with commas. If you use dashes, use them sparingly, since they tend to give an informal feeling to your writing.

8.4.2 Matters purely of style

TIP

Don't take it personally if you're asked to change your writing to take a client's or senior lawyer's stylistic preferences into account. The goal is to draft a document that is clear and suitable to its purpose, not to fight over the placement of an adjective or two.

Everyone's style is unique, but some written styles are more accessible and appropriate to legal writing than others. While it is difficult, and in many cases undesirable, to give up your own style of writing completely in favour of another approach, you can and should think about ways to improve your writing. Junior lawyers, in particular, need to be flexible in their writing style, since the senior lawyers with whom they work may have very strong ideas about how certain documents should be written. You may need to adapt your style to match that of the person with whom you are working.

It may be that you will be given conflicting instructions from the senior lawyers with whom you work. You probably have run across this phenomenon already at university and at school: one instructor tells you one thing while another instructor tells you the exact opposite. First, you need to distinguish whether the advice you have been given concerns mandatory rules of grammar (in which case, you need to do what is objectively right, regardless of what others say; remember, many people do not know the rules of grammar) or discretionary matters of style. Second, if the advice concerns a matter of style, you need to consider whether to follow that advice and to what extent. Sometimes you will need to make the change only once, for expediency's sake, on one particular assignment. Other times you may consider making a permanent change to your writing style. Remember, you can learn something from almost everyone – some lawyers are good at writing demand letters, others are better at writing memoranda of law, still others are better at writing fact summations. If you adopt the best aspects of each person's writing style, you will be well on the way to becoming a better writer yourself.

Following are a number of suggestions on how to improve your writing. Adopt or discard these suggestions as you wish, realising that none of them reflects a mandatory rule that cannot be broken. For ease of discussion, the advice has been broken down into three major points:

- word choice;
- sentence structure; and
- formatting.

a) *Word choice*

Under the heading of 'word choice' lies a multitude of issues, including:

- beginning sentences with 'and' or 'but';
- ending sentences with prepositions;
- using gender-neutral language;
- using 'as' for 'since';
- using contractions and hyphens;
- spelling out numbers;
- using jargon, acronyms and 'legalisms', as opposed to terms of art;
- using passive, wordy or verbose language rather than simple, direct phrases; and
- differentiating advocacy from inflammatory prose.

We will deal with each of the points in turn.

(1) Some grammarians insist that it is technically correct to begin a sentence with 'and' or 'but'. However, many readers find such constructions sloppy or overly colloquial. If you feel you must begin a sentence with one of these words, do so with the understanding that you may put off at least part of your audience.

(2) Just as the beginning of a sentence can cause problems, so too can the end of a sentence. The major concern involves prepositions. While it is perfectly acceptable for novelists and journalists to end sentences with a preposition, lawyers do not have the same freedom. Legal writing remains much more formal than fiction and journalism. When you find yourself faced with a sentence that ends in a preposition, you have three possible solutions: (1) you can place the preposition earlier in the sentence; (2) you can find some phrase to tack onto the end of the sentence,

thus embedding the preposition in text; or (3) you can rephrase the sentence to avoid the offending construction. For example:

Samuel wondered whom[14] *the letter was from. (ending in preposition)*

(1) Samuel wondered from whom the letter was.[15]

(2) Samuel wondered whom the letter was from and glanced at the return address.[16]

(3) Samuel wondered who wrote the letter.[17]

All of these techniques can work well, depending on the context. For example, while the first option sounds a bit too formal in the context of this simple sentence, it will often be acceptable in legal prose. Similarly, while the third sentence appears the best of the three options in this example, since it is the simplest and most direct construction, there will be times when you want to retain a passive verb form rather than shift to an active verb form.

(3) Certain problems associated with gender-neutral language have been discussed in earlier sections concerning subject-verb agreement. Basically, you should not use 'them' in reference to an antecedent noun when that noun is singular, even if you do so to avoid using the gender-specific 'he'. However, you may question the use of gender-neutral language altogether, preferring to use the simpler and more traditional approach of using 'he' or 'man' to refer to all persons.

In the end, use of gender-neutral language is a matter of style rather than a mandatory grammatical rule. It is not incorrect to use 'he' to refer to all persons. Certainly most statutes use 'he' to refer to all persons. However, this convention may be changing, since the Lord Chancellor has recently come out in favour of gender-neutral language. It may be that use of the older style will soon be seen as anachronistic. However, as you decide which approach you will use, you should be

---

[14] Note that the proper word here is 'whom', not 'who'. Generally, you should use 'whom' whenever you could use the word 'him' (ie to him, from him) and 'who' whenever you should use 'he'. It's easier to remember this trick if you use male pronouns rather than female pronouns, since the male pronouns demonstrate the he/who, him/whom parallel most clearly.

[15] Although this may sound a bit formal, particularly in the context of this simple sentence, you quickly become used to phrases such as 'from whom', 'to whom', 'of which', etc.

[16] This example reads somewhat awkwardly due to the simple sentence construction, but that need not be the case in all circumstances. If tacking on an additional phrase does result in a wordy or unwieldy sentence, however, you should consider using one of the other techniques instead.

[17] This is perhaps the best option of the three, since it uses a more active and direct verb form rather than a passive verb form.

aware that many people currently become irate upon seeing 'he' or 'man' to refer to all persons. If your aim is to avoid saying something that would make your reader disinclined towards you and your position, you should avoid gender-specific language.

(4) It is quite common to see people use the word 'as' instead of the word 'since' or 'because'. For example:

As he was a plumber, repairing the drain was a simple task.

While close inspection of the dictionary suggests that 'as' may be used in this way, some readers object strongly. Again, if your aim is to avoid alienating your readers, you may want to consider avoiding this type of construction, even if it is technically correct.

(5) Once upon a time, contractions were severely discouraged in legal writing. They were considered too sloppy and colloquial for the elevated practice of law, leading lawyers to avoid their use altogether. With the advent of the plain English movement in legal writing, lawyers are free to use less formality in their writing. The extent to which you use contractions in your writing is up to you, but be aware that legal writing still tends to be more formal than other types of communication.

Contractions refer to shortened words. However, hyphens can be used to extend the length of words, turning two words into one in order to show how the words relate to one another. These hyphenated words are called complex nouns or complex adjectives. The rules about hyphenation have changed. At one time, it was common to use hyphens to create longer words. For example, people used to write 'decision-maker' rather than 'decision maker', or 'sun-dried tomato' rather than 'sun dried tomato'. Some words that used to be hyphenated have now become single words: for example, 'life-like' is now 'lifelike'.

Although modern usage varies,[18] the general trend is to avoid hyphenation of distinct words except to avoid confusion. For example, there is a significant difference between the phrase 'man eating tiger' and 'man-eating tiger'. Use your common sense and consult a dictionary if you run into trouble.

(6) The convention about spelling out numbers is little-known outside publishing circles, but many readers can sense an error, even if they cannot say what the rule is. In all cases, you should always spell out numbers zero through ten. Some grammarians say that you should

---

[18] As is often the case, differences exist between American and British usage regarding spelling and hyphenation.

spell out numbers zero through one hundred, but there is not as much consensus on that particular convention. Unless you have a long series of numbers, fractions (three-quarters, two-fifths, etc) and rankings (first, second, twenty-seventh) are best in spelled-out form.

However, if you refer to several different numbers in the course of a discussion, you should be consistent: either spell out all of the numbers or none of them. The choice of whether to spell out or write the number is up to you unless one of the numbers falls in the zero to ten range, in which case you should spell out all the numbers.

(7) The most difficult thing to contemplate in the abstract is the overall tone of your prose. For the most part, you should avoid excessive use of jargon or acronyms, unless those terms are universally used. You are all used to reading legal opinions that are so overburdened with acronyms and abbreviations that the text is virtually unreadable. The same is true of student essays. Excessive use of acronyms can become confusing or lessen the persuasive power of the work.

In any case, you must remember to define your terms before using an abbreviation. If, for example, you throw 'UCTA' into a tort essay without further explanation, it may take your reader a while to understand that you are referring to the Unfair Contract Terms Act 1977. Similarly, you can abbreviate party names in a problem question, but be sure to define them first. Avoid beginning a sentence with an abbreviation, particularly abbreviations such as 's' or 'ch', which relate to sections of a statute or document. For a more complete discussion of this point, see section 9.4, which addresses formatting conventions relating to professional practice.

The difference between legal jargon and terms of art can be difficult to define. There are some legal terms that cannot be properly translated into plain English. Some of these terms are in Latin – for example, *res ipsa loquitur* – whereas others are in English – for example, duty of care or *Wednesbury* reasonableness. You must be able to use these terms correctly and precisely if you wish to convey your meaning. Failure to use the proper legal terminology can lead an examiner to conclude that you simply don't know the correct language. Don't worry about repeating the term too much; if it is the correct term, use it whenever it is appropriate. While some writing instructors encourage students to use 'elegant variations' rather than repeat the same phrase over and over, legal writing is different in that too much variation in terms leads to confusion, particularly when you are, for example, describing a legal principle or a contractually defined term.

Legal jargon refers to the type of overused legalisms that really add nothing to the discussion. For example, referring to 'the aforementioned' or 'the *res* in question' is pompous and unnecessary. Just name whatever it is you are discussing. Including unnecessary Latin phrases also puts the reader off – for example, there really is no reason to use the terms '*qua*', '*ex ante*' or '*de novo*'. The difference between legal jargon and a proper term of art is whether the word or phrase carries a specific legal meaning or is part of a legal test. If the term has acquired this type of official legal value, then it is usually a term of art. It is difficult to describe a fee simple or a constructive trust except as legal concepts. Fraud and misrepresentation are more difficult terms – they both carry purely legal meanings as well as popular meanings. You will want to be careful how you use those particular terms. If, however, the term is merely used by convention or tradition and does not carry a particular legal connotation – for example, 'heretofore' carries no legal meaning[19] – there's no real need to use it. Use your judgment, and remember that just because you've seen the phrases used in reported opinions doesn't mean that you should use them in your own work. Many of the cases you read are somewhat elderly, and legal writing has changed a lot in recent years. Similarly, not all judges can be considered good writers.

(8) Another misconception that students have is that hesitant or equivocal language is more objective and lawyerly than bold, unambiguous statements. Students will therefore litter their essays with terms such as 'it would seem' or 'it appears to be the case that'. Avoid these and any other phrases that demonstrate uncertainty on behalf of the writer. You are the expert. These are your conclusions and arguments; don't weaken them with seeming hesitance. If there is a split in the law or a debate about the wisdom of a particular course of action, then discuss both sides and offer your conclusion. Don't characterise your conclusions before you state them. In the end, you may not be able to persuade your reader to your point of view, but if you don't appear to believe in your own statements, the reader will be less likely to do so.

This is not to say that you should ignore real instances of uncertainty or cases which are too close to call definitively one way or another. There are times when you need to say that something 'appears' to be true or that one party will 'most likely' prevail. However, real splits in the authorities occur far less often than students think they do. Instead, students seem to believe that by appearing hesitant about their conclusions, they will hedge their bets and win more points in case they are wrong. In fact, your reader will not be fooled by this kind of language. Your conclusions are your conclusions; stand by them.

---

[19] There are occasional exceptions. Some contracts use 'heretofore' as part of the formula introducing terms and conditions or a party's warranties. For example, 'it is heretofore agreed between the parties that ...' While you should not introduce this kind of language into your essays, be aware that some practitioners you work with may require you to use these terms in formal documents. You would not need them, nor should you use them, in less formal documents such as correspondence.

Students also precede many of their statements by the phrase 'I believe' or 'I think', occasionally tossing in a 'this author believes'. This type of tip-off is unnecessary. The reader knows that your entire essay constitutes your own thoughts. The only time you might need to identify a thought or conclusion as your own is if the idea stands in close proximity to the report of another person's beliefs.

> **EXAMPLE**
>
> Jones writes that the royal prerogative is an outdated concept that should be replaced with a written code outlining the executive power, whereas Littleton advises caution in any reform attempts. Jones's position is unrealistic, given the British animosity towards codifying large swathes of the law, whereas Littleton's view is too cautious. I would recommend an intermediate step, wherein reform would progress piecemeal by codifying individual aspects of the prerogative one bit at a time.

> *** NOTE**
>
> Use an apostrophe followed by 's' to make a proper name possessive, even if the name – like Jones – ends in 's'. The only exceptions to that rule are the names 'Jesus' and 'Moses'.

In the above example, the 'I would' sentence could be changed to 'A better solution would be to adopt an intermediate course, wherein (etc)', thus avoiding the use of 'I' altogether. However, this is one of the few examples where you can adopt the first person without weakening your argument.

You can also slow down your essay by using too many words. Try to cut down the numbers of words you use and use short, simple sentences. One practitioner, well known for his powerful written communication, advocated the KISS rule: Keep It Simple, Stupid. Don't try anything fancy. Just say what you have to say and move on. In fact, experienced examiners know that students often use passive, wordy prose when they don't really know what they're saying. Someone who is overflowing with things to say writes in a tight, energetic manner. If you find yourself becoming passive and wordy in your prose, stop. Do you really know what you're trying to say? If you don't, neither will your reader. Sort yourself out before continuing to write. A short essay that speaks directly to the question is often far better than a long, meandering discussion that never really gets to the point.

> **TIP**
>
> *When in doubt, apply KISS.*

Often prose can be tightened up by using an active, rather than passive, voice, as described below. Also, instead of characterising something or some action by using the verb 'to be' plus a gerund (a verb acting as a noun) or an adjective, try using the gerund in its verb form or turning the adjective into an adverb. For example:

Mark is advocating reform.

Mark advocates reform.

Jennifer was nervous when writing her examination.

Jennifer nervously wrote her examination.

Essays also become wordy and vague when the writer spends too much time characterising an action or event rather than describing what occurred and why it is important. For example, a student may classify a particular case as 'radical' or 'ground-breaking'. These are empty phrases that add little to the discussion: unless those adjectives are immediately followed by the word 'because', you should eliminate them from your essay. Even worse is the word 'interesting', which has been so overused that it has lost its descriptive force completely. Your characterisation of the case, statute or event is not what is important: it is the content and/or impact of the case, statute or event. Move past vague, introductory language and say why you are discussing the matter. If you show your readers what you're thinking, they will form the same conclusion that you have. If you do not show them what you're thinking, they will not believe or understand your characterisations.

Sometimes passive language results when a writer uses a phrase that is accurate but that can be replaced by shorter words or phrases. For example, consider replacing the examples of passive language with those which are more active:

WRITING TIP

Show, don't tell, in your writing. Use strong verbs and examples instead of adjectives and adverbs.

Passive language	Active language
in order to, for the purpose of, with a view to	to
as a consequence, for the reason that, on account of, on the grounds that, in light of the fact that	because
in the event of, in case of	if
in spite of the fact that, irrespective of the fact that	although or even though
notwithstanding the fact that	even if
there can be little doubt that, it is indubitable that	clearly or undoubtedly[20]
until such a time that	until

[20] Be aware that many writers believe that the use of the word 'clearly' or 'undoubtedly' actually signals a fact or opinion that is anything but clear or undoubted. It is always better to show the reader something rather than tell the reader something. If the fact or opinion is clear or undoubted, demonstrate that with legal authority or a summation of the facts. Showing your reader how you have arrived at your conclusion is more powerful than merely assuring him or her that you are correct. Remember, your opponent is making precisely the same assurances in return.

Other phrases can be deleted altogether without losing the sense of the sentence. For example:

> *One should note that criminals often regret their actions.*
>
> > *Criminals regret their actions.*

> *The fact was that Simon didn't want to go cycling that day.*
>
> > *Simon didn't want to go cycling that day.*

Common offenders of this rule are:

> *one should note that*
>
> *it is important to note that*
>
> *the fact that*
>
> *it is true that*

There may occasionally be times when you need or want to use these phrases to add emphasis or to alter the tempo of the paragraph. Use them sparingly, however.

WRITING TIP

Don't overuse the thesaurus. Remember to KISS.

Finally, some people think that unusual, literary or polysyllabic words impress readers and demonstrate greater erudition and knowledge. Not true. Often big words slow the pace or confuse the meaning. Remember KISS – Keep It Simple, Stupid. Don't use a long word if a short one will do just as well. You can be an effective writer without wearing out your thesaurus.

(9) Sometimes the issue is not that a student's prose is too deferential or wordy, it is that it is too one-sided. Strong language is fine as long as you do not exaggerate the claims that you make on either the facts or the law. Learn to differentiate between advocacy and inflammatory prose. This is a problem that more often arises in professional practice, particularly if you are involved in litigation or dispute resolution, but sometimes students think that being persuasive means ignoring or belittling an opponent's argument. Instead, you should strive to make your case as persuasively as you can while still retaining some objectivity. If the other side has a valid point to make, you must acknowledge it. If you appear to be too one-sided, you will fail to persuade your reader. Readers tend to trust objective analysis more than one-sided rhetoric.

You need to be sure to address any gaps or weaknesses in your own arguments in addition to dealing with any valid points that can be raised by your opponent. You can persuade a reader to adopt your point of view by demonstrating how your argument is either more logical, more just or more in line with the authorities. Dismissing your opponent's argument out of hand or failing to address it at all carries no persuasive value. When offering advice to clients in professional practice, a lawyer must recognise points of weakness as well as points of strength. You need to do the same in your essays and examinations.

Another thing to look out for is excessive characterisation of positions, facts or legal arguments. As mentioned above, it adds very little to say that one of your points is 'devastating' or 'fatal' to your opponent if it is not, in fact, determinative. Similarly, describing a certain case as 'radical', without discussing why it constitutes such a sharp shift from the past, does not make your point. Showing your readers what you mean is much more persuasive than telling them your conclusions.

b) *Sentence structure*

The previous subsection concentrated primarily on word-choice issues. However, the type of sentence structure you choose also affects your writing. The most common error lies in the excessive use of passive sentence construction. When you write in the active voice, the subject of the sentence acts. When you write in the passive voice, the subject of the sentence is acted upon. Compare the following sentences:

Jane was treated by the doctor for influenza. (passive)

The doctor treated Jane for influenza. (active)

The roses were dug up by the neighbours' dog. (passive)

The neighbours' dog dug up the roses. (active)

Generally, the active voice is more direct and engaging to the reader. It is the preferred voice in all sorts of prose. However, there are times when the passive voice should be used, particularly by lawyers. For example, if you do not know who did something or if you want to emphasise that the act was done, rather than that it was done by someone in particular, you may need to resort to the passive voice. For example:

The flat was broken into at approximately 3:00 a.m. (you don't know by whom)

The New Year was rung in with great frivolity. (the emphasis is on the frivolity, not on the actors)

Unfortunately, the passive voice is often overused in legal writing. Students, and indeed many practising lawyers, operate under the mistaken assumption that the passive voice is more objective and lawyerly than the active voice. While the passive voice is one of the many tools available to a good writer, it should be used sparingly and only in suitable circumstances. The active voice will be more useful in most circumstances.

Another sentence construction that should be used sparingly is the rhetorical question. Although rhetorical questions can be effective in oral argument, they often fall flat in an essay or exam scenario because

TIP

If you're struggling to correct a small portion of a larger sentence or paragraph and just can't come up with a simple solution, try stepping back and rewriting that sentence or paragraph from scratch. Sometimes a full-scale change is faster and better than trying to salvage an irretrievably flawed sentence or phrase, no matter how much you like your original wording.

they conflict with the author's primary purpose. Rhetorical questions are not meant to be answered: the purpose of a law essay, however, is to answer the question set. You see the dilemma. Avoid rhetorical questions as a stylistic device as a general rule.

c) *Formatting*

Finally, it may help to include a few words about essay formats, meaning the mechanical production of your work. In most cases, you should be guided by your tutor and your own preferences. For example, some tutors prefer typed essays, whereas others do not care one way or another. You may find it easier to type your work, since you can revise it more easily than you can a handwritten essay, but you may also find it difficult to switch back to handwritten essays when it comes to time to take your examinations. If you have typed most of your written work during the term, be sure to practise a few handwritten essays before you take your examination.

Some tutors will feel strongly about whether you should single- or double-space your typed essays. Some will not care. There is no hard and fast rule. If you're concerned, ask your tutor.

You can use internal headings (outline numbers or text descriptions) if your argument is very complex or if you feel the need to help your reader follow your structure. Internal headings are often a good idea in long documents. For the most part, however, student essays are too short to need such internal organisation, but you should feel free to use headings if you wish. You should avoid bullet points, however. While bullet points are becoming more common in business and professional practice, they are inappropriate in a student essay which is being evaluated for its style as well as its content.

With the rise in word processing, many students go to great pains to italicise or underline case names and/or quotations and to include full case or statute citations in footnotes. Neither technique is absolutely necessary unless your instructor makes it a requirement. You can put case names in the text just as you would in a handwritten essay. Just be sure your references are clear. There is no need to switch font size or style for quotations, even though practitioners occasionally do so. The use of quotation marks (inverted commas) should be sufficient to indicate that you are citing an outside source. You should try to offset case names by underlining or italicising them, though.

The final point has to do with the visual layout of the paragraphs on the page. Most of you have read older decisions that seem to be one long paragraph. Nothing is more daunting than facing an unbroken page of type, and few things are harder to read. You all know that you should begin a new paragraph every time you begin a new idea, but there are

---

NOTE

If you do not already know how to touch-type (meaning typing without looking at the keys), consider taking a course during the holidays. Typing is an essential business skill for everyone these days.

WRITING TIP

You don't need to use fancy fonts to indicate quoted material, but you must use quotation marks. An unattributed quote constitutes plagiarism!

WRITING TIP

Control the amount of white space on the page to help the reader's understanding.

times when you may end up with one very long paragraph. Even though the paragraph may be correct as a matter of grammar, you should consider breaking it up into two or more paragraphs as a matter of style and thus increasing the amount of white space on the page. Doing so will undoubtedly increase your reader's understanding of your discussion and thereby increase the possibility of your receiving a higher mark.

When you begin a new paragraph, either skip a line (if you intend to place the first word flush against the left margin) or indent the first word one tab (usually five spaces). If you just use a hard return and then begin your next sentence flush left, it is difficult for the reader to see that you have begun a new paragraph, particularly if the last sentence of your previous paragraph runs close to the right margin. You may think this is a minor point, but if the purpose of writing is to communicate your ideas effectively to your reader, then you want to do everything possible to increase the reader's understanding. Breaking the text up into different paragraphs is one of the primary ways of facilitating communication in written prose, since a new paragraph signals a new idea. Don't lessen the effectiveness of your organisational structure by hiding the beginnings and endings of your paragraphs. Doing so will only confuse the reader and drop your marks.

The other formatting point concerns the end of sentences. Whenever you end a sentence, follow it with two spaces, not one. The additional white space helps your reader scan the page more easily and stops the text from looking too cramped.

8.5 Writing techniques: self-examination

You may wish to run through the following self-examination to see how well you know the mandatory and discretionary rules of writing. The answers may be found following the quiz.

Part one
Select the correct answer from the options shown.

1. The contraction of 'it is' is:
   a. its
   b. it's
   c. its'

2. The possessive of 'they' is:
   a. there
   b. they're
   c. their

3. A sentence fragment can be described as:
   a. a sentence without a verb
   b. a sentence without a noun
   c. a sentence without an object
   d. none of the above
   e. all of the above

4. A comma splice results when:
   a. you use one comma instead of two to set off parenthetical information
   b. you join two stand-alone sentences with a comma
   c. you use a comma when you should use a semicolon
   d. you introduce a quotation with the word 'that' followed by a comma

5. You should end a sentence with a preposition:
   a. sometimes
   b. always
   c. never
   d. it depends

6. A dangling participle is incorrect because:
   a. a sentence should never end in a participle
   b. it modifies the wrong part of the sentence
   c. both (a) and (b)
   d. neither (a) nor (b)

7. In legal writing, you should use contractions:
   a. sometimes
   b. always
   c. never
   d. it depends

8. Which of the following numbers should be spelled out in text? (circle all that apply)
   a. 102
   b. 7
   c. 17
   d. 1/2
   e. 3/16
   f. 3rd
   g. 14th
   h. 1,000,000

9. You may use a colon:
   a. to introduce a list of items
   b. to introduce a quotation
   c. both (a) and (b)
   d. neither (a) nor (b)

10. Which of the following terms should be capitalised? (circle all that apply)
    a. President Fox of Mexico
    b. the President of Acme Food Co Ltd
    c. Edith's Aunt
    d. the Court of Appeal
    e. the Local Court
    f. the Agreement between Supply Co and Builder's Co (the 'Agreement')
    g. a Legislative decision

11. You should use the passive voice:
    a. to sound more lawyerly
    b. to draw attention to the person doing the action
    c. to make your prose tighter and more energetic
    d. to focus the reader's attention on the act itself

12. Use rhetorical questions only when:
    a. you are sure the reader knows the answer
    b. you follow them with words such as 'because' or 'due to'
    c. you want to emphasise a certain point
    d. you need to speed up the pace of your writing

13. A block quotation does NOT:
    a. have fewer than 50 words
    b. have quotation marks (inverted commas) at the beginning and end of the quoted material
    c. have quoted material within the larger quote
    d. have a colon as its introductory punctuation

14. The word 'its' is:
    a. the possessive of 'it'
    b. the plural of 'it'
    c. the contraction of 'it was' or 'it is'
    d. 'its' is not a proper word

15. When altering a quotation, you should:
    a. indicate changed letters or words with parentheses ()
    b. indicate deleted words with ellipses (three full stops)
    c. both (a) and (b)
    d. neither (a) nor (b) – you should never alter a quotation

16. Parenthetical information can be:
    a. set off by two commas
    b. set off by one comma
    c. set off without a comma
    d. none of the above

17. Which of the following is NOT correct?
    a. a group of squirrels eats
    b. Mavis's apple cart
    c. the girls' book
    d. a herd of horses drink

18. A good writer:
    a. never acknowledges the merits of an opposing argument
    b. directs the reader's mind by characterising legal authority and arguments as 'strong' or 'persuasive'
    c. uses the active voice when at all possible
    d. uses lots of jargon to indicate an insider's knowledge of the law

19. An appropriate gender-neutral variation on 'he says' would be:
    a. one says
    b. he or she says
    c. people say
    d. they says
    e. (a) and (b) only
    f. (a), (b) and (c) only
    g. (a), (b) and (d) only
    h. (b), (c) and (d) only

20. When you begin a new thought, you should:
    a. begin a new sentence
    b. begin a new paragraph
    c. use an appropriate transition sentence
    d. all of the above

ANSWERS		
1. b	8. b, d, e, f, g, h	15. b
2. c	9. c	16. a
3. e	10. a, d, f	17. d
4. b	11. d	18. c
5. c	12. b	19. f
6. b	13. b	20. d
7. c	14. a	

Part two

The following discussion of religious rights in the UK contains numerous errors. Numbered questions relate to different parts of the text. See if you can spot the errors and improve the language.

TEXT

Because the United Kingdom does not have a single written constitution, it[1] addresses issues regarding religious rights piecemeal, rather than in a unified manner. Some jurists[2] believe that a country with an established faith must experience religious discrimination on some level, though others disagree. Certainly the Church of England enjoys protections and benefits not shared by other faiths, although in 1991 Purchas, LJ in the Court of Appeal stated that 'no distinction between institutions of the Christian church and those of other major religions would now be generally acceptable.'[3] The veracity of the statement, however, is questionable in light of the Court of Appeal's refusal to extend the law of blasphemy to cover non-Christian faiths in *R v Chief Metropolitan Stipendiary Magistrate*, ex parte *Choudhury* just a year before.[4]

The court in *Choudhury*[5] could decide as it[6] did because no specific prohibition on discrimination on the basis of religion existed in England and Wales until the passage of the Human Rights Act 1998. Prior to that time, practitioners and commentators had argued that the Race Relations Act 1976 could be used to address some types of religious discrimination, at least for those religions that were associated with distinctive racial groups, but courts were unpersuaded, the rationale being[7] that the Act was not intended to address purely religious discrimination.[8] Although the Supreme Court has relied on the 1976 Act to remedy some legal injuries related to religious discrimination, as seen in *R v Governing Body of JFS*, that ruling appears very limited in scope. Other jurists claimed that international instruments that have binding or influential power in the UK required the principle of non-discrimination on the basis of religion to be recognised explicitly at the domestic level.[9]

The only jurisdiction to address religious discrimination in the UK prior to the enactment of the Human Rights Act 1998 was Northern Ireland.10 The history of sectarian strife in that region made it necessary to enact specific legislation, particularly in the area of employment, prohibiting discrimination on the basis of religion and making it a criminal offence to incite religious hatred.[11]

Despite these admonitions,[12] discrimination still exists, most visibly and most symbolically in the requirement that the monarch may not be or marry[13] a Roman Catholic. In addition, it was only twenty-five years ago[14] that the office of Lord Chancellor officially became open to Roman Catholics. Employment rates in Northern Ireland show Catholic unemployment at approximately two and a half times that of Protestants.[15]

QUESTIONS

1. To what does the word 'it' refer? How might the sentence be improved?

2. Is the phrase 'some jurists' the best that can be used? How would you alter the text?

3. What is missing from this sentence?

4. What's wrong with this sentence?

5. Is this phrase correct?

6. To what does the word 'it' refer? How might the sentence be improved?

7. What do you think of the phrase 'the rationale being'?

8. What's missing from this sentence?

9. What's missing from this sentence?

10. Why did the author choose to use this type of sentence construction? Does it work?

11. Is a citation to a specific statute necessary here?

12. Is there a problem with this phrase?

13. Is a comma necessary here?

14. Why did the author choose to use this type of sentence construction? Does it work?

15. Does 'Protestants' need an apostrophe? If so, where would you put it?

TEXT

Immigration is another area where religious discrimination arises.[16] In *R v Home Department*, ex parte *Moon*, the Court[17] considered the Home Secretary's claim that he had denied Reverend[18] Sun Myung Moon, founder of the Unification Church (known commonly as the 'Moonies'), entry into the United Kingdom because:[19]

> the Unification Church, even if recognised as a religious organisation by the Charity Commissioners,[20] acts to the detriment of the families to whom its members belonged [sic][21]....[22] The Home Secretary considered the need to act in accordance with a wider obligation to respect freedom of expression and freedom of religion but has concluded that in view of the activities of the Unification Church and those of the Applicant as its head,[23] the exclusion is justified in the public interest.[24]

In the end, Sedley J ordered the Home Secretary to provide reasons for his[25] decision and allow Reverend Moon to respond, noting that 'it is precisely the unpopular applicant for whom the safeguards of due process are most relevant in a society which acknowledges the rule of law.'[26] However, the willingness and ability of the government to discriminate on the basis of religion, as demonstrated by this case, is disturbing.[27]

The UK's legal position regarding religious discrimination has changed, however, with the enactment of the Human Rights Act 1998. Although the applicability of the Act to private entities is indirect only,[28] parties involved in disputes in domestic courts[29] may now expressly rely on many of the provisions found in the European Convention, including its prohibition of discrimination on the basis of religion. In construing the various rights, courts are to take into account European decisions applying the European Convention.

QUESTIONS

16. Why is this sentence here? Is it necessary?

17. Should this word be capitalised?

18. Should this word be capitalised?

19. Do you need a colon here?

20. Should this term be capitalised?

21. What does 'sic' mean and why is it included here?

22. Why are there four full stops here?

23. Is this comma correct?

24. Why are there no closing quotation marks (inverted commas)?

25. Shouldn't this be 'his or her'?

26. Should there be a case citation here?

27. Would you use the word 'disturbing' here?

28. What's missing here?

29. Should this be capitalised?

ANSWERS

1. 'It' refers to 'constitution', not to 'United Kingdom', as the author intended. The author will need to rephrase the sentence so that the word 'it' refers to the proper antecedent.

2. It would be better to refer to specific jurists by name, rather than lump them together. The same is true of the word 'others' later in the sentence – the author should try to be specific when referring to commentators.

3. Referring to a specific judge by name demonstrates a very good facility with the materials, but the author has forgotten to name the case itself.

4. The beginning of the sentence ('The veracity of … in light of') is technically correct but somewhat wordy. The author should be more direct.

5. Yes. Although the author is referring to a specific court, the word 'court' is not being used as part of a title or official designation.

6. 'It' refers to 'the court in Choudhury'. The phrase is correct and sufficiently succinct to stand as it is.

7. The term is technically correct, but perhaps a bit stilted. How might you improve it?

8. The sentence is long but technically correct. Still, it might be better, as a matter of discretion, to break it into two parts, one dealing with practitioners and commentators and the other dealing with the courts.

9. It would be helpful to know which jurists made the claim.

10. The author seems to have chosen this construction to emphasise that Northern Ireland's approach to religious rights is the exception to the general rule. It may also be that the construction was used to give the following sentence the proper antecedent ('that region').

11. A specific citation would be helpful but is not necessary, since the provisions are described with sufficient detail for this discussion.

12. It is unclear what the author means by 'these admonitions'.

13. No comma is needed here since both verbs ('be' and 'marry') refer to the same subject ('monarch').

14. This sentence does not technically use the passive voice, since something is not being done to someone else. The wordiness is suspect, however, although the author is probably using this sentence construction to demonstrate how recent the change in policy has been.

15. No apostrophe is needed, since the possessive element is shown by the sentence structure: 'that of Protestants'.

16. The sentence provides a transition from the previous paragraph and is necessary to indicate that a new example is now being discussed.

17. The word 'court' should not be capitalised here, since the word is not being used as part of a title or official designation.

18. The word 'reverend' should be capitalised, since it is part of a title.

19. A colon is necessary here to introduce the block quote that follows.

20. It is unclear from the quoted material whether the term had been defined earlier in the source material; however, since it is capitalised in the quotation, the author has properly retained the capitalisation.

21. The term 'sic' (sometimes italicised as *sic*) is the Latin for 'so' or 'thus', and is used to indicate an error that exists in the quoted material. In this case, the verb 'belonged' appears to be incorrectly conjugated, but the author properly chose to retain the error with the word 'sic' following to demonstrate that the error existed in the original.

22. The author has used four full stops to indicate the omission of some quoted material (three full stops) and the end of a sentence.

23. The comma is technically incorrect; the sentence should either have no commas or two commas to indicate parenthetical information (one comma appearing here and the other appearing after the word 'that'). However, the error exists in the original material and is too minor to merit deletion (using an ellipsis for a single comma is unusual) or use of the word 'sic'.

24. The author did not use quotation marks (inverted commas) because it is incorrect to do so with quote blocks.

25. Although it is wise to use gender-neutral language, there is no need to do so when referring to a known person. Here, the Home Secretary was male and so can be referred to as 'he' even if his name is not used.

26. There is no need for an additional case citation, since it is clear from context that the quote comes from the previously cited case.

27. The characterisation of the government's actions as 'disturbing' is tricky. Some people would omit the phrase as unnecessary, whereas others would include it, since the basis for the author's conclusion has been made clear. This is one of those areas of discretion where there is no objectively right or wrong approach.

28. It would be nice for the author to slip in a citation to the seminal case on indirect horizontal application (Douglas v Hello!), but it's not absolutely necessary.

29. There is no need to capitalise the word 'courts' here, since the term is acting as a common noun.

This concludes our discussion of general tips on legal writing. Although there is a lot of information contained in this chapter, it can all be simplified to two basic rules:

(1) If you confuse your reader, you will not win top marks, no matter how brilliant you are.

(2) If you can't figure out what the rules of grammar would require in a particular circumstance or if a certain phrase just looks odd, change the sentence structure. That's usually the best and fastest solution. There's no reason why you have to retain your original approach.

As mentioned before, there are numerous books on writing, including some concerning legal writing in particular, and you should feel free to consult them if you have further questions. At this point, however, we will turn to the question of how to adapt the CLEO method for use in legal practice.

CHAPTER 9

Adapting CLEO for professional practice

Many students worry about the transition from academic law to professional practice. Although that fear is perfectly understandable, you should take comfort in knowing that you will receive lots of very specific guidance on how to write letters, memoranda, attendance notes, legal opinions and other types of legal documents once you get on your vocational course and start your pupillages and traineeships. In fact, it is helpful not to get too wedded to one particular model, since most firms and chambers have their own house style that you should emulate once you get into practice.

You are also well prepared to make the transition because you are now familiar with the way practitioners analyse the law and present their arguments in writing. Although you will have to adapt the CLEO method to some extent when you get into practice, you have a solid foundation from which to work. Many students arrive at their traineeships and pupillages without having anywhere near as strong a notion about how to proceed.

Although CLEO techniques will be helpful to you in numerous areas in professional practice, CLEO will not be of great use to you in those areas of law that rely heavily on the use of precedents. As you may know, a good deal of legal work is wholly original, in the sense that you create both the form and the content of the final document. However, some types of written work require you to adapt 'precedents', or model documents that provide the basic form and much of the content of the final submission. A precedent can relate to a common type of legal document between parties (such as an agreement for the sale of goods or services, a will or a trust) or a common type of document used in a court action (such as particulars of claim, defences, etc). Precedents can be found in various form books (ask your legal librarian) or can be given to you by your colleagues. While a precedent can be a great help, and is indeed necessary in many transactions where it would be impractical to create an entirely new document from scratch, you

> **❊ NOTE**
>
> Precedents, properly used, can help you avoid errors and minimise costs.

should never accept any precedent at face value, no matter how prestigious its source. Every case or transaction is different, and you must review your precedents each and every time you use them to make sure that the final document addresses all of your client's relevant issues. Some lawyers operate almost on rote, merely filling in the blanks of a model form without thinking about what they are doing. That is the road to malpractice and disciplinary proceedings; don't do it, not even if a more senior lawyer assures you that this is just a routine matter that doesn't need any special attention.

WRITING TIP

Do not use precedents by rote. Think about what you're doing.

This chapter will not discuss the art of adapting precedents, however, since those skills will be taught in your vocational courses and by your principals and pupil masters, once you graduate to the work-place. Adapting precedents is also very case- and transaction-specific and is thus difficult to discuss in the abstract. Instead, this chapter will focus on how to draft original documents that do not rely on precedents and on adapting the CLEO method to help you create those types of documents. This chapter will therefore discuss:

(1) what forms of documents you will encounter in legal practice;

(2) how to find the question in legal practice; and

(3) how to answer the question in legal practice.

The chapter will conclude with a short discussion of various formatting issues in professional practice.

9.1 Forms of legal documents

Although professional legal documents bear some similarity to the types of essays that you write in university, there are significant differences, both in style and content. These differences will be discussed in greater detail in your vocational courses and in your pupillage and traineeships. However, as you begin the on-the-job aspects of your legal training, you may find the CLEO principles helpful to you as you draft the following documents:

(1) letters;

(2) attendance notes;

(3) memoranda;

(4) briefs (instructions); and

(5) opinions.

Each of the types of documents listed above has certain unique characteristics. Letters, for example, are used to communicate with parties outside the author's own organisation. Legal practitioners write letters that go out not only under their own or their firm's name but also under their clients' names. Any or all of these letters can end up as exhibits in a litigation or arbitration, so you want to be sure that they are as accurate and precise as possible. To some extent, your firm or chambers will have a house style that you should adopt in correspondence. Similarly, there are certain formalities regarding formats, including the proper openings and closings (or 'tops and tails') that you should respect. Again, you should be guided by your supervisors or refer to other books that deal specifically with legal writing in professional practice.

Many lawyers now conduct much of their correspondence by email rather than through formal letters. You must be very careful about what you say in an email, even if it is only sent internally. Email can be forwarded to other parties very easily, and what you thought was only going to be seen internally can suddenly be sent to any number of unintended recipients. If you have a 'do not forward' function on your email system, consider using it. Another problem arises regarding the content of the email. Because email is more informal than 'proper' letters, people tend to write more colloquially and spend less time thinking about what they are saying. As a result, mistakes about legal matters can occur more readily. People also feel free to include jokes in their emails. Again, be careful. What you intend as a joke may not be read by the recipient as one. Even if the person who initially reads your email sees the humour in what you have said, the message may not seem as appropriate two or three years down the line when the email appears as an exhibit in a court case. Computer records, including email records, are disclosable under the rules of civil procedure, so don't be fooled into thinking that just because there is no hard copy of an email, no one will ever see it. Nowadays, courts will demand disclosure of electronic files, including back-up copies of documents or emails that were never communicated to others.[1] Essentially, everything that you type into your computer is recoverable by experts, no matter how hard you try to delete it or overwrite it.

Attendance notes memorialise conversations and meetings, setting forth the details of who attended the event, what was said, what was agreed and whether any documents were provided. A note can be quite short or quite long, depending on the circumstances. Sometimes, as you will learn, it is good practice to make a note of attempted telephone calls or in-person visits that did not result in any sort of

WRITING TIP

Draft all of your documents as if they will end up in court as exhibits. Who knows, they might.

WRITING TIP

Be sure to use proper spelling and grammar, even in electronic mail. Do not confuse a professional email with a Tweet or text message.

CAUTION

Watch what you say in emails. They are perhaps the most dangerous form of communication used in modern legal practice.

---

[1] In the coming years, disclosure and analysis of this 'metadata' will become increasingly important in litigation.

TIP

A note to the file is an excellent way both to cover yourself and make sure important facts and events are remembered.

✱ **NOTE**

Even so-called 'privileged' documents can sometimes show up in court.

conversation, just so that you can later establish your attempt to make contact. As with letters, attendance notes can end up as exhibits in a court case. You do not need to address an attendance note to anyone – a note to the file can be sufficient.

Memoranda involve communications within an organisation such as a law firm. Memoranda may convey the results of legal or factual research or provide a status report on an ongoing project. Because memoranda often involve legal analysis and are not disclosed to third parties, it is possible that they may avoid ending up as court exhibits due to legal privilege. Still, privilege can be lost (for example, if the document is shown to a third party) or waived (for example, if a client wishes to sue its lawyer), and not every memorandum meets the necessary requirements in the first place. Therefore, you should still be cautious about what you say in an ostensibly privileged document.

Briefs, which are also known as instructions, are the formal documents by which a solicitor asks a barrister for a legal opinion. In a brief, a solicitor outlines the facts of the matter and identifies the legal questions he or she would like answered. In addition to the specific questions posed, a solicitor should also ask for the barrister to give advice generally about the matter, just to make sure all contingencies are covered. In the opinion, the barrister provides an analysis of the solicitor's questions and offers his or her perspective and guidance on the problem. Solicitors may also draft opinion letters in the name of their firm. An opinion letter may be used, for example, in large corporate transactions where the parties need a high level of assurance about a particular legal issue before the deal is completed. The solicitor provides an opinion asserting the legal propriety or status of a certain aspect of the client's business, which gives the other party sufficient confidence to proceed with the transaction.

9.2 Finding the question in professional practice

One of the most difficult aspects of professional practice is figuring out what question you need to answer. Students have it easy: not only are they given the question that they must answer, but they are given a discrete amount of time in which to work. Practitioners have to identify the question themselves, although young lawyers are given lots of guidance by senior lawyers, particularly in the early days of a traineeship or pupillage. What is even more difficult is deciding when the question has been answered sufficiently. Some assignments appear to go on forever. When is the right time to call a halt to the research? The short answer is: when you have found the answer or run out of time.

The long answer is: when you have found the answer, run out of time or reached the point of diminishing returns on your investment of time and money. After a certain point, you will find yourself spending a lot of time without finding anything new. That is probably the point at which you can call a halt, since your client will probably not want to pay for you to continue past a reasonable point.

The problem of when to stop researching a question is something that you need to work out as a practical matter on each assignment. The more important issue, in terms of adapting your CLEO methodology, is how to identify the relevant question once you get into professional practice.

One of the things you will learn early on is that you must be flexible as you identify the legal question you must address. Sometimes the question will shift as a result of new factual discoveries. Sometimes it will shift as a result of your legal research. You should re-evaluate the scope and direction of your analysis on a regular basis to take the information you have learned into account. Do not be afraid of abandoning a line of questioning and picking up a new thread halfway through the exercise; no work is ever lost or wasted.[2] Often that information will become useful later. Keep your materials so that you can refer to them later.

> **NOTE**
>
> Be flexible when identifying the question you need to answer.

Often you cannot identify the legal question definitively until you have a full (or relatively full) set of facts. As you know from your academic work, the addition or deletion of a single fact can change the entire analysis. For example, all the facts may point to your client having committed battery on another person. All of your legal analyses may point in one direction until you learn that the other person shoved your client before the alleged battery. That shove changes the entire analysis: instead of battery, you are now dealing with self-defence. You could have learned about the shove as a result of good factual analysis (such as a rigorous question and answer session with your client regarding all the events leading up to the alleged battery) or as a result of a good legal analysis (for example, if your research into battery identified self-defence as a potential legal defence, which then led you to ask your client about the events leading up to the alleged battery). Either way, you need to know how the facts and the law interrelate in a question involving battery. Much of your law course focused on identifying basic principles of law so that you would be able to spot

---

[2] One of the questions young solicitors ask is whether they should bill the client for these abandoned lines of research. Consult with a more senior lawyer at your firm to find out your firm's billing conventions before you delete that time from your records. Different firms approach the question differently, and some may want you to account for all of your time, regardless of the outcome, since, as stated above, no research is ever truly wasted.

relevant issues once you got into practice. You also learned some of the basic rules of legal research. You will need to continue to perfect these skills once you get into practice. However, you will also need to learn how to undertake factual research, since the facts will help you identify the legal question at stake.

As you conduct your factual analysis, you need to keep an awareness of the potential legal issues in the back of your mind, and vice versa. It is similar, in some ways, to the second step of your CLEO analysis, where you were required to keep the facts in mind as you answered the legal aspects of the question. You had to be aware of the relevant facts, since, during the 'E' step of the essay, you would be evaluating the law in light of the facts. Problem questions in an academic setting were easy in the sense that you had a discrete set of facts and law and could figure out your issues relatively quickly. In practice, you have to do a bit of juggling, since you are identifying the relevant law at the same time that you are identifying the relevant facts. Solicitors spend a great deal of time investigating and reporting on the facts at issue. For example, a transactional lawyer has to do due diligence into the financial and legal condition of the company or companies that are being traded. A family lawyer has to learn about all the facts affecting the case at hand, whether it is a divorce or the drafting of a will. A litigator has to gather all of the facts relevant to the dispute.

Your vocational course and on-the-job training should help provide you with the skills you need to carry out a factual investigation. You need to learn how to frame your questions, whom to ask for assistance in your investigation and what information you (or your opponents) are entitled to receive. You will need to focus on information to be gained from witnesses as well as information to be gained from documents and other permanent sources such as computer databases. Because every investigation is carried out for a different purpose, it is impossible to identify, in the abstract, what questions you should ask and what documents you should seek. However, as a general rule, you should keep your investigation broad in the beginning, since you will need to gather information to help you formulate the scope of your legal inquiry. You don't want to foreclose any potentially relevant issue too soon.

9.2.1 Asking the right questions

One of the hardest things for a young practitioner to do is to know how to focus a factual investigation. This is one area where your training in the CLEO method can help you. As you recall, a claim in the CLEO system can be analogised to the cause or causes of action that your client may want to pursue or may need to defend against. If your professional practice involves litigation, you can do the same thing: figure out all the

TIP

The practice of law is an iterative process. Keep an open mind as you work.

✳ NOTE

To figure out what question you must answer in professional practice, you often have to juggle simultaneous investigations into the facts and the law.

potential causes of action that may arise in your particular action and start identifying what elements need to be established as part of the claimant's *prima facie* case. Also consider what defences may exist and what elements must be established for any particular defence to prevail. Then you need to search for facts to support or reject each of those elements.

You don't have to be working in a litigation context to use the CLEO method to help your fact-finding process. You can still think of what you wish to accomplish in terms of a CLEO-type 'claim', even in other areas of legal practice. For example, your client may wish you to draft a will for him or her. Therefore, if you think about your 'claim' in terms of what your purpose is in representing this client, you will see that you need to identify all of the factual issues that will affect the shape and content of the will, otherwise you will draft a will that is incomplete or that doesn't properly reflect your client's wishes. Among other things, you will want to know about your client's assets, dependants or other beneficiaries, charitable interests and tax status. Only then can you give proper legal advice and carry out your instructions.

To adapt the CLEO method to professional practice, you will need to modify the first step of the analysis (identifying the claim) to include both factual and legal matters. Therefore, the process of identifying the claim will require you to gather all the relevant facts whilst keeping in the back of your head all the matters that will have to be addressed as a matter of law. If you are working in a litigation context, the 'matters that will have to be addressed as a matter of law' are the possible causes of action and defences. If you are working on a will, the matters are the legal elements required to make a valid will and carry out your client's wishes. As difficult as this sounds, you are well prepared to consider both legal and factual matters simultaneously, since you have written numerous student essays in which you presented the law in one part of your essay while preparing your factual evaluation in your head. All that you must do now is pull back one step and carry out that juggling act as you identify the question that you need to answer.

Remember, the process of claim determination is a continuing one, since you cannot be expected to anticipate every possible contingency in your first interview with your client, nor will you be able to conclude all your legal research on the first attempt. Obviously you should try to identify the question and the claim as quickly as possible, but you must remain open to the need to shift to accommodate new facts and possible claims.

9.2.2 Drafting the factual summary

In your academic courses, you were given a fact pattern as part of a problem question. As a practitioner, you must draft your own fact patterns. Your drafting style will vary according to the purpose of your document. For example, if you are drafting instructions to counsel, you will not relate each and every fact known; you will only mention those that you believe are important to the legal issue on which you are requesting advice. You will not include any legal analysis in your instructions – after all, that is what you are asking the barrister to provide – but your legal analysis will nevertheless form the foundation of your factual discussion, since you will present only those facts that are or may be relevant to the barrister's decision-making process. While some solicitors downplay their legal skills and rely heavily on the judgment of counsel, you must remember that you, as a solicitor, have been trained in the law and are being paid to apply your knowledge to the question at hand. You cannot avoid using your legal know-how as you draft a proper set of instructions.

Other kinds of documents may require you to be more expansive in your discussion of the facts. For example, you may need to draft a memorandum to the file outlining your findings of fact. Since this document is intended to constitute the definitive description of the facts known at the time of writing, you will include virtually everything you have discovered, even if you have decided that something is ultimately irrelevant to the legal question at hand. Your analysis may change down the road, and you don't want to forget that titbit of information in case it helps your revised view of the case.

Regardless of whether you are drafting a narrow or broad summary of the facts, you should proceed in a logical manner. Chronological organisation is often best, although you can use another method if that makes more sense. Use the same kind of strong, decisive language that you used in your student essays and avoid characterising the facts or drawing unnecessary conclusions from them. State what happened and move on. It is often best to put your conclusions and surmises in a separate section so that your reader knows what is fact and what is conjecture.

Those of you who are intending to go to the Bar may not see how the previous discussion is relevant to you, since barristers are often not involved in the acquisition of facts, at least not in the early stages of a matter. However, a barrister cannot ignore the fact-finding endeavour altogether.[3] For example, an astute barrister may help a case along by referring factual questions back to the solicitor and asking the solicitor to pass the questions back to the client. In any event, barristers become very much involved in the facts at the later stages of a case, since the barrister will be the one presenting the facts to the court. Very often, solicitors will give barristers more information than is actually needed, since it is

---

[3] Indeed, as more and more barristers are turning to employment in law firms, more and more people who trained as barristers will become involved in fact-finding.

important to give counsel a full and complete view of the matter, and the barristers will cull through the information and choose the best and most persuasive bits to present to the court. Whether you are a barrister or a solicitor, however, you must remember that you have a duty to the court not to misrepresent the truth as to the facts or the law relevant to the case at hand. You may not omit evidence just because it is inconvenient or injurious to your case.

9.3 Answering the question in professional practice

Although the content of your legal document matters more than its physical layout, some lawyers become angst-ridden if a particular item does not look the way it is supposed to look. Since nearly every firm or set has its own way of doing things, rely on the advice of your colleagues about the visual format of your documents. The following discussion will focus more on the content of your professional submissions.

As you can anticipate, you will be asked to draft a variety of documents once you begin legal practice: letters, attendance notes, memoranda, opinions, etc. Each of these documents has a separate purpose and therefore contains slightly different types of information. Simple attendance notes and letters do not need to be mentioned here, since there is no need for you to apply a rigorous CLEO-type analysis. However, some of the more complex documents such as legal memoranda and legal opinions can benefit from a CLEO analysis. Although you should be guided by the senior lawyers at your place of work, you can anticipate that most of these complex legal documents will contain all or most of the following elements:

(1) question to be answered;

(2) executive summary;

(3) facts at issue;

(4) in-depth analysis;

(5) projected outcome and/or advice; and

(6) methodology and further questions.

We will discuss each of these elements in turn.

9.3.1 The question

As discussed earlier in this chapter, identifying the question is a major component of nearly every written assignment you will receive in practice. Going through the analysis can take some time and effort, but once you have figured out what the question is, the hard work is done. As with any CLEO-type analysis, writing up your ideas is almost mechanical in its simplicity.

When you move into practice, you should begin every document by identifying its purpose. Most pieces of writing have a dual purpose, one logistical and one substantive. For example, the logistical reason for writing a letter may be to respond to another letter. An attendance note may be created to summarise the content of a telephone call or the proceedings at a meeting, and a memorandum of law may be meant to answer a particular question given to you by a senior lawyer. It is often good practice to identify the logistical purpose of your document at the outset. Although the purpose is always clear to you when you write the letter, note or memorandum, it may not be as clear to the reader. As time passes, you yourself may forget why you wrote a particular document. Therefore, it's best to state what the document is meant to accomplish. This technique may seem unnecessarily pedantic at first, but you will see how useful it is when you look back at a piece of your writing two years later, with fresh eyes. The clarity of this approach will amaze you.

How you go about stating your logistical purpose is a matter of style and may vary according to the type of document. For example, a letter may begin, 'This is in response to your letter of X date,' although some people now consider that a rather old-fashioned convention. An attendance note may begin, 'This is to summarise the meeting of 23 May 2003 between Sandra McClintock, Bernard Whyte and Gillian Nixon,' again, setting forth succinctly the aim of the document. Take guidance from your colleagues as to the precise manner in which things are done in your workplace, but try to remember to set out the purpose of every piece of writing. In terms of language, be as clear and as concise as you were when you identified the claim in your CLEO essays. As you now know, there is no need to ease your reader into the discussion.

In addition to stating what your logistical purpose is in writing the document, you need to identify your substantive purpose. The substantive purpose is equivalent to the claim in CLEO: it is the legal question that you are attempting to answer.

Melding these two purposes into a succinct introductory sentence is not difficult, given your experience with CLEO essays in the past. For example, a senior partner at your law firm may ask you to draft a memorandum of law relating to a particular question that he or she has set. You could see the aim of your memorandum as either (1) a response to the partner's question or (2) a response to the legal question. You could begin your document in two different ways:

TIP

Know why you are doing what you are doing.

Option 1: answer the partner's question

> **EXAMPLE**
>
> I was asked by Alice O'Connor to research the boundaries of the doctrine of 'piercing the corporate veil' to identify whether our client, Joseph Williams, can be held personally liable for the actions taken in his capacity as director of Acme Food Company from May 1999 to August 2002.

This addresses the logistical question.

This addresses the substantive question.

Option 2: answer the legal question

> **EXAMPLE**
>
> This memorandum defines the boundaries of the doctrine of 'piercing the corporate veil' and discusses whether, on the facts set forth below, Joseph Williams can be held personally liable for the actions taken in his capacity as director of Acme Food Company from May 1999 to August 2002.

This only really addresses the substantive question.

You will more likely use the first option in purely internal documents, when you want to highlight the fact that the boundaries of the question have been set by a senior lawyer. You may also use the first option when you want to indicate that the work is being done at a client's request, thereby identifying on the face of the document the possibility that the work may be protected by some sort of legal privilege. You are more likely to use the second option in documents that will be shared with a client, since you are speaking on behalf of your firm. In that case, it is not as important to identify the request as originating from a particular lawyer, although you could reference the client's original request if you wished to do so. It can be good practice to reference a client's request for advice if the client has only given you limited information and you believe there may be other relevant facts that could affect your analysis. Doing so limits the possibility that your conclusions will be given more force than they merit.

Sometimes, in a very formal document, you will phrase the purpose of the discussion in the form of a question. Again, the question will resemble the claim in a CLEO analysis.

> **TIP**
>
> *If a document carries some sort of privilege, try to make that clear from the outset. Your designation of something as privileged is not determinative, but it will raise a red flag later and help avoid problems with inadvertent production.*

> **EXAMPLE**
>
> Can the doctrine of 'piercing the corporate veil' support an argument that Joseph Williams should be held personally liable for actions by him taken in his capacity as director of Acme Food Company from May 1999 to August 2002?

However you decide to proceed, remember that a quick, concise statement describing the aim of your written work – ie the question that you are seeking to answer – is as important in the professional realm as in the academic realm. Doing so defines the scope of the following discussion and helps your reader know what to expect.

9.3.2 Executive summary

The term 'executive summary' refers to a single paragraph that provides the response to the question posed – the 'yes' or 'no' answer – as well as an overview of why the question has been answered in that way. Notice that this technique contradicts what you need to do in an academic setting. When you write your CLEO essays at university, you should avoid conclusory remarks, meaning those phrases that omit the intermediate analyses and skip straight to your judgment call about how a matter of fact or law will be decided. In an academic setting, you must walk your reader through your analysis, step by step, and support every statement of law with some sort of legal authority. In practice, you will also be required to vdemonstrate your analysis and show legal support, but you will do that in the body of the document. The executive summary gives the reader a short outline of your basic argument; the arguments themselves will be discussed later, as will the legal authorities. While this kind of summary is a helpful tool in any piece of writing, the time and space restrictions on academic writing – particularly in a timed essay situation – preclude students from using this device.

WRITING TIP 🖊

Academic essays are too short to need an executive summary.

The length and content of the executive summary varies according to the type of document. For example, a short letter may be summarised in one sentence.

This identifies the 'question', ie the purpose of the letter.

This identifies the response in executive summary fashion: no information will be provided, for the reasons below. The letter is too short to require more.

> **EXAMPLE**
>
> This letter is in response to your letter of 24 August 2003, which requests our client to provide your client with information relating to all company directors' meetings from May 1999 to August 2002. For the reasons set forth below, we believe your client is not entitled to that information.

Often a letter such as this would go on to describe the reasons why the information will not be produced, but you should be aware that writing in a professional context is somewhat different than writing in an academic context. Sometimes, for tactical reasons, you may not want to provide the type of full and frank discussion that is expected in an academic setting. There may even be times when you will be purposefully vague when communicating with an opponent or third party. You should take guidance on these matters from more experienced lawyers, while always keeping in mind the relevant rules of responsible professional behaviour. Tactics should never outweigh ethics.

An internal document, on the other hand, or a memorandum for a client, would contain a longer executive summary which noted the key legal or factual issues and outcomes. You can even use explicit headings to separate each section of your work.

EXAMPLE

I. Question to be addressed
Can the doctrine of 'piercing the corporate veil' support an argument that Joseph Williams should be held personally liable for actions by him taken in his capacity as director of Acme Food Company from May 1999 to August 2002?

II. Executive summary
English courts hesitate to pierce the corporate veil and treat a director as the 'alter ego' of a company unless a high degree of impropriety exists. The concept is extremely limited in English law and the motive of the alleged wrongdoer is highly material. The appropriate test is whether special circumstances exist, making the company a mere façade for the wrongdoer. The company must be used as a puppet of the sole director before courts will go behind the corporate structure to hold the director personally liable. Because our client's activities cannot be said to rise to this level of wrongdoing, it is unlikely that he will be held personally liable for his actions as a director of Acme Food Company.

9.3.3 The facts

In this section of your document, you relate the relevant facts. As indicated above, you must adapt your drafting style to suit the document. A memorandum summarising an interview with your client or your review of documents will need to relate everything you have learned in its entirety, whereas a memorandum of law or a letter to a client or third party will not. Recall how problem questions were drafted when you were on your law course. Every sentence bore some relation to the legal issues that you then discussed. While your recitation of the facts may be longer than that found in a problem question, you should strive for a similar level of clarity and relevance. Remember, you are the expert on the subject matter of your

WRITING TIP

Make every sentence in your factual discussion count, just as the problem questions on your law course did.

WRITING TIP

Make sure your documents are correct and readable.

TIP

When drafting law essays and exams under the CLEO system, you demonstrated legal judgment not only by what you included in your essay, but by what you excluded. The same is true in practice.

document; you know what is relevant and what is not. If you are unsure about whether a particular fact will become relevant, put it in a separate 'questions' section.[4]

Putting potentially irrelevant information in the 'facts' section gives rise to two problems. First, you lengthen what should be a short summary into a longer, less persuasive section. Sometimes people who are (or who think they are) familiar with the facts will skim quickly through a fact summary, particularly if it is on the long side. Other people will skip it altogether (always dangerous and not to be recommended, since the reader may not know certain key facts disclosed in the summary or may, on the other hand, be able to correct the author on certain points). If you keep the discussion short, you are more likely to keep the reader's attention.

Second, putting extraneous information into your fact summary can end up hiding potentially important points. If you think something is critical to your analysis, make sure it stands out. Use separate headings and distinctive formatting (including different fonts and typeface, if necessary, though you should use this feature sparingly, lest your document end up looking like a tabloid newspaper). Not every fact is of equal value; use your discretion and omit those items that are not of great weight, just as you omitted minor arguments and legal authorities in your CLEO essays at university. The result will be a stronger and more readable factual summation.

Because the structure and form of each fact summary depends on both the information available and the purpose of the document, it would not be helpful to provide a full example of a fact summary here. However, when drafting a fact summary, you should remember to focus not only on content but also on style. Sometimes it will be appropriate to use a neutral, objective tone, whereas at other times it will be appropriate to use a more persuasive or advocate-orientated approach. The best way to learn what works and what doesn't is to read the work of a more experienced lawyer. Find someone whose writing you admire and then ask if you can read through some of his or her old papers. Writing is much easier if you know what you're trying to accomplish.

9.3.4 In-depth analysis

At this point, you are ready to undertake your normal CLEO-type analysis. You will have already identified the CLEO claim: it is the same as the substantive question you asked at the beginning

---

[4] Recall that you had a similar 'queries' section in the case summaries that you did as part of your note-taking as a student.

of the document. Now you need to proceed to the 'L' and 'E' steps of the discussion, remembering always to keep your discussion relevant to the question you are addressing. You have more scope for discussion here than in an academic essay, but you should still apply the same analytical method. For example, a strong CLEO essay always puts case references into context rather than just dropping a case name in at the end of a sentence. The same is true in practice. Take your time and explain what you are doing and why. Keep the length of your analysis within reason, but realise that you may be covering legal points that your reader has not considered since he or she left university or parsing through a very detailed statutory provision or judicial opinion. Take as much time as is necessary to convey your meaning.

One reason you can and should spend more time discussing the details of the cases and statutes that you cite is because those cases will be even more relevant to your particular issue than the materials you used as support in your academic essays. When you are on a law course, you are given a limited number of general legal authorities that you then use to support your arguments as best you can. Once you move into professional practice, however, you have access to a much wider range of cases and statutes and will seek out those materials that are most relevant to the problem you are discussing. Because they bear so heavily on the question you are answering, you will want to parse through those cases in greater detail and identify how they relate to the issue you are researching, since they will determine the advice that you will give at the end of the day. As always, you want to show your reader how you came to your conclusion. It may be that your reader weighs the information differently or draws different insights from the materials, which could lead to fruitful discussions.

Although you should be sure to include both 'L' and 'E' steps in your analyses, you will need to adapt your writing style to conform to the needs of the document. Most letters will be very short, for example, although a 'letter before action' may be somewhat longer, since its purpose is to set forth a claimant's theory of liability before initiating a cause of action. Attendance notes will probably not include an analytical section, since their purpose is to provide a memorial of a meeting. Instructions to counsel will also omit any sort of analysis, since that is precisely what the solicitors are asking the barrister to provide.

Therefore, you are most likely to have to draft an analytical section in memoranda of law, legal opinions and some letters. Even among this group of documents, the format and approach can vary greatly.

Again, the best way for you to learn how to write a good analytical section is to ask senior colleagues to lend you some of their old papers as models. While you must adapt the models to suit your needs, you will start to get an idea about how to put these documents together. You can also get some good ideas from documents received from your opponents in the course of your practice, but be aware that sometimes organisations have their own way of doing things, both substantively and stylistically, and you should conform your writing style to match that of your supervisors. Sometimes there will be great variation in approach even within the same organisation, so you will need to ask each person you work with how he or she wants a document to appear. Again, ask for models, since they are your best guide to how things should look.

9.3.5 Projected outcome and/or advice

In your CLEO essays, you were told to anticipate the outcome of the dispute in question. You were told to keep your conclusions quite short, since that is what is done in litigation. Keeping your final statements quite short also suited the restricted format of an academic essay.

Now that you are in professional practice, you can take slightly more time to describe how you envision the particular problem playing out. Very often, you will be required not only to anticipate the resolution of a particular question, but to provide advice on how to proceed as well. For example, you might want to describe ways to remedy or mitigate the problem. Alternatively, you could suggest further legal or factual research that needs to be done. How you phrase your conclusion depends, as always, on the type and purpose of your particular document, but you need to remember that you are now acting as a professional. While you will still have to analyse a question, as you did in your academic work, you are now being asked to go beyond simple analysis and use your best professional judgment to advise your reader about the appropriate measures to be taken as a result of the analytical process.

You should set forth your projected outcome and advice in a separate section, so that anyone who is in a hurry can flip to it right away. As always, aim to be clear and concise, and separate different types of action tasks from one another.

NOTE

You may need to adapt your writing style not only to suit the type of document that you are creating, but to accommodate the individual quirks of the person requesting the document.

NOTE

Barristers are not the only ones who provide advice. Solicitors do as well, though perhaps of a slightly different nature.

WRITING TIP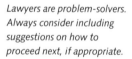

Lawyers are problem-solvers. Always consider including suggestions on how to proceed next, if appropriate.

EXAMPLE

V. Conclusions and advice

As the above analysis suggests, it is unlikely that an English court will 'pierce the corporate veil' to hold Joseph Williams personally liable for his actions as director of Acme Food Company. However, this analysis is based on the facts set forth above. As suggested in section III, there are several areas that require further investigation before the threat of an action based on 'piercing the corporate veil' can be dismissed.

Further inquiries:

- Are there any contemporaneous documents showing that Mr Williams suggested Resolution 115 as a means of reducing tax to the company, rather than increasing dividends paid out to shareholders, including himself?
- Is there any truth to the allegation that Mr Williams's personal stock portfolio had just suffered a large loss at the time he suggested Resolution 115?
- Did Mr Williams follow the proper corporate formalities when introducing Resolution 115?

In addition, there are several steps that should be taken to minimise the likelihood that Mr Williams will find himself subject to these kinds of charges in the future.

- We should advise Mr Williams of the importance of following proper corporate formalities when acting as a director.
- We should look into whether the corporate charter and/or by-laws should be amended to clarify the procedures that need to be taken when introducing resolutions regarding dividend distribution.
- We should look into whether additional directors should be created to ensure a measure of objectivity in the decision-making process.

9.3.6 Methodology and further questions

Because many legal matters stretch out over several months or years, you should take the time to explain your research methodology in some of the documents you create. For example, in a formal opinion you will want to list which documents you reviewed so that someone cannot come back later and claim that you overlooked an important fact contained in a particular letter or report. If you were not given the document, you cannot be held responsible for not knowing the fact. Similarly, if you have been focusing on legal, as opposed to factual, research, you will want to identify what types of searches you have done so that the work will not be duplicated if there is a need for supplemental research at a later date.

TIP

Laying out your methodology helps you remember what you've done so that you don't accidentally repeat the same steps later.

> **EXAMPLE**
>
> The preceding research involved an all-text search on Westlaw and
> LexisNexis and the 'words and phrases' digest for the phrase 'corporate
> veil'. I also reviewed the subject digest under 'director's liability'. Due to
> the press of time, I did not have time to review journal articles or treatises,
> although I believe some follow-up in this area would be helpful. No statutes
> appeared to be relevant to this analysis.

Some people believe that the methodology section should appear at
the beginning of a document rather than at the end. Ultimately, where
you put this information is a matter of personal choice, as long as
your approach is logical and easily understandable to the reader. Just
remember to include the information somewhere if yours is the kind
of document that would benefit from a methodology section. Alternatively, you can put the information in a note to file if it is inappropriate
to include it in the document itself.

9.4 Formatting issues

Earlier chapters discussed the use of footnotes and full case citations
in academic essays. The suggestion there was that you did not need to
include either footnotes or full case citations unless your instructor
required you to do so. The brevity of academic essays, as well as the
problems associated with remembering even case names in an examination scenario, obviated the need to use formal citation methods.
When you enter professional practice, however, you will need to use
proper citations, including the full names of cases and statutes as well
as references to the law reports.

WRITING TIP

*Draw up a list of citation
forms for the sources that you
use most often in your work
and pin it up by your desk for
quick reference.*

You will also need to include the paragraph numbers for more
recent decisions, in accordance with the Lord Chancellor's direction.
Citation style can vary according to which reporting series you use,
so be sure to check first. Your law library should have a reference
guide available. Every little detail matters. For example, you may not
care whether a certain reporting series puts the year of the decision in
square brackets [ ] or parentheses (). Other people will, however. Use
the right form to avoid appearing uninformed or unprofessional.

The question of where to put citations is a tricky one. Some people
are comfortable putting the reference in the text if the document is
short or informal, whereas other people put all citations into footnotes, regardless of the length of the document. As usual, be guided by
common sense and the advice of those with whom you work.

Earlier in this book, you were cautioned not to begin sentences with an abbreviation, particularly 's' for 'section'. The same is true in practice: spell out any word that begins a sentence. Indeed, you should try to avoid the use of 's' and similar abbreviations (art, ch) when the reference appears as part of a sentence rather than as a citation following a sentence. For example:

Section 11 of the Unfair Contract Terms Act 1977 raises the issue of 'reasonableness'.

The issue of reasonableness is raised by section 11 of the Unfair Contract Terms Act 1977.

'Reasonableness' is defined by statute (Unfair Contract Terms Act 1977, s 11).

Other formatting issues generally adhere to the rule of common sense. Practitioners are busy people and appreciate the use of standard formatting devices to organise written material visually. In a long document, use numbers and letters to break your text into sections. A shorter document can be organised through various headers, set off by different fonts. Bullet points have also become common in business documents and correspondence, although they are used less in formal legal documents such as court papers or contracts. As mentioned in earlier chapters, use white space to assist the reader.

While you should not get too elaborate in your text design, many readers appreciate the use of **bold** type to highlight different section headings. Practitioners often use *italics* to indicate quoted material, whether it is inserted in a sentence or offset in a block. Sometimes the typeface of an italicised block quotation is reduced, though this is not necessary. Remember to use inverted commas in accordance with the rules discussed in the previous chapter, even if you use italics, and always include a citation to the source of the quoted material, including the precise paragraph and/or page. Aside from these general conventions, you should avoid using special fonts to try to cure weak writing; it is generally more effective to redraft the text.

You now have an overview of how to adapt the CLEO methodology to legal practice. You will also receive a good deal of guidance on these issues during your professional or vocational training. However, making the transition from law student to legal practitioner can be difficult at times. Therefore, you should not hesitate to ask the senior lawyers with whom you work for assistance, even if you occasionally feel awkward doing so. It is part of their job to provide pupils and trainees with guidance. At the same time, it is not just up to supervisors

WRITING TIP

Breaking up a long discussion into subparts not only helps you organise your thoughts, it helps readers follow your argument.

TIP

Do not overuse special fonts. It can be distracting, particularly to judges, senior lawyers and older clients who grew up in a time when such 'bells and whistles' were considered unnecessary.

TIP

Don't be afraid to ask questions. It can save you a lot of work.

to offer advice; it is also your responsibility to seek help and feedback on your work. It's far better to take ten minutes at the beginning of a project to go over the scope of the assignment than to show up at the last minute with a ten-page memorandum that doesn't answer the question properly.

This chapter has focused entirely on issues that arise in professional practice. However, one cannot progress to professional and vocational courses, and eventually to practice, without doing well on one's law course. Therefore, the following chapter will provide detailed comments on six different student essays so as to further solidify your understanding of the basic CLEO method.

Worked questions

The preceding chapters should give you a good idea on how to write a CLEO essay in response to either a problem question or a 'discuss' question. However, writing is difficult to learn in the abstract. What an apprentice writer needs is examples. The problem with many writing guides, however, is that they only provide perfect, seemingly unattainable writing samples. Students become discouraged when they read essays that they don't believe they can reproduce. Perfect writing samples are also problematic because students also don't know why the essays are as good as they are. As mentioned in earlier chapters, good writing is often noted more in its absence than its presence. Therefore, there is little educational value in providing a single sample and saying 'just do this'.

What seems more helpful is to provide you with essays written by current law students along with detailed commentary indicating the essays' strengths and weaknesses. None of these essays would be given a first-class mark, although some come quite close. The commentary will indicate how the mark could be improved. Read through the essays and the discussion points to learn how to improve your own essays. There are some tips contained in this chapter that are not included in the previous chapters, so it is worth your while to work through all of the examples.

Remember that not every comment will apply to every student. For example, some writers are quite wordy, whereas others are naturally succinct. If you tend toward the concise, don't read a comment aimed at another writer and think that you need to become even more terse. Brevity can be taken too far. However, if you fall into the former category, then you should take the suggestions on how to make your writing more concise to heart.

You should also be aware that every university has its own standards concerning student essays. Similarly, every tutor has his or her own ideas about what a student should include in an essay. Some universities or tutors may want to see a lot of black-letter law, whereas other institutions or instructors may prefer to see a deep discussion

NOTE

This chapter contains tips not found in the previous pages.

TIP

Be judicious in deciding which corrections to apply to your writing. Not everyone has the same issues to address.

of legal theory in response to every question. You must find out the standards by which you will be judged, since you cannot meet (or exceed) those standards unless you know what they are.

This chapter contains six student essays, four in response to problem questions and two in response to 'discuss' questions. The first two essays are in response to the same question, so you will see how two different writers grappled with the same issues. Those two essays are in contract, as is the third essay, which responds to a different problem question. Following the contract questions are two tort questions, one in response to a problem question and one in response to a 'discuss' question. The last student essay relates to a jurisprudence 'discuss' question. General comments and a class mark follow each of the essays. For the most part, the comments will not refer to the students' discussion of the substantive law, since your syllabus may differ from that given to the students who wrote these essays. In any event, this book is not about teaching the content of the law; it is about teaching you how to write good essays. Use your skills and judgment to determine whether the sample essays describe the law accurately.

As noted, none of the student essays can be considered first class. Having a first-class essay can be helpful, though, both as a guide to your own work and as a standard by which to judge the student essays. For those reasons, a partial sample from a first-class essay in tort appears before the student essays. Use this sample as a model, by all means, but realise that you do not have to emulate the style exactly in your own essays. The goal here is to improve your individual writing style, not to force you to adopt a whole new style.

10.1 First-class model in tort

Following is an excerpt from what would most likely be a first-class essay in tort. The problem was assigned very early in the course, so the author did not have very many cases or issues to consider, but the essay uses a first-class style of thinking and writing. In any event, the excerpt will give you an idea of how succinctly a CLEO essay can be written. This is by no means the only way to answer this particular question, and there may very well be other quotes or cases that apply, but in this short sample you can see how well the author implements each of the steps in the CLEO analysis.

As you see, the author has broken the answer into three sections marked (a), (b) and (c), tracking the organisation of the question. This is often a good technique to use, since it appears logical to the reader (who, in all likelihood, wrote the question). This type of organisation also allows you to incorporate earlier discussions of the law by reference,

TIP

To the extent you can, ask your examiners what they are looking for, both in terms of substance and style. The best essays conform to the reader's expectations and desires – not the author's.

QUESTION

Several young offenders resided at an open youth custody centre and escaped one night. The centre had suffered several such escapes over the course of the preceding year, and members of the local community had complained on several occasions. However, the authorities did nothing to increase security at the centre. After their escape, the boys found their way to the nearby home of Daniel, where they stole various items of food and clothing as well as an expensive Faberge egg that had been in Daniel's family for generations. They also smashed up the house for a bit of fun and then started a fire which gutted the house. One of the boys travelled over 250 miles to find Edward, who had given evidence at the boy's trial. Edward suffered severe injuries when the boy assaulted him with a kitchen knife. Another boy with a history of convictions for petty theft carried out several daring cat burglaries around the country before being located and returned to the custody centre.

Do (a) Daniel, (b) Edward and/or (c) any of the victims of the cat burglaries have a cause of action against the Home Office, based on its supervisory power over the youth custody centre? Would your answer change at all if the custody centre's officers had not locked any of the doors and windows on the night of the escape, based on recent Home Office instructions stating that the boys' interests would be served best if they were placed on trust day and night?

ANSWER

a) The issue is whether Daniel can pursue a claim in negligence against the Home Office for the losses he suffered when the boys in question escaped from the youth custody centre. To prove negligence, a claimant must establish: a duty of care by the defendant to the claimant; breach of that duty; factual causation ('but for' causation); legal causation; and damages. Defences such as contributory negligence may be raised in some cases. The claimant has the burden of proof and must prove his/her case beyond the balance of probabilities.

In this fact pattern, the major question arises concerning duty of care. Many courts litigate duty of care as a preliminary matter, since, if a duty is not found as a legal matter, there is no need to litigate the other elements of negligence, which are factual in nature. Therefore, we will address duty of care in this question first.

A duty of care is owed by a defendant to a particular claimant – there is no 'general duty' of care owed to the world. In the current situation, we are investigating whether the Home Office owed a duty of care to Daniel, a person living near the youth centre. *Dorset Yacht* is the case most on point.

continues

ANSWER continued

There, the House of Lords ruled that the Home Office, which was operating a borstal, owed a duty of care to a nearby yacht owner whose boat was damaged by boys who escaped from the borstal. Even though the boys' actions might have been considered independent causes of injury, Lord Reid noted that 'although one of the connecting links [to harm] is deliberate human action, the law has no difficulty in holding that the defendants' conduct caused the plaintiffs' loss.'

In *Dorset Yacht*, the Home Office was liable because the officers of the borstal had a duty to keep the boys from escaping but were negligent in their duty to do so. The Home Office might have had discretion in how it ran the borstals (which would protect it, normally, from civil liability), but in that case it did so so unreasonably as to be 'no real exercise of discretion which Parliament had conferred'; therefore the Home Office was acting outside of its area of statutory discretion. This is distinct from *East Suffolk* and *Stovin*, where public bodies were held to be not liable for their actions because they were acting within the area of discretion. *East Suffolk* might have found that a particular claimant was foreseeably harmed by the public body's lack of action (certainly Lord Atkin thought so in his dissent in that case), but the majority found otherwise.

One reason why the yacht owner in *Dorset Yacht* was able to recover was because there was reasonable foreseeability that his chattels would be damaged; Lord Pearson noted that there was no general duty to all persons for harm caused by escaped juvenile delinquents. It was the physical proximity of the plaintiff in *Dorset Yacht*, combined with the fact that the boys had escaped before and were known to be likely to steal transportation, that helped the House of Lords hold that a duty could exist.

The facts of the current hypothetical are very close to those in *Dorset Yacht*. The boys were known to be willing and able to escape, Daniel lived close by, and the officers of the custody centre did nothing to tighten security. Although doing nothing is similar to the delay/lack of action in *East Suffolk* and *Stovin*, the similarities of the current facts with *Dorset* suggest that the Home Office will be held to have a duty of care.

The defendants in our fact pattern might try to rely on *Smith* as part of their defence. In *Smith*, vandals broke into an empty cinema and started a fire that affected the building next door. The owner of the cinema was held to have no duty to his neighbours. Although *Smith* was not a case concerning a public body, it does demonstrate that there are situations where defendants will not be held liable for the actions of others. However, there was no prior relationship between the vandals and the owners of the cinema in *Smith*, nor was there any knowledge on the part of the owners that vandals might cause harm to the plaintiff's property. Because our hypothetical includes a prior relation ship

continues

ANSWER continued

and prior knowledge of the predilections of the boys, *Smith* can easily be distinguished and should not be considered persuasive.

Because a duty of care exists, further investigation is necessary. The standard of care here is that of the reasonable custody centre. Obviously, as there had been previous escapes and the officers 'did nothing to tighten security', something any reasonable custody centre would do, there is a breach of the duty of care. There is 'but for' (or factual causation), since the harm to Daniel follows directly from the boys' action. There is also legal causation, either under the *Wagon Mound* test of reasonable foreseeability or under the (now largely outmoded) directness test of *Re Polemis*. Finally, damages are evidently present, as Daniel has suffered loss in the form of food, clothing, the Faberge egg and damage to his home. No defences appear to exist (common defences include contributory negligence, *volenti*, illegality, etc), so Daniel should be able to recover all of these property damages from the Home Office.

b) The issue in the second part of the hypothetical is whether Edward has a cause of action in negligence against the Home Office. The five elements of negligence are the same as noted above, as is the standard and burden of proof.

As was the case with the preceding question, the major controversy will be over whether there is a duty of care. This issue will be addressed preliminarily, as a court would do in real-life litigation.

[The excerpt stops here but you would normally continue with the analysis of duty of care.]

[Also be sure to answer section (c) and the second question regarding the instruction to put the boys on trust.]

> ✳ **NOTE**
>
> If no duty of care existed, you could stop after the first sentence and say 'because no duty of care exists, there is no need to address the other four elements of negligence, since the claimant cannot prevail.'

thus helping you move through the subsequent discussion much more quickly. However, if the question does not give you sub-questions to answer, you will need to organise your response by some other means. Often the best way to do so in a complex fact pattern is to break your analysis up according to different claimant–defendant pairings or different claims. Be sure to read the question, however, since you don't want to waste time answering a question that isn't asked. Also remember that this sample related directly to the defendant's duty of care – other questions may have one or more different controversies for you to address. You don't always have to treat duty of care in this much detail.

10.2 Contract problem question one (author one)

Following is the first of two student essays responding to the same problem question in contract. Compare the two responses to see the different ways in which people view the same question.

Overall, this first essay lacks distinction. While the organisational structure is adequate, the author has missed several major substantive areas of discussion. There is also a shortage of legal authority, and the cases that have been introduced are repeated too often and

---

QUESTION

Phil Philanthropist, an architectural buff residing in the historic village of Muddleton, decides to repair and renovate the quaint but structurally unsound village courthouse, which is owned by the Muddleton Parish Council. He puts the job out to tender, and Overeager & Co., a company based in a neighbouring village, puts in a bid for £50,000, which is approximately £25,000 less than that of any other contractor. Phil, not wanting to pay more than he has to, makes an offer to Overeager to complete the work for £50,000, which is accepted. No date is set for completion of the work, but the contract specifies that renovations are intended to return the courthouse to working order. The court is currently closed for its annual summer break.

The work proceeds slowly due to the unexpected presence of groundwater. Nathaniel, the principal of Overeager & Co., approaches Phil, telling him that more money is needed to shore up the foundation of the courthouse to overcome problems associated with the groundwater. He asks for an additional £20,000, which Phil agrees to pay on the condition that Overeager & Co. makes every effort to complete the renovations by the end of the month, when the court returns to session and when the BBC will be doing a news segment on Phil's philanthropic work. Phil, being a modest soul, does not mention the television programme to Nathaniel, although Phil anticipates receiving a number of donations to a charity he runs as a result of the renovated courthouse's appearing on the programme.

It soon becomes apparent that Overeager & Co. will not finish the work by the end of the month, partly because it has started work on another project in Muddleton. Advise Phil about the ramifications of taking each of the following possible actions:

(a) asking Overeager & Co. to vacate the courthouse so that Quick & Competent Ltd. can finish the job by the end of the month. Overeager & Co. has already been paid £30,000 under the original contract; Quick & Competent Ltd. estimate that it will take £60,000 to complete the work in the required timeframe.

(b) allowing Overeager & Co. to complete the work as quickly as possible, recognising that the completion date will overshoot both the BBC filming date and the first day of the new court session. Muddleton Parish Council estimates that it will cost £4,000 a week to rent other accommodations suitable to carry out the business of the court.

(c) terminating the contract with Overeager & Co. and walking away from the project.

RESPONSE (paragraph one)

The facts that surround the problem faced by Phil Philanthropist in his renovation of the courthouse raise many issues of contract law, and it is necessary to advise Phil on three possible courses of action.[1] Either he can ask the original firm to vacate the premises and engage the alternative firm to finish the work, allow them to continue with the work or abandon the project and terminate the contract.[2] Each one of these raises different issues, and accordingly, each one will be dealt with in turn.[3]

COMMENTS (paragraph one)

1. This sentence is too wordy and mostly unnecessary. The author should cut the excess prose and begin the essay: 'Phil has three possible courses of action', or, better yet, 'Phil has three potential claims in contract' or 'actions in contract'.

2. First, this sentence constitutes a sentence fragment. It would be grammatically correct if introduced by a colon (since it constitutes a list of possible actions) but it cannot stand alone. Second, the sentence basically repeats the facts given in the question and is therefore unnecessary. The sentence should thus be deleted.

3. The idea here is good, but the prose can be cut down to 'Each claim will be considered in turn.'

NOTE: The author intends this paragraph to constitute the 'C' step in CLEO, but he has written far too much. This is a waste of time, particularly in an examination scenario.

RESPONSE (paragraph two)

Turning first to the scenario where Phil requires Overeager and co. LTD to vacate the premises and engages Quick and Competent LTD to finish the job off, the issues are first, whether he is legally allowed to do this and, assuming that he is, what the extent of his claim against Overeager and Co. Ltd could be.[4]

COMMENTS (paragraph two)

4. The author has decided to organise the response according to the fact pattern, taking each possible outcome in turn. This is perfectly legitimate, although there are other ways to organise one's response, as the next sample essay will demonstrate. There are several problems with this sentence, though. First, it is very long, somewhat wordy and and stands as its own paragraph. Second, it contains several typographical errors. Third, it contains very little substance – the phrases 'legally allowed to do this' and 'extent of his claim' don't really define what legal issues are at stake. The author should be less general and more specific about why Phil can or cannot take the action noted.

RESPONSE (paragraph three)

Two possible alternatives present themselves in law here, the first of which is the argument of no consideration, and the two most important cases on the subject are those of *Stilk v. Myric* and then the seminal decision of *Williams v. Roffey Bros and Nicholls Ltd.*[5] In the former case it was ruled that a captain who had promised his crew extra wages could not be bound by this engagement as there was no consideration for the promise.[6] However, the *Roffey* case, which concerned a firm of builders asking for more money to complete a job, presents a more liberal notion of consideration in the form of practical benefit.[7] The court of appeal ruled that the claimant had gained a practical benefit in having the work completed, so this was sufficient consideration.[8] In short, this case broadened the notion of consideration.[9]

COMMENTS (paragraph three)

5. First, this is a run-on sentence (also known as a comma splice). The sentence could well be ended after 'here' (and the phrase 'in law' could be cut as well); the next phrase could be made into a proper sentence and the third phrase containing the case citations could be made into a third sentence. Second, the organisation is problematic – the author mentions a 'first' but does not make the second point clear (it appears two paragraphs later). The case names are also misspelled. On the positive side, the author has begun introducing substantive case law and has thus begun the 'L' step of the CLEO analysis relatively quickly.

6. The phrasing is somewhat wordy and passive ('it was decided' – by whom? The author could say '*Stilk v Myric* held that a captain …' to avoid the problem of passive construction), but the analysis is good. There are sufficient facts to identify the case and contextualise the legal holding, which is contained in the same sentence.

7. This is good. The author compares the ratio in *Roffey* to the ratio in *Stilk,* while still contextualising the *Roffey* case factually. The factual references are short and the focus is on the legal points. This is precisely what is called for in a law essay.

8. The term 'Court of Appeal' should be capitalised, but the sentence itself is good, since it relates the facts of the cited case to the legal holding, which will help lay the groundwork for the third step in the CLEO analysis, the evaluation. The sentence also keeps the focus on the primary issue noted in the first sentence in the paragraph: that of consideration.

9. Again, a good sentence. It is concise and gives the final answer on how the two cases cited relate to one another. It would be helpful to have more case law on this point, but the author has identified the two major cases and analysed them succinctly.

RESPONSE (paragraph four)

An application of this rule to the present case suggests therefore that the *Roffey* case all but condemns this argument.[10] Admittedly there are differences in the facts between that case and the present, but it would not be the most likely submission to succeed.[11]

COMMENTS (paragraph four)

10. The author begins a new paragraph to evaluate the law introduced in the previous paragraph. As you will see from the next paragraph, this is an example of a CLELEO type analysis – rather than introducing all law relating to one claim, the author evaluates each sub-issue before moving to the law for the next sub-issue. However, this sentence is somewhat odd and the reader is left wondering what the author means.

11. This sentence is also a little strange. The author's evaluation is not being made clear – the essay needs to state why the claim will not succeed. Mere factual differences are not enough to allow a court to disapply a precedent.

RESPONSE (paragraph five)

The alternative, and more optimistic route for Phil is to establish that Overeager and co. have breached a condition of the contract.[12] In law, a contractual term is either a condition, a warranty or an innominate term. Breach of a condition gives rise to a right to either termination of the contract by the victim of the breach and a claim in damages, or affirmation of the contract and a claim in damages. On the other hand, the breach of a warranty only gives rise to a claim in damages, whilst the remedy for breach of an innominate term is dependent on the seriousness of the consequences caused, or likely to be caused, by the breach, as set out by Lord Diplock in *Hong Cong Fir shipping v. Cawasaki*.[13] However, it must be clear that the parties meant the term to be a condition in a technical sense, and in *Couchman v. Hill* this was defined as a term going to the heart of the contract, as reaffirmed by *Schulla Machine Tools v. Whickman*.[14] The

COMMENTS (paragraph five)

12. Again, a typo in the text, and the comma after 'alternative' is incorrect. The word choice of 'optimistic' is unusual, but the gist of the sentence – that Phil can claim a breach of contract – is correct and well noted. Note that this paragraph presents the law concerning the second argument Phil can make – again, the author is using a CLELEO analysis.

13. This is a good, concise summation of the law regarding conditions. More cases and fewer typos would be helpful, but the author is basically correct. However, the author should be careful not to overstate the law regarding damages available upon termination of a contract: damages may be available, but not always. Be precise in your language.

14. Typos detract from the strength of this sentence, as does a slightly wordy sentence structure (the author should use two sentences, with a full stop following 'sense' and the next sentence reading '*Couchman v Hill* defined a condition as going to …'). The author should also note whether the test for the parties' intention is objective or subjective.

parties can also make it clear that time is of the essence.[15]

15. The author is correct, but a case and description of what 'time is of the essence' means would be better.

RESPONSE (paragraph six)

Applying these rules to the facts of this case leads to the following conclusions: the original contract stated that the work was for the purposes of renovation of the coutrhouse for use, and although time was not made of the essence, it seems clear that this should have been done by the start of the new session.[16] In any case, the modified contract was accompanied with a request to overeager and co. to make every effort to finish the work by the end of the month, it would be clear to b both contracting parties that time was of the essence of the contract. In addition, the fact that Overeager and co. have taken on other work, thereby incapacitating themselves from finishing the work on the courthouse, phil therefore has a right to ask Overeager and co. to leave.[17]

COMMENTS (paragraph six)

16. This paragraph evaluates the law contained in the previous paragraph. The author does a better job explaining the reasoning behind these conclusions. However, the failure to identify precise case law relating to 'time is of the essence' issues has led the author to an incorrect conclusion – one cannot merely assume from the circumstances surrounding a contract that both parties knew time is of the essence. The requirement must be explicit.

17. This statement is rather conclusory and therefore unpersuasive. The author needs to link this evaluation/outcome to the law introduced in the 'L' step. The author may be right, but he has missed an opportunity to show legal judgment and discretion.

NOTE: How the typos throughout detract from the persuasive value of the essay.

RESPONSE (paragraph seven)

The issue now becomes the extent of Overeager and co.'s liability in a claim in damages, which of course Phil is entitled to pursue.

COMMENTS (paragraph seven)

This sentence constitutes a transition into the remedies relating to the first claim. The idea is good, although a single-sentenced paragraph is unadvisable. Typos still exist. Substantively, the author has not explained what those damages would cover, thus raising the spectre of double recovery. You must be precise in your language and not overstate yourself. Look out for all possible ambiguities. This author knows full well that double recovery is impermissible but has not said so. It's what's on the page, not what's in your mind, that wins you marks.

RESPONSE (paragraph eight)

The case of *Haddley v. Baxendale*, containing the remoteness rule for contractual damages, held that contracting parties were liable for damages that are in the reasonable contemplation of the parties.[18] Similarly, the obligation to mittigate his loss, as laid down by the ruling in the *Dunlop Pneumatic tyre co* case, lies with the victim of the breach, and failure to do this has a resultant effect on the eventual damages awarded.[19] Finally it must not be forgotten that as the Victoria Laundry ruling shows, profits that could not be in the reasonable contemplation of both parties cannot be recovered in damages.[20] As for expenses already paid, restitution of these may only be an option in the case of total failure of consideration, as stated by the ruling in *Whincup v. Hughes*.[21]

COMMENTS (paragraph eight)

18. A reasonably clear statement of the rule in *Hadley v Baxendale*, although there is obviously more that could be said about the case. When discussing damages, you must bring up *Hadley v Baxendale*; know it and its elements well.

19. Lots of words to say not much: it's good that the author is supporting the various propositions with law, but the analysis is sticking to surface issues for the most part. Also, the issue of remedies and the quantum of damages is a relatively minor one in this question, which has lots of substantive points of law to discuss. This portion of the essay suggests that the author has either misread the question or is trying to disguise a lack of knowledge in other areas of the law by a lengthy discussion of damages.

20. Again, the author is a bit wordy and is basically restating the rule in *Hadley v Baxendale*. It's not clear why the *Victoria Laundry* ruling is being introduced here and how it expands or redefines the rule in *Hadley v Baxendale*.

21. The author here touches on the issue of partial payment, a substantive legal concern that should be discussed even outside the realm of remedies. This is one of the issues that the author has overlooked, and though this one citation is helpful, it does not overcome that deficiency.

CONSIDER: How typos and misspellings again detract throughout. Note for your own benefit that 'mitigate' has only one 't'.

RESPONSE (paragraph nine)

The facts of this situation therefore indicate that Phil may not recover the £30000 he has already paid to Overeager and co. However, the argument that he has mittigated his loss is persuasive, given the situation he found himself in. He would therefore be able to recover at least the £20000 extra that he had to spend on engaging a new contractor.[22] As for the charity and television segment, these could not be expected to be in the reasonable contemplation of both parties, given that they were not mentioned by Phil, so he could not recover any potential profits from Overeager and Co.[23] Phil's chances of £20000 damages are, therefore, strong underr this course of action.

COMMENTS (paragraph nine)

22. The author here lumps the 'E' and the 'O' step together, thereby losing an opportunity to persuade and demonstrate good legal judgment.

23. This sentence demonstrates a much better evaluation of the facts, since the author correlates the facts (the television segment which was not mentioned by Phil) to the law discussed previously, even bringing in the language used by the court ('reasonable contemplation') to help identify the proper standard. This is strong and persuasive writing.

RESPONSE (paragraph ten)

If, in the alternative, Phil decides to allow Overeager and co to continue the work, exercising his right to affirm the contract following the breach of a condition, the, the issue is once again the liability of Overeager and co. to Phil in damages.

COMMENTS (paragraph ten)

The author has again given the reader a single-sentence transition paragraph. The use of the phrase 'in the alternative' does not make it clear, however, that we have now moved into the second factual scenario, nor does the characterisation of the claim as one regarding the affirmation of a contract give the reader much insight into the legal discussion that is to come. Typos again detract.

RESPONSE (paragraph eleven)

The legal rule in *Haddley v. Baxendale* is once again of undoubted relevance as it articulates the remoteness principle by which damages are assessed, and the breacher can only be liable for the losses naturally flowing from the breach that would have been in the reasonable contemplation of the parties. From this it also follows that the principle in *Dunlop* of mitigating one's losses is also greatly important.

COMMENTS (paragraph eleven)

The author here is struggling. The only two cases that are cited have been cited before in the discussion of remedies. Although it is perfectly acceptable to refer to cases mentioned before and to incorporate previous discussions by reference, any time you have new or different facts in a complex fact pattern question, you are going to have to present new law precisely because the legal issues will be different. No two parties are ever situated in exactly the same way in a problem question.

BE AWARE that 'breacher is not a legal term – use the phrase 'breaching party'.

RESPONSE (paragraph twelve)

These two decisions are sufficient to decide the issue of Overeager's liability: by choosing this course of action, Phil can be said to have taken reasonable steps to mitigate his loss, as it may prove less expensive than employing a new contractor.[24] In any case, it could not be said to be unreasonable, so it is likely that Phil could recover the £4000 for each week of the new session for which the courthouse would be unserviceable, always assuming that he is the one footing the council's bill.[25]

COMMENTS (paragraph twelve)

24. The evaluation here is of a reasonable type, but the paucity of case law in the preceding paragraph means that there is little of substance to discuss.

25. The author here alludes to a subject that should be treated much more expansively: that of rights of third parties such as the council. The author touches on the subject later in the essay, but it seems to be an afterthought. Had the author taken more time considering the claims before starting to write, the third party issue might play a larger role in the essay.

RESPONSE (paragraph thirteen)

The final option is for phil is to terminate the contract and walk away from the project. It has already been established that there is a right to terminate the contract, but does Phil have the right to leave the project and, if not, what are the legal consequences of such an act?

COMMENTS (paragraph thirteen)

Here, the author is making the transition to the third factual scenario and the third issue. Again, the generality of the language and the failure to define the legal issue narrowly means the author has lost an opportunity to demonstrate his knowledge of the law as well as an opportunity to persuade the reader.

RESPONSE (paragraph fourteen)

The rule that one must take all reasonable steps to mitigate one's loss as laid down in *dunlop* has already been discussed ans is once again of importance to decide this question.[26] However, what is also important is the contracts (rights of thirrd parties) act 1999, according to which, where the benefit of a contract is for a third party, the third party can sue on the contract, avoiding the doctrine of privity. Moreover, if McKendric and Treittel are correct in stating that the act applies without express reference thereto in the contract, this is certainly a significant development.[27]

COMMENTS (paragraph fourteen)

26. Again, the author has relied on case law introduced earlier in the essay. While that is not a problem of itself, the author has failed to notice the different legal posture of the third factual scenario and has therefore failed to introduce the appropriate case or statutory law.

27. The author here makes a brief reference to the Contracts (Rights of Third Parties) Act 1999 but does not adequately discuss its significance or relationship to the facts in this case. Similarly, while the author has done well to mention the work of commentators, the references here are too vague and general to increase his marks significantly. Note that the phrase 'significant development' is rather empty, since the author does not go on to indicate why or how the development is significant.

RESPONSE (paragraph fifteen)

On this basis it would appear unwise for Phil to walk away from the project leaving it unfinished. Not only would there be absence of mittigation of loss, but the council may well be able to act under the 1999 statute and sue Phil despite there being no contract between them.

COMMENTS (paragraph fifteen)

The author here combines the 'E' and 'O' steps in rather cursory fashion. In addition to undertaking a more detailed evaluation (which is difficult, given the lack of legal authorities in the preceding paragraph), it would be helpful to include a summation of the other two outcomes, particularly since the question asks the author to advise Phil, a direction which implicitly demands a weighing up or comparison of the various options.

EXAM TIP

Know your law so that you can spot your claims.

are too general to allow for any sophisticated discussion. The primary problem arises at the very beginning of the essay, in the claim-spotting stage: the author does not see all the various issues that need to be discussed. The failure to spot all the claims leads to vague language and an inability to introduce different cases relating to the different legal nuances. It then becomes impossible to evaluate the facts in light of the law, since there is no law. The author seems to know how to carry out the evaluation step when necessary, but he cannot do so to the extent necessary, given the problems in the earlier stages of the analysis. The lesson here is to know your law so that you can spot the claims in the first step of your analysis.

The essay also has problems on a stylistic level. First, there are a significant number of typographical errors that detract from the substance of the essay and suggest that the author has not taken the time to proofread the essay. While there are fewer grammatical errors, the language can get wordy when the author is struggling for content. Compare the paragraph discussing conditions in contract (paragraph five) with almost any other paragraph and you will see an immediate difference in style and impact. The author can be direct and straightforward in the right circumstances. When there is a shortage of content, however, the writing style disintegrates.

WRITING TIP

Wordy prose results when you don't have anything substantive to say.

This essay would earn a low 2:1 or, more likely, a 2:2 mark. Notably, the problems here lie with this particular essay, not with the author, who has obtained first-class marks on other essays in the past.

10.3 Contract problem question one (author two)

Because writing styles vary widely, it is helpful to see how another student addressed the question posed in the preceding example.

QUESTION

Phil Philanthropist, an architectural buff residing in the historic village of Muddleton, decides to repair and renovate the quaint but structurally unsound village courthouse, which is owned by the Muddleton Parish Council. He puts the job out to tender, and Overeager & Co., a company based in a neighbouring village, puts in a bid for £50,000, which is approximately £25,000 less than that of any other contractor. Phil, not wanting to pay more than he has to, makes an offer to Overeager to complete the work for £50,000, which is accepted. No date is set for completion of the work, but the contract specifies that renovations are intended to return the courthouse to working order. The court is currently closed for its annual summer break.

The work proceeds slowly due to the unexpected presence of groundwater. Nathaniel, the principal of Overeager & Co., approaches Phil, telling him that more money is needed to shore up the foundation of the courthouse to overcome problems associated with the groundwater. He asks for an additional £20,000, which Phil agrees to pay on the condition that Overeager & Co. makes every effort to complete the renovations by the end of the month, when the court returns to session and when the BBC will be doing a news segment on Phil's philanthropic work. Phil, being a modest soul, does not mention the television programme to Nathaniel, although Phil anticipates receiving a number of donations to a charity he runs as a result of the renovated courthouse's appearing on the programme.

It soon becomes apparent that Overeager & Co. will not finish the work by the end of the month, partly because it has started work on another project in Muddleton. Advise Phil about the ramifications of taking each of the following possible actions:

(a) asking Overeager & Co. to vacate the courthouse so that Quick & Competent Ltd. can finish the job by the end of the month. Overeager & Co. has already been paid £30,000 under the original contract; Quick & Competent Ltd. estimate that it will take £60,000 to complete the work in the required timeframe.

(b) allowing Overeager & Co. to complete the work as quickly as possible, recognising that the completion date will overshoot both the BBC filming date and the first day of the new court session. Muddleton Parish Council estimates that it will cost £4,000 a week to rent other accommodations suitable to carry out the business of the court.

(c) terminating the contract with Overeager & Co. and walking away from the project.

RESPONSE (paragraph one)

According to McKendrick, 'English law would rather pay damages and let parties go off on their own separate ways as opposed to keeping parties together when a breach occurs' (Lecture, Oxford). In this case, two parties entered into a contract and party, Overeager (O), breached the modified contract.[1] This essay will argue that 1) Phil (P) legally tendered to contract with O; 2) The modified contract had consideration; 3) P is advised to terminate the contract and claim damages for £20,000.[2]

COMMENTS (paragraph one)

1. This author has never felt comfortable beginning an essay with a straightforward presentation of the claim. Instead, he is more comfortable easing the reader into the essay with a few introductory sentences. Judge for yourself whether this paragraph is necessary. Do note, however, that the author has taken pains to define terms properly.

2. Although this author has set up a good organisational structure, these three points are an unusual choice. It might be better to follow the three factual scenarios in the question (as the previous author did) or to choose three legal issues that control the dispute. For example, all of the factual scenarios are affected by: (1) the question of time being of the essence (an issue which could also be described as relating to the purpose of the contract); (2) the alleged modification to the contract; and (3) the possibility of special damages. You might want to make those your three major headings, since the determination of those points will affect each of the three potential courses of action described in the question.

RESPONSE (paragraph two)

A. The Claims of the Parties
P has three options that he might take. Phil will claim that he had the right to terminate the contract with O. He will likely sue O for damages (reliance costs), after mitigating his loss. O will counter-claim saying that P did not have the right to terminate the contract. O will then try to sue for the remainder value of the contract or at least the total value of the labour (save the £30k paid) or reliance costs for tools bought for the job.

COMMENTS (paragraph two)

This is an odd paragraph. On the one hand, it seems to set out the claims that will be addressed in the essay, even though the preceding paragraph already seemed to do that. On the other hand, the paragraph seems to set out the procedural sequence of events. While the author has very clear language and structure, his purpose is unclear. The paragraph headings are in the original and help organise the essay.

RESPONSE (paragraph three)

B. The legal issues surrounding this case Tendering is governed by the law of contracts.[3] When a party has decided to accept bids, he is inviting to treat (*Harvela Investments*).[4] An offer is made by the highest or lowest bidder (*Harvela Investments*). In addition, according to *Blackpool* (1990), the tenderor has a 'duty to consider' the tenderee that best suits the criteria set out in the stipulations of the tendering agreement.

COMMENTS (paragraph three)

3. While this sentence is strictly true, it's not clear how it advances the argument or introduces the law section of the essay.

4. The references to *Harvela Investments* here and in the next sentence are a bit cursory, but the author has done well to include case citations for even these basic propositions. The language is nice and crisp, however, and shows a good understanding of the concepts, even if the cases are not discussed in detail. The author should strive for gender-neutral language, however.

RESPONSE (paragraph four)

Once a contract is agreed upon, it can be amended, but they must have consideration in common law.[5] Consideration according to *Currie v Misa* is the reciprocal exchange of promises (there is no need for exchange to be of equal value, *Chappelle v Nestle*).[6] As set out in *Williams v Roffey Bros* (1991), consideration can be made in a modified contract based upon a 'practical benefit' (Purchas LJ). This decision is controversial because it re-allocates *Stilk v Myrick* as a duress case (as opposed to case on consideration).[7] This means that modification of an agreement for an additional promise is acceptable consideration. In addition, *Roffey Bros* is important because while it doesn't make mention of *Foakes v Beers* (coming from *The Pinnals Case*) with regard to acceptance of partial payment.[8] While Lord Blackburn's dissent in *Myrick* was more in line with 'practical benefits', the case ruled that consideration was not given for payment less than what was contracted. If an amended agreement does not have consideration, then a party can claim that the opposing party was estopped for denying that a agreement was made, when claimant acted on it to their detriment (*Macfarlaine v Gatty*).[9]

COMMENTS (paragraph four)

This paragraph is quite good – lots of law, tight prose, proper use of legal terms such as 'practical benefit' and good analysis of the relevance of the cases to each other.

5. The word 'they' is incorrect in number and does not refer to the correct antecedent.

6. The author should use commas after 'consideration' and after '*Misa*' to set off the parenthetical information.

7. This sentence seems a little off-point unless the author has an unexpected argument coming up in the 'E' section.

8. This is a sentence fragment – something needs to follow 'because while it'. Also, the reference to *Pinnals* appears to be a bit of name-dropping. Historical background is good, but only if it has relevance to your argument.

9. This statement appears to be true, but it is a bit muddled when compared to the other sentences. Also, the first clause could be tied in to the other case references a bit better.

RESPONSE (paragraph five)

Once a contract is made, the law requires that payment be given upon the entire completion of comprise (entire obligations rule).[10] While the doctrine of substantial performance (*Hoenig v Issacs*) and divisibility (*Sumpter v Hedges*) have mitigated rule, it is not acceptable in common law to leave a garage half build and expect to be paid for it unless expressly stated.[11]

COMMENTS (paragraph five)

10. The phrase 'completion of comprise' seems a bit archaic. If the author has pulled that from a source, it should be identified.

11. The sentence has a few typographical errors and is a bit of a non-sequitur, but the reader can generally anticipate where the author is heading.

RESPONSE (paragraph six)

If a clause in a contract is breached, a party may terminate it and claim damages.[12] It is important to note that only conditional clauses will allow termination.[13] While the words need not say 'condition', the court will construe such a intention.[14] If damages are to be claimed, mitigation, remoteness and causation need to be established. If a party is claiming reliance costs (because profits would be impossible to assess, *East Anglia TV v Reed*), a party must he mitigated his loss (*Brit Electric v Underground* (1912)) but not too much that it changed nature of promise (*Plkington v woods*).[15] The party may be required to accept an offer to continue with contract for sake of economic efficiency (*The Solholt*). Remoteness states that in *Hadley v Baxendale* (1854) (Anderson J) that breaching party must have reasonably contemplated this loss.[16] If not, loss cannot be claimed (*Victoria Laundry* (1949)).[17]

COMMENTS (paragraph six)

12. It is not clear whether 'it' refers to the clause or the contract. Also, the author needs to explain more precisely what type of damages are available to avoid the issue of double recovery.

13. The phrase 'it is important to note that' can be deleted, and the phrase 'conditional clauses' can probably be replaced with the simple word 'conditions'. There is far less need for elegant variation of terms in a law essay than in other types of writing.

14. The courts will construe an intention if what conditions exist? Why? The sentence is grammatically correct but needs more substance.

15. There are a few typos in this sentence and the case references are a bit cryptic, but the author obviously knows the law and is doing well to substantiate each point with authority.

16. The phrase 'remoteness states that' is rather odd. Also, the author is rushing and is therefore missing out words here and in the previous sentence. While that is understandable, try to avoid it, as it does not give an aura of poise and competence.

17. The author needs to explain this point a bit better – special damages is what is at issue.

RESPONSE (paragraph seven)

C. Combing Claims and the Law
In this case, P successfully tendered for building contract. O offered – and offer was accepted – by P based upon the stipulations (albeit unknown to me) of the tender. Contact was agreed and amended. The amendment had consideration because O accepted an additional sum and P received a new promise which was to finish job at a specific time. This can be interpreted as a practical benefit, as per *Williams*, because P needed the building finished in order host the BBC. O did not force P into paying more money (duress), but rather sought to renegotiate based upon the additional cost working with the unexpected groundwater. Therefore the second promise was not the same as the first (this being the opposite claim in *Stylick* v *Myrick*).

COMMENTS (paragraph seven)

The header here helpfully indicates that we are now in the third step of the CLEO analysis. Note that the typographical error is the type that will slip past your computer spell check, demonstrating that there is no substitute for proofreading. Overall, however, the evaluation in this paragraph is good – it relates the facts to the cases and uses legal terms appropriately. The author may go too far in stating that the promise was to finish the job at a specific time, but the promise that was given might still qualify as consideration.

RESPONSE (paragraph eight)

O's promise was to finish the work by a specified date.[18] Being that P knew that his promise would not be fulfilled, he had two choices: 1) terminate and look to another builder to finish job; 2) allow O to finish job (albeit breaching time aspect of modification) and then sue for reliance cost of not using facility (£4000 per week times X number of weeks); or 3) terminate and leave the building unfinished.[19] First, if P chooses choice one, then will likely face a claim that O didn't breach a condition of C; therefore damages are due O.[20] This author believes that while P did terminate unlawfully (which means that O will probably claim reliance costs of tools bought for job (being that he was already paid £30,000), P will win damages of £20,000 because O partially performed contract and this was not acceptable (like getting half a garage, its useless) and P mitigated loss by hiring Quick [paid 30k, amended contract 70k (70−30=40), contract

COMMENTS (paragraph eight)

18. The author needs to be careful here. Whenever you start discussing specific dates in contract law, you need to consider whether time was of the essence. Because we are now in the 'E' step of the analysis, it seems that the author has missed the opportunity to introduce any law on this point. While references to legal authorities can, of course, be introduced at any time, it is best to do so in an orderly fashion in the 'L' step.

19. This sentence is a little long, but the internal numbering gives it sufficient organisation (although the author does give three options after noting that Phil has two choices available to him). The phrase 'being that' is a little awkward, however, and the missed words also detract from the overall persuasive value of the writing.

20. This sentence is a bit vague and conclusory.

with Quick 60k $(60-40=20)$.[21] P would have difficulty claiming value of charitable donations because it is unlikely that O 'reasonably contemplated' such an outcome.[22]

21. Several things are going on here. First, the phrase 'this author believes' is unnecessary and can be deleted. 'Its' also needs an apostrophe. Second, the author is bringing in facts not at issue in the problem (the tools). Don't add to the hypothetical – the question usually has more than enough to discuss on its own. Third, the author is turning this question into a question regarding damages calculation. Seldom will you have to do a detailed calculation of damages in contract (you will have to do so in tort, especially relating to damages arising from death). By misreading the question and turning it into something else, the author is missing a lot of opportunities to win marks.

22. This sentence is a good evaluation of the facts under *Hadley v Baxendale* principles. Note the appropriate use of legal language.

RESPONSE (paragraph nine)

Second, P could keep O on job but due for breach of modified contract's 'time' clause. Damages would be reliance costs of using another facility (once again it would be difficult to claim charitable donations because O did not contemplate it). This solution would be legally sound if it was more economically efficient to keep parties together, as per *The Solholt*.[23] This author disagrees with this chose of action because P is not getting the promise he asked for in contract.[24] He is accepting a lesser alternative, which the doctrine of mitigation would oppose (*Pilkington v woods*). Therefore I would advise the first solution because P is getting the outcome his contracted for in the first place.[25] He will not be too disadvantaged by terminating contract with O (may have to pay for tools).

COMMENTS (paragraph nine)

Typos and skipped words detract from the argument. Don't make the readers work this hard.

23. This sentence is good because it relates the evaluation to the case law introduced above, something that the previous sentence does not.

24. This sentence is good because the author indicates why he is concluding as he is.

25. One could also discuss whether there was a total lack of consideration resulting from the failure to deliver the renovation on time. The idea would work nicely with the doctrine of partial payment, an issue that this author has not considered in any detail.

RESPONSE (paragraph ten)

With regard to choice 3, it is the worst one of the three because if P just terminates and doesn't look to mitigate, then O will sue for damages against unlawful termination and P will have an unfinished building that he could not sue O in order to have him pay for the completion of the building. This chose will cost P £30,000 + tools + cost of finishing building at later date (if desired).

COMMENTS (paragraph ten)

The paragraph begins somewhat awkwardly and doesn't follow the style of the previous paragraphs. If you begin a series with 'first, second, third', stick with that form. Don't suddenly change to 'choice three' (which should be spelled out, by the way). More generally, the first sentence doesn't make much sense, and the author appears rushed for time. It is good to try to get something on paper, even if you are rushed, since it is the only way to win marks, but obviously you will want to be as clear as you can. Again, typos mar the presentation.

RESPONSE (paragraph eleven)

D. Conclusion

This case has demonstrated that a party can alter a contract under the law when additional promises are created. In addition, damages are due when a party partially performs a contract regardless of an unlawful termination. The law of contracts looks to facilitate commercial society. This result shows, as Mc Kendrick mentions, how it is more efficient to separate parties and allow them to go separate ways.

COMMENTS (paragraph eleven)

It is good that the author is trying to present a unified outcome, but it would be better to tie the conclusion in to the three specific scenarios contained in the question. The author does demonstrate a nice stylistic touch by referring to the commentatary introduced in the opening paragraph.

This essay contains some very good elements. The presentation of the law is perhaps the strongest of the four CLEO steps, demonstrating a good knowledge of the cases and a good ability to write concisely and precisely. The evaluation is a bit spotty at times, varying between strong analysis (for example, when the author ties the facts to a specific case or to specific language) and vague supposition. Far too much time is spent on the evaluation step, particularly when compared to the law section. The problem, however, is that the author has failed to spot a number of claims, which means that he does not give himself the opportunity to present the law concerning those issues. For example, the author might consider discussing the subjects noted in the comments to paragraph one: (1) time of performance/purpose of the contract (this might include some discussion of anticipatory breach, recovery of money paid for part performance and/or

> **NOTE**
>
> If you don't spot the claims in the first place, you can't present the law properly. Take your time in the 'C' step and be broad in your thinking.

the ability to recover the £60,000 from O); (2) modification of the contract; and (3) special damages (the author touched on this point, though he didn't discuss the recovery of the money to be earned from the television show) and mitigation of damages (for example, the costs incurred as a result of the breach, including the £4,000 monthly rent). Unfortunately, the author spent too much time on tangential issues such as tender/offer and acceptance and on the calculation of damages point.

Stylistically, the author wins marks for a good clear structure and some strong writing but then loses marks for typographical errors and inadvertently omitting words. Although the examiner knows that the author is writing under time pressure, presentation matters, subconsciously at least. Presentation alone will not pull a paper down a mark, but it could be the deciding factor if the paper falls on the edge of two marks. Other students will be able to produce excellent content and excellent writing, even under time pressure. Strive to do the same.

This essay provides a very good example of how some things can be done well. Unfortunately, the author missed too many substantive points to earn more than a high 2:2 mark.

10.4 Contract problem question two

Following is a different problem question in contract, written by yet another student.

QUESTION

Adam agreed to sell his residence, a converted church, to Bob for £400,000. The price was somewhat higher than might be expected for a building of that sort, but the area was becoming more commercial and both parties knew that Bob was intending to convert the building into a themed nightclub called 'Bats in the Belfry'. Neither party knew at the time that the local council had just decided to list the building on the historical register, meaning that no further conversions would be possible.

When Bob found out about the council's decision, he put the building back on the market at the going price of £300,000. When taking prospective buyers through the house, Bob found that entire sections of the wooden floor – which were covered by rugs and furniture during earlier inspections – were suffering from dry rot, which would force him to drop the purchase price by an additional £50,000. Adam had not mentioned this problem prior to the sale. Bob also discovered that a small local airport offered classes in helicopter flying and that students practised hovering manoeuvres within earshot. When Bob had asked about any possible noise coming from the airport, Adam had said that the building was not in the flight pattern for planes that were landing or taking off. Bob had not thought to ask about helicopters.

Advise Bob of any claims he may have against Adam.

RESPONSE (paragraph one)

There are three main issues to be dealt with during the course of this problem.[1] Firstly whether Bob is enable to rescind the contract as being void for mistake because of the fact that neither party knew that the local council had just decided to list the building on the historical register meaning no conversion of the building was possible?[2]

COMMENTS (paragraph one)

1. A good, concise opening sentence, though 'during the course of' can be shortened to 'in'.
2. The concept of this sentence is acceptable, but there are grammatical problems. First, it is a sentence fragment, albeit a wordy one. Second, there should be a comma after 'firstly'. Finally, there should be a full stop rather than a question mark at the end, since the structure is that of a sentence rather than a question.

RESPONSE (paragraph two)

Secondly, whether Bob has any claims in respect of the condition of the wooden floor through any misrepresentation as to the condition that may have been made? Thirdly, whether the omission to state that helicopters hovered overhead was again a misrepresentation?

COMMENTS (paragraph two)

It is not clear why the author has separated these two claims into a new paragraph. Again, each claim constitutes a sentence fragment that needs to be corrected, and the question marks need to be changed to full stops. Substantively, each of the claims should be worded more as a type of action, just as the first claim is (rescission as a result of the contract's being void for mistake). The claims here are a bit too fact-based; they would be improved by reference to legal actions, terminology and remedies.

RESPONSE (paragraph three)

The law of mistake has historically developed over the past fifty years into two categories. Firstly, mistake at common law (*Bell v Lever Bros*). It was said that common law took a very narrow view of mistake and could only provide a remedy where the new facts made the contract something different in kind from the contract in the original state of facts. Such a mistake would render a contract void and therefore both parties would be able to rescind the contract.

COMMENTS (paragraph three)

The author has now begun the 'L' step of the essay. While a historical approach is often not advised, it is appropriate in this case, since, as shall be seen, a recent case has altered the existing law considerably. The second sentence in this paragraph is a fragment, but is used as an introductory device and is thus less problematic. Although there are a few problems with wordiness ('it was said that ...' could be shortened to 'the'), the analysis of *Bell* is succinct and to the point.

RESPONSE (paragraph four)

Equity then stepped in, and Denning LJ in *Solle v Butcher* relying on the earlier case of *Cooper v Phibbs* and giving a strict interpretation to *Bell*, gave relief to a landlord who had claimed recission of the contract on the grounds that the mistake as to the maximum payable rent on the flat was fundamental to the contract.[3] Denning LJ stated that in this situation the courts can give relief in equity so that the contract becomes voidable rather than void, and therefore only terminates when an election is made by one party to cease the obligations under the contract by one party (being a party who is not relying on their own mistake).[4]

COMMENTS (paragraph four)

Overall, this paragraph contains a strong description of the law, based on legal authority.

3. This sentence is long but understandable. A comma should be placed after '*Butcher*' so that the parenthetical phrase (ending in '*Bell*') is properly offset from the rest of the sentence. The facts of *Solle* are appropriate and succinct.

4. Another long sentence, but this one makes less sense. It is not clear how the 'therefore' clause follows or relates to the first part of the sentence. 'Cease the obligations' is also a rather odd phrase, as is 'being a party'.

RESPONSE (paragraph five)

However the law of mistake has recently been restated in the case of *Great Peace Shipping Ltd. v Tsavliris Salvage (International) Ltd.*.[5] There Lord Phillips MR disapproved of Denning LJ's reading of the authorities that gave rise to the suggestion that equity had a separate jurisdiction in this respect. Lord Phillips MR found that there was no separate equitable jurisdiction, that the two tests laid down in *Bell* and *Solle v Butcher* were in fact indistinguishable, and that the authorities Denning LJ had relied upon in formulating *Solle v Butcher* which included *Cooper v Phibbs* did not suggest an equitable jurisdiction that was beyond the boundaries of the common law doctrine of mistake.[6]

COMMENTS (paragraph five)

5. This sentence is very good structurally, since it calls attention to a recent, and thus very important, case in the Court of Appeal. Two minor errors pop up: there should be a comma after 'however', and only one full stop is necessary, even when the sentence ends with an abbreviation.

6. These two sentences are excellent. They show a good understanding of the *Great Peace* and the relationship of that case to previous case law. They use legal terminology appropriately and assure the reader that the author knows the subject well. This is precisely the kind of writing to which every law student should aspire.

RESPONSE (paragraph six)

The ongoing debate as to whether there is such an equitable jurisdiction could prove fundamental to the resolution of the first issue. If the mistake does not fall within the

COMMENTS (paragraph six)

A good paragraph, but marred slightly by (1) odd word choice ('fundamental' and 'being void' are awkward, and the word 'debate' suggests that the decision by the Court of Appeal is still in narrow common law doctrine (therefore being void enabling the parties to rescind) then we would have to look at the equitable jurisdiction (*Associated Japanese Bank* per Steyn J) to see if the contract is voidable, however this is in doubt following *Great Peace Shipping*.

dispute) and (2) grammatical errors (there should be a comma after the parenthesis following 'rescind' and after the word 'however', and the comma following 'voidable' should be a full stop to avoid a run-on sentence). The reference to *Associate Japanese Bank* is also a bit cursory. We also are beginning to lose the overall structure. Where are we going next? To more law or to the evaluation step?

RESPONSE (paragraph seven)

The question in this instance in relation to the common law doctrine of mistake is whether it applies in relation to the quality of the subject matter rather than its actual existence.[7] *Kennedy v Panama* suggests there would not be. There the plaintiff relied on a statement in the prospectus that they had obtained a valuable contract to carry mail for the NZ government in buying a number of shares.[8] Blackburn J held that this mistake only went to the quality of the subject matter and that the plaintiff had still got what he contracted for, the shares that were the substance of the contract.[9] In *Bell v Lever Bros* Lord Atkin stated that a mistake as to quality would have to make the contract essentially different that the thing that was believed to be contracted for.[10] In that case the House of Lords refused to nullify an agreement to terminate a contract on the basis that the employers could have terminated the contract anyway without the payment of compensation as laid down in the agreement.[11] Lord Atkin held that the parties got what they contracted for, the termination of the contract of employment and it was immaterial that they could have got this by another method.[12]

COMMENTS (paragraph seven)

7. This sentence is rather confusing – lots of 'in relation to' references – and it's not clear what the purpose of the paragraph is. The reader doesn't know whether the author is continuing the 'L' step, and if so, in what direction. The following case reference does not clear up the matter, either.

8. There's a pronoun problem in this sentence – 'they' cannot refer to a single plaintiff.

9. It's unclear to what 'this mistake' refers. Although the author seems to know what he is talking about, he leaves the reader somewhat confused. The phrase 'still got' is awkward as well. Finally, the clause following the comma creates a run-on sentence as it stands; to cure the problem, the author could insert an 'ie' (meaning 'in other words') after the comma. A comma should always precede and may follow both 'ie' and 'eg' (meaning for example). You may also use full stops in 'i.e.' and 'e.g.', if you wish, but whatever form of commas and full stops you use, be consistent.

10. Here, there's a typo ('that' for 'from') and omitted punctuation (full stop to abbreviate *Bros.* and a comma following *Bros.*).

11. The author needs a comma following 'case'.

12. The author needs a comma after 'employment'.

RESPONSE (paragraph eight)

In the case of *Associated Japanese Bank* Steyn J found the non-existence of machines did make the contract void where the subject matter of the sale and lease back agreements were the machines themselves. In that case Steyn J stated that rules as to the quality of the subject matter are designed to deal with the impact of unexpected and wholly exceptional circumstances on apparent contracts and repeated the ratio of *Bell*.

COMMENTS (paragraph eight)

Substantively, it is not clear how this case expands or contracts the holding of *Bell* or, more importantly, the *Great Peace*. When discussing a line of cases, it is important to compare the significance of each case to the others. Otherwise, what should be an explanation of the shape and direction of the law reads more like a list of unrelated cases. The author here knows the building blocks of the law: he just needs to put them together in a more cohesive manner. Note that there needs to be a comma after '*Bank*' in the first sentence and 'case' in the second.

RESPONSE (paragraph nine)

In *Great Peace Shipping* the parties contracted a ship on five days hire in order to ensure the safety of a crew on a vessel that was subject to a salvage operation, but the ship was 415 miles away rather than 35 miles as the parties believed.[13] The Court of Appeal held that the case did not fall within the common law doctrine emphasising that the question to be asked was whether the new position essentially different from that to which the parties had agreed.[14] Here the contract was still possible to perform some days of escort could still be achieved although not as many. Lord Phillips MR emphasised that the common law doctrine of mistake was not there to alleviate the consequences of a bad bargain.[15]

COMMENTS (paragraph nine)

13. There should be commas after *Shipping* and '35 miles'. It would be helpful for the first sentence to relate the *Great Peace* to the preceding cases and note whether there had been any criticism of the existing approach to the issue of mistake. Doing so might allow for a brief discussion of legal commentary on the issue of mistake, something examiners want to see.

14. There should be a comma after 'doctrine', and 'different' should be 'differed'. The author should also make clear which common law doctrine he's discussing.

15. These two sentences make sense, although they contain awkward phrasing. What is not clear is why the author is repeating the discussion of the *Great Peace* at all, since there was a very good summation of the case earlier in the essay.

RESPONSE (paragraph ten)

Therefore in this instance could the loss of the ability to convert the converted church into a themed nightclub change the contract into something that was essentially different than the thing believed to be contracted for.[16] The subject matter of the contract, the building itself still existed therefore the case would appear to align itself to *Kennedy v Panama*.[17] The parties contracted for the sale of a building. It could be argued that the fact that Bob planned to convert it into a themed nightclub was irrelevant to the subject matter, the building itself. Also the fact that the decision was taken before the sale, a decision that Bob could have found out for himself through the public records, simply made the sale a bad bargain, as suggested in *Great Peace Shipping*, and a bad bargain in the sense that Bob paid over the market price for the building.[18]

COMMENTS (paragraph ten)

16. This is a question and should be punctuated as such. The sentence is a bit wordy, but commas before and after 'in this instance' might help clarify the meaning. You should consider whether it is proper to end the phrase with a preposition. On a functional level, the sentence works relatively well, leading the discussion into the evaluation step.

17. Again, the lack of commas is making the sentence difficult to understand. The author should add commas after 'itself' (because it is a parenthetical phrase) and after 'existed'. The author might want to make the connection to *Kennedy* a bit clearer, but it is good to link the evaluation directly to the cases cited.

18. These two sentences are a bit long, but the proper use of commas makes the meaning clear. Here the author is doing a good job of applying the facts to the law and noting how the different arguments could play out. As the author clearly understands, the outcome of the case will depend largely on how the subject matter of the contract is defined.

RESPONSE (paragraph eleven)

On the basis therefore that the common law doctrine could not assist Bob, Bob could then attempt to rely on the equitable jurisdiction.[19] In light of *Great Peace Shipping* this would be unlikely to prove a fruitful course of action.[20] However in *Solle v Butcher* the contract was viewed as voidable where there was a common mistake as to the legal position under the 1939 Rent Act as to the maximum rent that was payable by the tenant.[21] Likewise in *Grist v Bailey* the mistake in the contract of a sale of a house that it was a protected tenancy thereby reducing its value was one that made the contract voidable. In *Magee*, the court found that a contract of insurance

COMMENTS (paragraph eleven)

19. The point gets made eventually, but this sentence is a bit awkward. Commas around 'therefore' might be helpful, and the phrase 'then attempt … jurisdiction' could be replaced by 'invoke equity'.

20. Again, the author makes his point, but in a roundabout way. Lots of words can be cut here.

21. The author seems to know what he's saying, but the various 'as to' phrases make it difficult for the reader. There are some commas missing in this and the next sentence.

was voidable where the details were entered in such a way that the insurance company would never have dreamed of entering into the contract in the first place.[22]

22. The references to *Grist* and *Magee* are not perhaps as helpful as they could be because the author is not making clear what relevance (meaning legal relevance) these cases have to each other and to the *Great Peace*. This is unfortunate, because the author obviously has a good reason for introducing these references; it's just that no marks can be given unless the rationale is clear to the reader. Remember, the 'L' step requires you to do more than list cases: you must persuade the reader that your presentation of the law is correct and complete.

RESPONSE (paragraph twelve)

Aligning the problem with these cases, the contract of sale would probably be set aside for mistake in equity. The parties would not have entered the contract if they had known the true position (*Magee*) and the contract of sale was made on the basis it could be converted and this was fundamental to the contract (*Grist v Bailey/ Solle v Butcher*).

COMMENTS (paragraph twelve)

Although the phrase 'aligning the problem with these cases' is rather odd, it is clear that the author has begun the evaluation step. He does a good job of linking the analysis to the cases cited above, albeit in a slightly cryptic manner. Still, the analysis and conclusion are apparent to the reader.

RESPONSE (paragraph thirteen)

If the claims of common mistake for Bob failed, then he would have to look to claims for misrepresentation that induced him to enter into the contract and that would make the contract voidable.

COMMENTS (paragraph thirteen)

This is a transition paragraph which does a good job indicating that we have moved on to Bob's alternate claim, even if the paragraph is only one sentence long.

RESPONSE (paragraph fourteen)

The two main issues here are whether there has been a misrepresentation as to conduct, and whether there has been a misrepresentation by an omission to speak i.e. a duty to disclose.[23] A misrepresentation is generally regarded as a misrepresentation of fact, that is addressed to the party misled and which induces the party to enter into the contract.[24]

COMMENTS (paragraph fourteen)

23. Comma errors: there should be no comma after 'conduct' (since it splits the object clause from the subject and verb), and there should be commas surrounding 'i.e.'
24. There doesn't need to be a comma after 'fact' and the author should be consistent in using either 'that' or 'which' to introduce the subordinate clauses. A case citation to support the proposition would be helpful as well, since we have begun another 'L' section.

RESPONSE (paragraph fifteen)

The first question to ask is whether in each case there was a misrepresentation of fact?[25] A misrepresentation of fact can sometimes be found through conduct. In *Gordon v Selico* independent contractors covered up dry rot in a house instead of eradicating it, and both they and the vendors were held liable for it to the purchasers. Even though there was no statement made by the vendor he was still liable for not pointing out the dry rot. Jessel MR in *Redgrave v Hurd* also decided that there it is not sufficient to say that the purchaser had an opportunity of discovering the truth of the situation, but did not avail himself of the opportunity.[26]

COMMENTS (paragraph fifteen)

25. Again, this is a sentence, not a question, based on the sentence structure. When you say, 'The question is X', you are not asking a question: you are making a statement. The author should use a full stop. The phrase 'in each case' is also somewhat ambiguous in this context.

26. These three sentences are relatively clear and indicate the direction in which the author will be moving. Commas continue to be a problem and should appear after 'Selico' and 'vendor'. Finally, the final sentence is also grammatically incorrect. The author should be careful of using 'he' generically.

RESPONSE (paragraph sixteen)

With regards to a duty to disclose, there is no duty at common law to disclose facts (*Smith v Hughes*). However it has been suggested that there is a partial duty to disclose, in other words, a duty not to give a misleading statement.[27] In *Notts Patent Brick Co. v Butler* a misrepresentor was held liable for not all the relevant information had been disclosed. In that case there was a sale of land.[28] The vendor's solicitor stated he was not aware of any restrictive covenants on the land, whereas in fact there were some that prevented the use of land as a brickyard as the vendor's client had told him. It was held that the vendee could rescind the contract despite having paid the deposit money and clauses to the effect that nothing could annul the contract. In this instance Adam as vendor knew what purpose Bob had in asking whether any noise came from the airport, and although the statement by Adam had been literally true, Adam had failed to disclose the relevant information when asked.[29]

COMMENTS (paragraph sixteen)

The author is doing a good job of introducing legal authority here and in the previous paragraph.

27. These two sentences are concise and well written, although there is a comma missing after 'however'. In addition, the author should consider rephrasing the second sentence. Anytime you say 'in other words' you are being repetitive. It's better to say what you have to say once and move on.

28. This sentence is a bit confusing. The author needs a comma after '*Butler*' and might rephrase the latter part of the sentence to read 'liable for not disclosing all of the relevant information regarding a sale of land'. The next sentence can then be deleted.

29. The author here is evaluating the law, although the phrase 'in this instance' is a bit confusing as a transition, since the reader is not sure what 'this instance' means. There is also a problem with verb tenses – it might be better to say Adam's statement 'was' true instead of 'had been' true. The evaluation is a bit conclusory, but does relate to the law introduced previously.

RESPONSE (paragraph seventeen)

Since the representation was clearly addressed to the party misled the next question to ask is whether the misrepresentations induced Bob to enter into the contract? *Edgington v Fitzmaurice* held that the misrepresentation need not be the sole factor in inducing entry into the contract and *Barton v Armstrong* went further stating it need only be a factor even if the contract would still have been made. However *Smith v Chadwick* made clear that it would not be an inducement where the representee regards it as unimportant. Therefore Bob needs to establish in each instance whether it was at least one factor that induced him to enter into the contract of sale.

COMMENTS (paragraph seventeen)

Basically, this is a strong paragraph, showing lots of law and analysis. The errors are minor. The first sentence needs a full stop, not a question mark. Commas should be placed between 'contract' and 'and' in the second sentence and after 'further', 'however' and 'therefore'. Antecedents are also problematic in the last two sentences. What do the two instances of 'it' refer to in the penultimate sentence and what does 'each instance' and 'it' mean in the last? Nevertheless, the author has done a good job presenting the law, which is the most important part of this paragraph.

RESPONSE (paragraph eighteen)

It is clear that the fact there was no dry rot was a factor in inducing Bob to enter into the contract since the fact that the value would have been reduced by £50,000 alone is a reason to believe that Bob was induced to enter into the contract at £50,000 above what might otherwise have been paid. However it is less clear cut with regards to the representation as to noise. The purpose of the purchase by Bob was to be a themed nightclub. It may be taken from the mere fact that he asked that he regarded the representation as a factor inducing him to buy, but it may well be asked how noise from overhead planes flying or helicopters hovering could disturb the noise emanating from a nightclub.

COMMENTS (paragraph eighteen)

The analysis verges on the circular at times in this paragraph, but the author has gone through the trouble to evaluate the facts in light of the law and set down the analysis explicitly. For that, marks are deserved and given.

RESPONSE (paragraph nineteen)

The last question to determine is what remedies the claimant may have under the contract for the misrepresentations once established. A misrepresentation entitles the misrepresentee to the option to rescind the contract being a voidable contract (*Car v Caldwell*). In this instance since the house has not been put onto the market then there are no third party rights to deal with from a bona fide third party purchaser for value then title remains with Bob and recission remains possible in this aspect (*Car v Caldwell*).

COMMENTS (paragraph nineteen)

Again, this is a good paragraph, well organised and well written aside from a few minor errors that you can note for yourself. The author loses his focus in the last sentence when he brings in a third party who is not in the hypothetical, but this is a relatively minor transgression.

RESPONSE (paragraph twenty)

However one possible bar to recission remains where the court has discretion to award damages in lieu of recission under s2 (2) of the Misrepresentation Act 1967. In this instance Adam may wish to claim that s2 (2) applies because he can then only pay Bob £50,000 in damages for the fall in value of the converted church resulting from the dry rot, and any damages resulting from the noise from the airport, which principally again would be a fall in value of the converted church. This may still be less than rescinding the contract which would cause the parties to be restored to their original position and the return of the £400,000, whereby Adam would have to place the converted church back onto the market at the going rate of £300,000 thereby losing £100,000 overall. If Bob wished to avoid this consequence then his only exception would be to claim fraudulent misrepresentation under *Derry v Peak*, which requires proof that the misrepresentor either knew that his statement was false or was reckless as to whether or not it was false, or claim that it is not equitable to do

COMMENTS (paragraph twenty)

Substantively, this is a good paragraph. Bringing up the Misrepresentation Act 1967 shows a good understanding of the law of misrepresentation, although the author could bring up some more case law. Because the author evaluates the law immediately after each legal authority, he loses the opportunity to compare and contrast different legal arguments. The essay is quite long, however, and it may very well be that the author is running out of time. Stylistically, there are a few problems. Using 's' as an abbreviation for 'section' in text is awkward, and the author continues to omit commas after introductory phrases ('however', in this instance). Some of the sentences adopt a stream of consciousness approach and, though technically correct, continue longer than they should as a matter of style. Examiners will not consciously mark you down for these types of errors, but you will not give the impression of having written a first-class essay.

so in these circumstances. The court may be inclined to award damages in lieu of recission here, because to do other would be to allow Bob to get out of what has become a bad bargain by reason of paying well above the market value of the converted church originally. The fact that the contract would then be upheld and the converted church would be useless to Bob now in light of the decision to list the building has nothing to do with the misrepresentation argument falling instead under common mistake which would make the contract void.

RESPONSE (paragraph twenty-one)

If Bob achieves recission then in this instance he would not need to claim additional damages because under whatever heading the misrepresentation is classified, there would be no further loss.

COMMENTS (paragraph twenty-one)

This one-sentence paragraph is a bit cryptic, and it's not quite clear what the author is driving at, although he obviously knows what he wants to say.

RESPONSE (paragraph twenty-two)

Therefore Bob has two methods of enabling the contract to be rescinded whether through mistake or misrepresentation. Both would make the contract void ab initio and therefore result in the return of the £400,000 and avoidance by Bob of the bad bargain but in the case of misrepresentation, by virtue of s2 (2) of the 1967 Act, this may be changed to damages if the court feels it is equitable to do so.

COMMENTS (paragraph twenty-two)

The author is now identifying the combined outcome of his analysis, which is a good procedural step. The language is not as clear as it could be, but the basic meaning comes through.

WRITING TIP

Try to find more than one case per point.

This is a solid essay with some very good case law and statutory language, even though there is very often only one case introduced to support a particular point. Try, as best you can, to find areas where disputes occur so that you can weigh up conflicting lines of case law. That is how you demonstrate a sophisticated understanding of the law. Also, when you discuss lines of cases, be sure to link each of the cases to each other rather than just listing them seriatum; while it may be clear in your mind why you are naming these cases in this order, you must explain yourself to your readers. State how the standard of law is narrowing or developing – that will show a good, nuanced understanding of the law.

The language throughout this essay is a bit awkward. At times, it is clear that the author is working under time pressure and doesn't have the opportunity to improve the prose, but it does make a difference to the reader's understanding. This author obviously knows what he is trying to say, but his knowledge doesn't always make it onto the paper. Keeping the sentence structure simple and straightforward would serve the author better than longer, more complex sentences. Remember, you are trying to persuade your reader, both by the content of your argument and by your presentation. You want to give the impression that you are cool, calm, collected and capable. Appearing rushed and harried destroys the vision of you as a competent lawyer and is thus counterproductive.

WRITING TIP

Sometimes students become flustered when they write because they think the written word has to be formal or elevated. If you're having trouble expressing yourself, try explaining your point out loud and write down what you said. Usually you'll make your point simply and concisely when you speak.

The author has done a very good job of identifying most of the major substantive points of law, and that is saying a lot in a problem this complex. The only real problems arise out of the language and occasional shortage of cases and statutes. If the author were to express himself more concisely, he would improve the essay immensely and bring it up to a first-class standard. As it currently stands, this essay would likely receive a high 2:1, even though the author appears to have a first-class understanding of the issues. However, because the author's knowledge is not on the paper, the examiner cannot give it a first-class mark.

> ✳ **NOTE**
>
> Examiners want to give you points, but they can't do so unless they see your knowledge on the paper.

10.5 Tort problem question

We will now move to a problem question in tort to see how CLEO works in a multi-party dispute.

QUESTION

Priscilla is an aspiring actress trying to break into the film world. Her publicist, Quarrell, thinks her image is a bit too innocent, so he makes arrangements for Randy, an aspiring actor known more for his sordid love affairs than his talent, to accompany Priscilla to a film awards show. The red carpet outside the theatre is wet from a recent downpour and Randy slips, falling against Priscilla. Sam Snapshot, a professional paparazzo, takes a picture of the accident that makes it look as if Randy is attacking Priscilla and she is slapping him. He sells the photo, without any explanation of what really happened, to Trouble! Magazine, who print it with the caption, 'Prudish Priscilla Rips into Rowdy Randy At Premiere'. Trouble! Magazine does not contact Priscilla directly, but does speak to Quarrell who, believing that no press is bad press, coyly denies any personal knowledge of the affair. Quarrell does not mention the matter to Priscilla.

Priscilla, who is a religiously devout person whose beliefs forbid her to engage in violence, suffers severe emotional distress as a result of the publication of the photo and leaves the country for two months, missing an important audition. Priscilla tries to get Randy to issue a joint statement with her, attacking Trouble! Magazine's characterisation of the photo, but he refuses, saying it's good press for him.

Priscilla's parents live in a very isolated part of the country and do not see or hear anything about the event until Nosy Nora, their nearest neighbour, shows them her copy of Trouble! Magazine. Priscilla's mother is a minister whose congregation votes to oust her as a result of Priscilla's violent behaviour.

Advise Priscilla and her parents.

RESPONSE (paragraph one)

The issues to identify in this problem are whether Priscilla or her parents can bring any claims for the damage suffered as a result of the episodes following the actions of Sam Snapshot, Trouble! Magazine, Randy, Quarrell and Nosy Nora which eventually led to the publication of a photo that Priscilla may allege was disparaging to her reputation. Who can bring claims against whom and what form would these claims take? I will first deal with the claims that Priscilla may establish and then move on to discuss Priscilla's parents' options.

COMMENTS (paragraph one)

The opening paragraph does a good job in trying to jump straight into the identification of the claims but spends a bit too much time summarising the facts and identifying the individuals. Nevertheless, the last sentence in the paragraph sets out the order of analysis.

RESPONSE (paragraph two)

Priscilla's main claim would be one of defamation. Defamation is a tort whose aim it is to compensate for the loss of reputation to the claimant that may result from the publication of material which result in the claimant be lowering in the esteem of right-thinking people (*Sim v Stretch*).

COMMENTS (paragraph two)

This is a very good paragraph – it gets straight to the point and identifies, with legal support, the elements that must be established to make out a *prima facie* case in defamation. The language can be tightened up or corrected in places (for example, one might say, 'Defamation compensates the claimant for the loss of reputation …'), but wordiness is not a major problem here.

RESPONSE (paragraph three)

Within defamation there are two forms of claim. Firstly, there is libel that is said to occur where the defamatory statement is written and in a permanent form. Secondly, there is slander that is said to arise as a result of defamatory statement that are oral and therefore temporary in form. The main purpose behind distinguishing between these forms of defamation is that in libel the claimant does not have to prove special damage whereas in slander the claimant does have to prove special damage unless he falls under one of four historical exceptions, the only relevant one here being that the imputation was directed to disparage the claimant in the way of his calling. In neither case however does the plaintiff have to actually prove that the defamatory statement was false. Once the elements of liability are established the defendant is presumed to be liable unless he can set up a valid defence.

COMMENTS (paragraph three)

While this is a well written paragraph and is true in all that it says, it is only tangentially relevant to the question. The distinction between libel and slander is not a major issue in this problem, and therefore the author cannot win a lot of marks for this discussion, as well crafted as it is. As you read through this essay, ask whether it would be diminished in any significant way if this paragraph were deleted. If it would not, then the paragraph is unnecessary.

RESPONSE (paragraph four)

Can it be shown here that the defamatory statement took the form of a libel? The material published was in the main a photo alongside a caption. In *Youssoupoff v Metro-Goldwyn* the plaintiff sought damages for a film that had been published by the defendants that suggested Rasputin had seduced her. Slesser J found that the photographic part is permanent and visible, and that it had to be taken with the speech as part of one complex. Additionally in *Charleston v News Group* a picture of the plaintiffs that had been taken from a computer game and which had the plaintiff's faces superimposed onto naked bodies performing sex was treated by the House of Lords as potentially libellous statements. This would suggest that the statement is libellous rather than a slander.

COMMENTS (paragraph four)

Here the author is taking an unusual approach to the 'L' and 'E' steps. Having introduced the general principles regarding libel and slander without any legal support in the previous paragraph, he now introduces a series of cases to define what a libel is. Again, the author's prose is excellent and the analysis is quite good, but the need to go into great detail about the difference between slander and libel is dubious. The cases can be used as general support to identify what constitutes defamatory material, but that is not the author's purpose in introducing the material. He will win some marks for knowing the cases defining defamatory material, but not first-class marks, since he is focusing on the wrong points.

RESPONSE (paragraph five)

The three key elements to establishing a claim in defamation are that the subject-matter of the action was actually defamatory, that it referred to the claimant and that it had been published to a third party. The defendant then has an opportunity to rely on a number of defences that include justification, fair comment, and qualified privilege. In addition either party may apply for the proceeding to be dealt with under a summary disposal by way of Defamation Act 1996, ss8–10. These will all be dealt with further below.

COMMENTS (paragraph five)

This paragraph has merit, although the information might have been introduced earlier (perhaps in paragraph two). While the first sentence obviously constitutes the general description of the elements of the tort of defamation, some sort of legal authority would be helpful, just as the defences could use some support. Although some people may believe that it is good to describe briefly the general elements of a tort before cluttering the prose with case references, you don't have a lot of time to keep going over the same points, particularly when those points are introductory in nature. The author here shows that he can write clearly and concisely, and it is likely that he can introduce the appropriate case references in his first discussion of the law without confusing the reader.

RESPONSE (paragraph six)

Is the statement here defamatory? As already mentioned the test is that which Lord Atkin laid out in *Sim v Stretch*, that the words have tended to lower the plaintiff in the estimation of right-thinking members of society. *Bryne v Deane* confirmed that the test is to be applied to society generally and not just to those persons to whom the statement may have had a particular impact upon in making the statement appear defamatory. There are two methods that the plaintiff may adopt in proving that a statement is defamatory. These rest on the connotations that the words may be said to have and rest on the idea that the words convey a hidden message or type of innuendo that ordinary people will perceive. Firstly, there is the true or legal innuendo. This is where the plaintiff tries to prove the innuendo based on external extrinsic facts so that to the persons who viewed the statement as defamatory did so, not on their ordinary meaning of the words, but together with the extrinsic facts (*Cassidy v Daily Mirror*). The second type, and the one that Priscilla may find most useful here, is the false innuendo. This is where the plaintiff relies on the ordinary and natural meaning of the words or a meaning that the words are capable of having. In *Lewis v Daily Telegraph* Lord Hodson found that it is for the judge to determine whether such a meaning is capable of being held before it is put to the jury (also see *Alexander v Arts Council*).

COMMENTS (paragraph six)

The opening to this paragraph reads well, even though it repeats points made earlier in the essay. Although it works here, you want to be careful of using this technique too often, since repetition wins no additional marks. The paragraph closes with a slightly odd phrase that may just be a typographical error. Taking the pargraph as a whole, however, it seems odd to spend so much time distinguishing between false and true innuendo, even though the discussion is well written and perfectly correct as a matter of law. It may be that the author believes a major controversy exists as to whether these words are defamatory at all, but the way he is introducing that controversy seems a bit unusual. However, it may be best to reserve judgment about the need for this discussion until one sees how the whole argument plays out.

RESPONSE (paragraph seven)

The requirement that the defamatory statement refers to the plaintiff (*Newstead v Express Newspapers*) is not in dispute here, but will be referred to later in considering the claims which the parents may have. The requirement that it has to be published may also be considered to be fulfilled since there has been a clear publication in a magazine that has been circulated to the general public.

COMMENTS (paragraph seven)

This is a good, concise paragraph demonstrating how to evaluate elements that are not in contention. More may need to be said about *Newstead* in the later discussion, but the author has done a good job in indicating to the reader that the point will not be lost.

RESPONSE (paragraph eight)

If Priscilla does manage to prove the above elements of liability, liability may still not exist if the defendant can establish any one of a number of defences. Justification may be raised if the defence wishes to show that the allegations or defamatory statements made were in fact true in fact. This includes both the facts on which comments made and the actual comments and inferences drawn therefrom. Although this could be pleaded, it is less likely to succeed than the defence of fair comment outlined below. The defence of qualified privilege may be raised and is mostly dealt with in relation to newspapers by s15 and Schedule I of the Defamation Act 1996. They may also be the defence of absolute privilege in relation to certain publications concerning special proceedings, mostly those of the legislature and court. Finally there is the defence of consent where the plaintiff had contracted to consent to the publication (*Chapman v Ellesmere*).

COMMENTS (paragraph eight)

We seem to have arrived at the defences section rather quickly, and the reader may wonder whether the defamatory nature of the publication has been fully proven. Nevertheless, the author's intent and direction is clear, and that is a plus. However, the discussion of defences suffers from the same problem as the earlier discussions do: even though this is the 'L' section of the essay, there are very few cases or statutes mentioned. While the statements made are true as far as they go, they do not demonstrate a sophisticated understanding of the issues involved but instead merely skim the surface of the relevant law. Occasional typos mar the presentation.

RESPONSE (paragraph nine)

The first defence that concerns us in particular here is fair comment. The defence of fair comment may arise where a defamatory statement is made on basic facts that are true and that the comments although not necessarily true were fair. In order to make such a fair comment the defendant must also prove that the fair comment was one that was in the public interest. In *London Artists v Littler* the House of Lords, reversing the decision of the judge, found that comments regarding the ending of a successful play, where it was alleged a plot had occurred to bring the play to an end, were ones in which the public were legitimately interested. In doing so the court took a fairly wide view of what could constitute the public interest.

COMMENTS (paragraph nine)

Another basically straightforward paragraph with a few grammatical errors and awkward phrases, particularly near the end. It seems as if there are a few too many facts regarding the *London Artists case*, but the author may show those details to be necessary when it comes time to evaluate the law. The reference to *Kemsley* is somewhat unclear, as is the proposition that is being advanced by that case.

Further, in that case the court held that, although it was in the public interest the defendants had failed to prove that the basic facts of the allegations against the plaintiffs were true, that there was in fact a plot. There are here two requirements therefore, that the public should be legitimately interested in a fair comment and that the basic facts upon which the allegations were made were true. It is also not necessary for all the facts on which the comment is made to be indicated as long as the subject matter is indicated with sufficient clarity and one that justifies comment such as an honest though prejudiced man might make (*Kemsley v Foot*).

RESPONSE (paragraph ten)

However the defence of fair comment can be reversed where the plaintiff can show evidence of malice from the defendant towards the plaintiff since a comment actuated by malice cannot be deemed to be fair (*Thomas v Bradbury*). In *Horrocks v Lowe* express malice was defined as a case where the defendant knows the statement to be false or is reckless as to the truth.

COMMENTS (paragraph ten)

The language in the first sentence is a bit awkward and occasionally incorrect, but it conveys the author's meaning, and the two cases regarding malice are a welcome sight.

RESPONSE (paragraph eleven)

The second defence that may be offered is under ss2–4 of the Defamation Act 1996. The publisher of a defamatory statement may offer to make amends under s2(1). In this instance the apology may be general or refer to a particular defamatory meaning which the person making the offer accepts that the statement conveys (s2(2)). The requirements of the offer are detailed in s2(3) and must be complied with. Under s2(4) the aggrieved party is also entitled to such compensation as the parties may agree and it must be made before a defence is

COMMENTS (paragraph eleven)

There are two main problems with this paragraph. First, its detailed summary of a statute appears to be more of a memory exercise than a critical analysis. For the most part, you don't win top marks for recounting a statute this way; it doesn't show your powers of analysis in any way. Second, this paragraph focuses on procedural matters that are not primarily at issue in the question. It may be that some defamation questions need you to consider the ability to make amends under the 1996 Act or the summary judgment served in defamatory proceedings relating to the subject-matter. Following the offer the claimant may accept the offer under s3 if he wishes and if he does but the terms cannot be agreed various mechanisms are laid out in order for the court to compel agreement. If the claimant chooses not to accept the offer, s4(2) provides that the publisher may rely on this as a defence subject to s4(3) that provides if the publisher knew of the nature of the defamatory statement and that it referred to the aggrieved party, the defence would not lie. Also under s4(4) if the publisher decides to rely on this defence then he cannot rely on any other defences but may nevertheless be relied on in mitigation of damages whether or not another defence has been submitted (s4(5)). It should be noted that these sections only apply as against the publisher. s3(7) makes it clear that accepting an offer does not affect any cause of action against another party.

procedure, but there is nothing in this question to suggest that either discussion is particularly relevant. Therefore, this paragraph constitutes yet another example of well-written prose that conveys correct legal information but that fails to win the author major marks. Note the incorrect use of 's' as an abbreviation, especially at the beginning of the last sentence.

RESPONSE (paragraph twelve)

As regards damages, it is for the jury to award damages in cases of defamation. However there has been a general trend for damages to be reduced following some extremely high awards. In *John v Mirror Group* the plaintiff had awards for damages and exemplary damages reduced from £75,000 to £25,000 and £275,000 to £50,000 respectively. The reasons given by the court were that the allegations made by the defendant did not attack the plaintiff's personal integrity or damage his reputation as an artist in relation to the general damages claim. Furthermore, the exemplary damages should not exceed the minimum necessary, and in order to establish such damages the jury had to be satisfied that the defendant had no truth in the statement and that he was cynically motivated.

COMMENTS (paragraph twelve)

This paragraph is good, since the quantum of damages may very well be at issue in this case. Another good point is that the discussion focuses primarily on legal issues contained in the *John* case rather than factual issues. Because this paragraph focuses on pertinent legal tests, it makes the relevance of the discussion more aparent to the reader. This amount of detail will make the evaluation step easier as well.

RESPONSE (paragraph thirteen)

Who then can Priscilla sue under these circumstances? Her main claim would be against the author, publisher and editor of the magazine in question as defined by s1 of the Defamation Act 1996. All three can be liable for its publication as *Watts v Times Newspapers* show. In this instance the author would include Sam Snapshot, and the publisher would be Trouble! Magazine, the editor being the editor of that magazine. Any claims against Quarrell or Randy would be subject to the defence under s1(1) that they did not take responsibility for the publication.

COMMENTS (paragraph thirteen)

The intent behind this paragraph – namely to begin the evaluation process by identifying the proper defendants – is good. The execution is not quite as successful, since the paragraph is repetitive and the reference to *Watts* glancing. Although Randy may well be able to avoid liability by reference to section 1(1) of the 1996 Act, Priscilla might be able to construct a decent argument against Quarrell. Remember, no two parties are ever situated in exactly the same manner; look for the differences between two defendants and discuss them. In this case, Priscilla might consider a claim against Quarrell based in agency or negligence. In addition, the author has missed a potential defendant: the printer of the magazine. Although the printer has an easy defence under section 1(1) of the Act as a person not responsible for the publication, it is good to identify the printer as a potential party, since it shows creative legal thinking.

RESPONSE (paragraph fourteen)

Both parties can if they wish apply to the court if they wish for a summary disposal of the case. Under s8(2) the court may dismiss the plaintiff's claim if the court believes that it has no realistic prospect of success. Under s8(3) the plaintiff may be granted summary relief if the judge feels that there is no defence to a claim that might otherwise have a realistic prospect of success. However under these circumstances it is unlikely the court would grant summary relief to either party since the claim is a good one, with a prospect of a defence.

COMMENTS (paragraph fourteen)

Again, the author has omitted numerous commas and used 's' instead of 'section', but the major problem lies with the focus of the paragraph. Lots of time is being spent describing statutory provisions that relate primarily to procedural matters not at issue in the question. The author has to do a better job of weighing the relative merits of the different claims and focusing on the ones that are most in contention as a matter of law if he wants to achieve a first-class mark. As a side note, the author needs to remember to use the word 'claimant' instead of 'plaintiff' when referring to a contemporary action: 'plaintiff' is no longer correct except in a historical sense.

RESPONSE (paragraph fifteen)

It would appear that the necessary elements are present for libel, alleviating the necessity to prove special damages. It would also appear that the best plan for the Priscilla would be to prove a false innuendo under *Lewis v Times Newspapers* since the persons to whom the photo and caption were published did not know of any extrinsic facts that might make the material more defamatory. The innuendo must therefore be said to arise from the natural and ordinary meaning of the words. As stated it appears the other elements of referring to plaintiff and publication are present in Priscilla's case.

COMMENTS (paragraph fifteen)

The evaluation here is somewhat superficial, especially since much discussion could result from whether a suggestion that Priscilla slapped someone is defamatory. For example, the author could have introduced 'eggshell claimant' cases to discuss whether her particular sensitivity allowed relief or not. The problem in this paragraph is not that errors or bad writing are obscuring the author's meaning: the author has simply failed to grasp the deeper issues in this question.

RESPONSE (paragraph sixteen)

The defences however must be dealt with on an individual basis. In the case of Sam Snapshot, the photographer, he was actually aware of the incident and witnessed. Furthermore he made the incident out to look like that which it was not. He then passed on the photo without a qualifying explanation. It is arguable his defence of fair comment would fail because the defendant can show that there is express malice. On the part Trouble! Magazine and the editor, the defence of fair comment has a better chance of succeeding. Although they did not contact Priscilla directly, they contacted her agent who was supposedly working for her, who gave a reply that he knew nothing of the incident. It may be arguable that the defendants in those circumstances should have attempted to contact Priscilla directly but malice would still be harder to prove and would fall under the reckless element. The fact that Randy refuses to issue a joint statement as to the event goes to whether the incident was itself defamatory. Clearly Randy did not regard it as such. The

COMMENTS (paragraph sixteen)

The author is following the CLEO method and trying to evaluate the facts in light of the law, which is good. Unfortunately, he didn't introduce the law in a sufficient amount of detail. Therefore, the legal analysis cannot support a sophisticated factual evaluation, and the author is left to merely recite the facts and offer conclusory statements. The author does a good job of analysing whether malice exists with respect to Trouble! Magazine's attempt to contact Priscilla, but the discussion would be improved if the author was able to relate the evaluation to specific legal language contained in the case or statutory law. To the author's credit, the discussion is well written and logical, as far as it goes, but does not have sufficient content to allow an examiner to award top marks.

issue is one for the jury to decide according to the test of the ordinary right-thinking people in society generally if the judge decides it is so capable of having a defamatory meaning.

RESPONSE (paragraph seventeen)

Priscilla may also claim both general and exemplary damages for the way in which she was treated. Once again this would depend on the motivation of the defendants and would be for the plaintiff to prove malice.

COMMENTS (paragraph seventeen)

The author is doing well to follow the 'L' discussion through, step by step, and evaluate each of the constitutent elements, but the analysis here is superficial and too speculative. You are the expert: you need to come to some decision about the merits of the arguments. Don't leave the conclusions up in the air.

RESPONSE (paragraph eighteen)

As stated earlier the publisher may offer an apology to the plaintiff before the defence is submitted. To avoid litigation this may the easy way out and may keep the action out of court. If Priscilla can also get a good settlement under the compensation provision this may also be her easiest option. It is also unlikely that this is such a clear cut case as to lend itself to a summary disposal.

COMMENTS (paragraph eighteen)

The prose is generally straightforward and understandable. Again, it is the content that is a problem. The author is focusing on procedural matters and failing to come to solid conclusions.

RESPONSE (paragraph nineteen)

In the case of Priscilla's parents, the key question is whether the libel refers to them? The other factors including who to sue, other elements of defamation, defence and damages would apply as stated above, therefore the question comes down to whether the parents can establish a claim at all? Once again here the test is whether the ordinary person, possessed with the relevant facts would understand the defamatory statement to be defamatory of him. In *Morgans v Oldhams Press* the relevant fact was that the persons who read the article knew the man in the

COMMENTS (paragraph nineteen)

The author does a good job of incorporating previous discussions by reference (although he should be slightly clearer which aspects he is citing), but needs to use full stops rather than question marks for his first two sentences. The statement 'the question is' is a statement, not a question. Therefore, it needs a full stop. Substantively, the author is using a circular argument: the publication is defamatory because the congregation ousted Priscilla's mother and it wouldn't have done so had it not considered the publication defamatory.

photo and would therefore implicate him in a kidnapping. In this case the relevant fact is that the congregation knew Priscilla to be the parent's daughter. Clearly the congregation regarded it as defamatory of her and referring to her from their subsequent vote to oust her as their minister, but as stated above the test of being defamatory is the ordinary person in society generally (*Bryne v Dean*) and, in this instance, with knowledge of the fact that the parents are Priscilla's daughter. It is therefore arguable whether it refers to the parents or not. There is a possibility that Nosy Nora may have republished the material here by showing Priscilla's parents the magazine, but this can be easily dismissed by *Slipper v BBC* where Bingham LJ states that where republication is proveable, foreseeable and natural even intentional then no reason why effects should be ignored, and the original parties would remain liable.

However, the legal test for defamation is slightly more complex than an ends-justified analysis and needs to be discussed in greater detail. The reader is also shortchanged by the omission of the further discussion of Newstead that was promised in paragraph seven. Similarly, Nosy Nora's role deserves more attention. Overall, this paragraph gives short shrift to a number of important claims, probably due to a lack of time.

RESPONSE (paragraph twenty)

Therefore both Priscilla and Priscilla's parents have arguable cases in defamation for damages. Once both parties have overcome the hurdle of proving a false innuendo and Priscilla's parents, that it refers to them, then they need to establish that the plaintiffs cannot rely on the defence of fair comment either by showing the basic facts were incorrect, that it was not a fair comment, that it was not in the public interest or that it was actuated by malice.

COMMENTS (paragraph twenty)

Here the author is attempting to tie up the various loose ends and provide a single outcome, but you see how speculative his conclusions are. Saying what the parties need to establish is not the same as saying whether or not they will prevail. The latter is the better approach to take.

This essay demonstrates some very good points. It is, for the most part, well written and clearly organised. It also contains a great many true statements about the law and a number of legal authorities. All of these qualites bode well. Unfortunately, they are not enough to earn the author a first-class mark. The major problem is that the essay fails to identify and discuss the sub-issues that are most in contention. The major claims were correct – can Priscilla and her mother pursue claims in defamation – but the author didn't distinguish between important and unimportant sub-issues. For example, far too much time was spent on statutory summaries (not analyses) and procedural points, thus leaving too little time to discuss whether the publication really was likely to lower Priscilla in the esteem of right-thinking people, whether Quarrell was a proper defendant and whether Priscilla's mother could be defamed by a publication that did not identify her or her relationship to Priscilla. Nora was a minor issue and didn't deserve much attention, but the other points should have received better coverage. Similarly, the author might have spent more time on the defence of qualified privilege, which was mentioned in passing but not discussed in any detail. Overall, this paper will probably win a 2:1 mark, even though the author seems to have the skill to earn a first-class mark.

10.6 Tort 'discuss' question

Having considered several problem questions, it is now time to turn to some 'discuss' questions.

> **QUESTION**
>
> How can one justify the existence of strict liability torts in a civil compensation scheme that relies primarily on the element of fault as the motivation for economic redress?

RESPONSE (paragraph one)

Often seen as the domain of civil wrongs, tort law defines the circumstances when individuals are to be held responsible for their actions and the extent to which they must make good any damage done.[1] The reluctance to be seen as a form of punishment (which is best left to the realm of criminal law) allows the notion of tort to be tied to a civil compensation scheme.[2] However, tort law in itself should not be constrained to mere compensation. It is thus in the other justifications for a law of

COMMENTS (paragraph one)

1. Opening sentences are hard in 'discuss' questions, but this author does a good job in easing into the topic, although the word 'often' is incorrect: tort always relates to civil wrongs.

2. The reference to 'reluctance' is odd – reluctance by whom to do what?

torts that one can see strict liability torts slotting in comfortably.[3]

RESPONSE (paragraph two)

A Victorian legacy left in tort is that due to moral reasons, compensation is only due when a link can be established between the plaintiff and defendant. Fault must be apportioned. However, the 'fault' assumption is often confined to the tort of negligence. As soon as one looks beyond that, for example to product liability and the rule in *Rylands v Fletcher* amongst others, a stricter form of liability emerges.

COMMENTS (paragraph two)

The opening clause comes across as confusing, but the paragraph improves as the author continues. The final sentence is quite good, in that it reverses the assumption that underlies the question (ie that fault is the norm in tort) by providing several examples to the contrary.

RESPONSE (paragraph three)

One must begin by looking at the faults of the law of negligence in order to understand why the torts of defective products, *Rylands v Fletcher* etc fall under a different form of liability.

COMMENTS (paragraph three)

It is not clear why this sentence deserves its own paragraph. It might be better to combine it with the following thought. The sentence is also slightly wordy ('one must begin') and lacks proper punctuation ('etc.' should be given a full stop and preceded by a comma – also, be very cautious about using 'etc.' in your prose, since it can become a lazy habit). 'Faults' may not be a good word choice here (perhaps 'flaws'?), given the special meaning that is attributed to 'fault' in the question.

RESPONSE (paragraph four)

Firstly, negligence's need for fault relies on a significant burden of proof on the plaintiff. This evidential burden – the chain of causation must be proven.

COMMENTS (paragraph four)

At this point, the reader doesn't know where the author is heading with his argument, even though the author obviously believes himself to have set up a structure. The author needs to be more explicit, earlier on, about what he intends to argue. Note the second sentence is a fragment.

RESPONSE (paragraph five)

In order to establish liability in negligence, one has to firstly prove that a duty of care existed between the claimant and applicant. Although *Donoghue v Stevenson* proclaimed the 'neighbour principle', the duty of care has been confined to circumstances where the two parties are in reasonable proximity to one another. In the simple cases, this principle holds no great problems. However, as shown in the case of *Murphy v Brentwood Council*, the courts are reluctant to expand negligence to such a wide degree and the plaintiff is denied a remedy. One can look for hope in the case of *Junior Books*, where the defective quality of a product was in question. Here a duty of care was found between the purchaser and a sub-contractor. But that case has not been followed.

COMMENTS (paragraph five)

The author is doing well to bring in three different cases, but his purpose in doing so is not yet clear. We're well into the first page of the essay, but don't have an idea of what the author is trying to say. By this stage, we should know what the thesis is and how the author intends to prove that thesis.

RESPONSE (paragraph six)

As soon as one starts to apply the duty of care idea in the area, for example, of defective products, it begins to stretch the neighbour principle further than has happened thus far. The courts would be reluctant to create a fiction where a producer is liable to an indefinite number of potential end users – in effect a duty to everyone.

COMMENTS (paragraph six)

This paragraph begins to develop the author's argument and tie his ideas in with the law introduced previously (the neighbour principle), which is good. The selection of defective products as an example is a bit unfortunate, of course, because *Donoghue* itself involved a defective product. The final sentence describing the problems associated with an indefinite duty extending to an indefinite number of potential victims is a well-known concept and should be discussed in greater detail and attributed to the appropriate commentator.

RESPONSE (paragraph seven)

Secondly, even if a duty is established need to establish a breach in that duty and factual causation. A breach can only occur when reasonable care was not taken in exercising the given duty. Using the example of the Thalidomide tragedy, the individuals affected were unable to get over this hurdle. The fact that the producers of the product were not themselves aware of the risk, due to the lack of medical evidence available, prevented a breach of the duty from forming.

COMMENTS (paragraph seven)

The author may be on to something here, but the meaning is not clear due to missing words and vague construction. The author is using terms of art (breach of duty, factual causation) but is not using them to best effect. The terms need to be tied more closely to cases and statutes to make sense and give the kind of detail that 'discuss' questions require. For example, the final sentence might be improved by a specific reference to the design defence in the Consumer Protection Act 1987.

RESPONSE (paragraph eight)

Factual causation often revolves around the 'but for' idea. However, even in negligence this can be a problem in the case of medical treatment, not knowing whether the patient would have been any better off for not having the negligent treatment. In relation to product liability – the test of negligence is once again a heavy burden, especially with medical products.

COMMENTS (paragraph eight)

The run-on sentence in the middle of this paragraph doesn't help the reader understand what the author is trying to say, nor does the general reference to the 'heavy burden' of negligence convey what's in the author's mind. The author obviously has some sort of argument that he's trying to construct, but because he has divorced his discussion from the building blocks of legal argument – cases, statutes, commentary – he has problems conveying his thoughts to his readers, let alone persuading them that his theory is correct.

RESPONSE (paragraph nine)

Therefore the standard of proof is often very high in relation to negligence and considerably difficult in some circumstances.[4] In the limited case of defective products, it seems inequitable to require 'fault' based principles in order to impose liability. In order to accept that principle, there must be a recognition that all torts are not the same. Negligence and indeed intentional torts e.g. assault, are based around the conduct of the individual.[5] But other (limited) torts need to be looked at

COMMENTS (paragraph nine)

4. The reference to the 'standard of proof' as being high is confusing, since the balance of probabilities is not a very stringent standard at all. Similarly, the 'considerably difficult in some circumstances' phrase is vague and empty – it adds nothing concrete to the argument.
5. This is a good concept, although the author needs to put a comma before and possibly following 'e.g.'

differently – liability on the basis on an event or a fact.[6] For example vicarious liability is based on the factual relationship between an employee/employer – fault is only relevant in establishing liability of the employee, not the employer.[7]

6. The reference to a 'limited' tort is unclear, though it sounds like an interesting idea.

7. The concept makes some sense, but it is not clear how it relates to the first sentence in the paragraph. Each paragraph should be used to develop a single idea; it is difficult here to identify the theme that is running through the paragraph. The author also needs to insert a comma after 'for example'.

RESPONSE (paragraph ten)

Yet, this inherent difference in some torts to one another may not be a sufficient reason in itself.[8] If these torts are to be seen as an exception, what is the underlying justification for the perpetuation of this exception.[9]

COMMENTS (paragraph ten)

8. Again, the author seems to have a good idea in his head, but the vague and sometimes problematic language (no comma after 'yet', and 'inherent difference to' is rather odd) fails to convey his meaning.

9. Here, the meaning is lost due to vague antecedents (does 'these torts' refer to 'some torts' or 'one another', and which torts are at issue anyway?) and high-sounding but empty phrases ('underlying justification for the perpetuation of this exception'). This sentence also needs to end with a question mark.

RESPONSE (paragraph eleven)

One must remember that tort is a balance between the interest of the plaintiff (the one to whom interest has been damaged) and that of the defendant's wrongdoing.[10] In that balancing act (assessing grounds of liability and thus compensation) it is better in some circumstances, instead of asking 'who is at fault?', to ask 'who is better placed to redress any damage done?'.[11]

COMMENTS (paragraph eleven)

10. The opening phrase is a bit wordy and there is a lack of parallelism between 'the interest of the plaintiff' and 'that of the defendant's wrongdoing'. The author needs to frame both ideas in terms of interests or actions.

11. If you use a question mark as internal or end punctuation, you do not need to add any additional punctuation – the question mark is sufficient by itself. Also, the author has added an extra space mid-sentence and following the opening parenthesis. Watch your spacing as much as your spelling. The most common error is only putting one space instead of two at the end of a sentence (either a full stop or a question mark). Use correct punctuation; not everyone will notice, but some people will and judge you accordingly. In terms of

substantive content, this sentence makes sense, but rehashes a concept that is well known in the commentary. Again, the analysis would be improved if the author referred to a specific source, not only to show a facility with the materials but because a specific reference would make the language tighter and more precise. Also, this point does not appear to have been included in the introductory paragraph. Remember, you should try to indicate the direction of your essay at the beginning; that way the reader is not surprised by new points halfway through the paper.

RESPONSE (paragraph twelve)

For example with defective products, the traditional doctrine was that of caveat emptor, buyer beware.[12] The consumer would thus always be bearing the risk, and if the product did in some way cause damage, they would have no recourse in tort.[13] *Donoghue v Stevenson*'s narrow ratio was a turning point in this, as Lord Atkin established that the ultimate user may have a case against the producer. Increasing social changes saw this to be too harsh on individuals, and in the modern world the presumption is that the producer is in a better place to bear the costs of any damage resulting from their product.[14] This is reflected in the 1987 Consumer Protection Act (a result of the 1985 EC Directive).[15]

COMMENTS (paragraph twelve)

12. This paragraph follows the preceding thought well, in that it is a specific example of the idea introduced previously, but the author needs to develop the idea in a more sophisticated manner – perhaps with citations to commentators – to do well. There's also a missing comma after 'example'.

13. There's a spacing problem at the end of the sentence as well as an antecedent problem due to incorrect use of gender-neutral language ('they' cannot refer to 'the consumer'). Although the concepts are good, the author should find some authority to support them.

14. It is good to cite to a leading case, even if it is as well known as *Donoghue*, but the author must develop the ideas further, with references to more specific authority. In addition, the antecedent of 'this' is unclear and the author seems to have stated the reverse of what he meant. The reference 'their' again mistakenly refers to a single antecedent ('the producer'). The number of either the first or second noun or pronoun needs to change.

15. The author here does a good job in trying to bring a statute into the discussion, but he needs to identify specifically what aspects of the 1987 Act demonstrate his point. There is also a spacing problem, and the reference to the 1985 Directive appears gratuitous.

RESPONSE (paragraph thirteen)

Hence the conclusion one can draw from this is that one of goals of tort law is to consider to whom it is better to allow the economic loss to fall on.[16] In some torts, fault may be the best way to provide a link between act and compensation. However, in other torts, the inequity of relying on fault, allows a gap to be formed, which is filled with strict liability.[17]

COMMENTS (paragraph thirteen)

16. The author is trying to avoid ending the sentence with a preposition but has used 'to whom' when 'on whom' would be the correct way to structure the sentence (the author would then delete the final 'on'). The author has also done a good job of directing the reader to the purpose of this paragraph, which is to draw conclusions from the previous discussion. The problem is that the previous discussion didn't provide a sufficient foundation for futher conclusions, since it suffered from a lack of clarity and detail. The author has an argument in his head, but it's not getting down on paper. Because there isn't enough detail, the author is also becoming repetitive and circular in his reasoning in this and the following sentences.

17. Here the author has a few too many commas. He can delete those following 'fault' and 'formed'.

RESPONSE (paragraph fourteen)

Yet as much as tort is about allocating 'blame and spreading the risk of activities, it is also based on the idea of individual responsibility.[18] Fault based torts requires an element of foresight.[19] Unless you were able to be in a position where a reasonable person could have prevented the act, liability is imposed.[20] However, some activities (non natural user e.g. keeping a reservoir) are so inherently risky that if one chooses to engage in such an activity, then one should also consider all the potential liabilities.[21] It is a highly normative

COMMENTS (paragraph fourteen)

18. This point is true, but it is quite basic. The author needs to advance more sophisticated arguments. The author should also delete the single inverted comma before 'blame'.

19. There's a subject-verb agreement problem here – the author should use 'require', not 'requires'.

20. The use of 'you' is a bit colloquial, and it is unclear how this sentence advances the argument.

21. There are some awkward and technically incorrect elements in this sentence, but the thought is interesting. However, the vagueness of the language means the author runs the risk of suggesting that liability based on *Rylands v Fletcher* is associated with dangerous or high-risk activities, which is not true.

suggestion.[22] But one based on a conception of tort that is not only about compensation in economic terms, but also about promoting/ prohibiting particular ways of behaviour.[23]

22. This sentence sounds good, but what is it really saying?

23. This sentence is actually a fragment, despite its length. The author appears to have a good idea, but the idea remains in his head rather than coming out on the paper.

RESPONSE (paragraph fifteen)

It is perhaps the harsh overtones of strict liability responsibility that has led to an attempted dilution of the rule in *Rylands v Fletcher*. Such an example is Lord Goff in *Cambridge Water* making the suggestion that some element of 'forseeability of risk' is needed in that tort.

COMMENTS (paragraph fifteen)

These are good points, but they should have been made earlier. Note how much more persuasive the text is when the author cites authority and uses the precise language of the case. There are, again, a few grammatical errors that slow the reader down, but the basic sense comes through.

RESPONSE (paragraph sixteen)

Therefore in conclusion, tort – the way civil compensation is primarily is given, does indeed have fault at its heart. But fault is limited to certain torts, and it is the exceptions to those – *Rylands v Fletcher*, defective products that one begins to see a broader picture of justifying compensation. Responsibility and a fairer allocation of risk provide adequate supplements to the notion of fault.

COMMENTS (paragraph sixteen)

The author obviously knows what point he is trying to make, but the various grammatical errors obscure his meaning and lessen the persuasive power of his conclusions. Also, this paragraph does not seem to be adding anything new to the discussion – it is just repeating points made earlier, with the same degree of generality. While you do not need to include new information in the conclusion, the final paragraph does need to serve some function, such as tying together the strands of the argument or identifying the outcome of the dispute.

WRITING TIP

If you don't have the building blocks of an argument (ie the law), your structure is irrelevant.

This essay demonstrates some positive elements. It includes a few citations to cases and statutes, which is difficult to do in 'discuss' questions, and it refers to the ideas of esteemed commentators, although those commentators are not named and are not quoted with a sufficient amount of detail to help the author formulate his argument. Without the building blocks of legal argument – ie cases, statutes and commentary – it is impossible to write a strong, persuasive essay. You need to use precise language and detailed citations to legal authorities to make your meaning clear. Vague and general language leads to confusion and circular argument. The author obviously has some good ideas and is a competent writer, but he has not succeeded in constructing a cohesive argument here.

The other major problem relates to the organisation of the essay. Even though 'discuss' questions do not follow a strict CLEO methodology, the various elements do need to exist. Here, the author fails to identify the claim (ie his primary point) at the beginning of the essay, forcing the reader to scramble to identify the major themes without assistance. There are elements of the 'L' and 'E' steps throughout, but the lack of detail in the legal analysis leads to a faulty and overly vague evaluation. The 'O' step also suffers from excessive generality, which is to be expected, since the preceding elements don't provide sufficient support. Remember, even a 'discuss' essay needs an overall structure and purpose and must be more than a string of unrelated points.

Overall, this essay falls somewhere between a 2:1 and a 2:2 mark. The precise placement would depend on how well other students handled the question.

10.7 Jurisprudence 'discuss' question

> **QUESTION**
>
> John Finnis attempts to base his version of natural law and natural rights on a number of goods that are 'self-evident'. Can one say that what is 'self-evident' will vary from culture to culture and that therefore Finnis's version of natural law is nothing more than a justification for the status quo, masquerading behind the veneer of a more universal framework of rights?

RESPONSE (paragraph one)

'Unscientific' was the word that Kelsen, in his development of the theory of the basic norm, used to sum up and resoundingly denounce the natural law doctrine in general, as these theories made no attempt to frame a definition of law round a formula that would work for all legal systems.[1] Kelsen was of course a positivist, and like Austin before him, and to a lesser extent Hart and Raz since, he believed in a value-free description of law, meaning that values that were 'self-evident'

COMMENTS (paragraph one)

1. The essay starts strongly, giving a definite and detailed perspective on the general area of law under discussion by a well-known commentator.

were not an issue that should be dealt with by a concept of law.[2] However, the natural docdtrine was resurrected by Finnis in his work, 'Natural Law and Natural Rights', and in the debate between positivists and non-positivists, Finnis firmly placed himself in the camp that admits values into a definition of law.[3] Yet the inevitable question that follows from this is simply that if values are to be admitted, values that are 'self-evident' or common, whose values are they to be and how can a theory encompassing all forms of legal system be arrived at?[4] In assessing whether natural law as postulated by Finnis is indeed little more than a justification for the status quo, the first task is naturally to examine the merit of this critique, but even though the ultimate conclusion must be that the criticism has a degree of justification, it would be an incomplete assessment that did not then enquire as to whether a better alternative presents itself.[5] A starting point will therefore be an analysis of the content and essence of Finnis' Theory.[6]

2. The qualification of Kelsen's comment is useful. However, the references to Austin, Hart and Raz appear to be a bit of name-dropping, since the author does not indicate how those commentators relate to the subject of this essay.

3. This sentence speaks the obvious, to some extent.

4. The author here seems to be trying to frame the claim of the essay but ends up repeating the question a little too much. The use of the question also diminishes the impact of the sentence, since a question gives little indication of the author's own viewpoint.

5. This sentence is far too wordy and circular in its reasoning. The author should just identify the points he is going to make and move on.

6. It is good to indicate how the author will begin the analysis, but the author should avoid the random capitalisation of the word 'theory'.

RESPONSE (paragraph two)

In constructing the natural law theory, Finnis makes clear his aim to depart from the valuefree accounts of law as advocated by the positivists. Indeed, he denounces the positivist accounts of law as descriptiv, whereas an account of law should in his view be prescriptive. At the heart of the theory lies the notion of the common good which, according to finnis, all legal systems and all men as individuals in society should strive to attain. The perfect legal system that conformed with Finnis' theory would have certain features, such as the eight disiderata of the rule of law, allowing individuals to plan their lives free from unjustified coercion, an authoritative force which would solve co-ordination

COMMENTS (paragraph two)

Aside from a few typographical errors, this is a well-written paragraph. The author is clear and precise in his prose and demonstrates a very good facility with the materials. The amount of detail is good and the content is correct, despite some typographical errors. As the reader progresses through the paragraph, however, it starts to read like a mini-treatise on Finnis. There seems to be something missing, namely a link to the question. It may be that the author will use this material in support of a larger argument, but because the essay's overall theme was not made clear at the outset, the reader starts to worry whether the author will address himself to the point at issue.

problems whilst conforming always with the law, and by having such traits it would assist the quest for the common good. Yet of course it would be unrealistic to admit that all legal systems would meet these requirements, and Finnis is quick to acknowledge this. The perfect legal system as described above is labelled the central case by Finnis, and legal systems that contain these essential traits to a lesser degree are the more peripheral cases. The quality of the case in question is determined through practical reasoning from the point of view of the person who would use practical reasoning in a reasonable way, and not, for example, from the point of view of the anarchist.

RESPONSE (paragraph three)

In addition, all legal rules should be made in furtherance of the common good according to the theory. To take a specific illustration, Finnis recognises that not every individual will work towards the common good in society. The criminal will, for instance, subordinate the interests of the common good to those individual profits and gains that are the reason behind his deviation from the accepted course. From this formulation it follows that the mechanism of punishment is used to restore the common good, not only by expressing the social dissatisfaction with the behaviour of the recalcitrant, but also by encouraging the offender not to work against the common good again. The effect of this framework of goods is, as Endicott has stated, to impose a duty on every individual not to infringe another's good, for to do so would be to deviate from the path towards the common good.

COMMENTS (paragraph three)

Again, a very good and well-written paragraph, although the failure to use gender-neutral language here and in the preceding paragraph could annoy some readers. The citation to Endicott is very good, since it shows a familiarity with commentators other than Hart, Finnis and Raz. The only problem is that there is no direct link to the question posed. It may be that the author has a connection in his mind, but that connection is not obvious on the paper. We are now well into the essay and have no idea where the argument is going, although we are confident about the author's facility with Finnis. If the author wants to receive a first-class mark, he needs to focus more on the question.

RESPONSE (paragraph four)

These, then, are the main elements of the theory, and already it can be seen that Finnis is not merely trying to justify the status quo.[7] The central case and peripheral case structure that he lays out, which follows a similar line to that taken by Aristottel when he used it to define friendship, is without doubt encouraging those thinking about law and its content to do the very opposite, and not without success.[8] By constructing this framework of cases, or instances of legal rules, Finnis encourages those seeking to assess a legal system to make a comparison between what the rule that is the subject of the assessment is, and what it ought to be.[9] Moreover, the same system can be used to assess the attitudes of the law subjects, for just as one can have a central case of a legal system, one can also have a central case of a law-abiding citizen. This way of thinking overcomes the obstacle that Hart's practice theory of rules and Raz's claim that law claims authority were less able to circumnavigate, for Finnis is able to distinguish between the good citizen who obeys the law for the purposes of the common good, and the anarchist who obeys the law because he is hoping it will help him violate it some time in the future. Inevitably such an exercise is complicated, and must admit of values, but as Finnis rightly states, the notions of simplicity such as a command, sanction and threat, most notoriously used by Austin in his account of law, miss the point as the legal theories which they produce are merely descriptive. At the very least, therefore, it can be said that Finnis, by constructing the theory of the central case in which the legal system contains all the essential features and strives to attain the common good, renders it inevitable that subscribers to the theory will always have

COMMENTS (paragraph four)

7. The purpose of the preceding paragraphs have now become clear: they were intended to summarise Finnis's theory of natural law and natural rights. While it is good to make sure that everyone is operating from a similar place of understanding, the author here spent a bit too much time going over general aspects of Finnis's work. The question has focused the student on one aspect of Finnis's theory: that is the aspect that deserves attention. General summations are, for the most part, not necessary or desirable. The second half of the sentence is too conclusory, however, since the preceding paragraphs did not demonstrate anything about Finnis's approach to the status quo.

8. This sentence is confusing, as is the reference to Aristotle (which is misspelled).

9. No comma is necessary after 'is'.

in mind the goals and direction which rules that form the legal system must take, and such a forward-looking perspective does not suggest a theory that serves only to justify the status quo.[10]

10. The remainder of this paragraph describes how the author views Finnis's theory as not supporting the status quo. Note how the substance of this essay compares to the previous one. The content here is much stronger and more direct because the author has linked the argument to the specific statements of commentators. The author needs to be careful of two things, however: (1) he should not just toss in names of commentators as a matter of course, since irrelevant references slow down the argument, and (2) he should make sure that all references to commentary relate to the larger argument. He does a relatively good job of that here, although the discussion is quite dense and one may disagree with his conclusions. Still, the approach is good.

RESPONSE (paragraph five)

Yet the problem still remains that although the structure of the central case, and the necessity to further the common good, are well-intentioned notions, the very question of what the common good contains is by no means straightforward to answer. Finnis states that the common good contains goods that are evident to the good man, or more correctly, the central case of a citizen who obeys the law, as opposed to the anarchist who obeys it most of the time. For the purposes of this discussion, this stance is of great significance, for it is clear that from culture to culture values will differ. By way of illustration, the example of punishment or deterrence can be taken: it has already been stated that, according to Finnis' theory, the recalcitrant is punished by society for his own good, and to re-establish the equilibrium by restoring the promotion of the common good which the recalcitrant interrupted by his unlawful act. Although Finnis quite rightly is very

COMMENTS (paragraph five)

This author has a very dense style of writing, and it may be helpful for him to break his sentences and paragraphs into shorter segments to aid understanding. There are a few minor errors throughout, but they do not detract from the meaning of the prose. The more pressing problem, however, is that the author is only now getting to the heart of the question, namely that the question of the common good (or self-evident goods) is not straightforward. The author begins to tie his previous points regarding the anarchist and the central case of the citizen together, but only now acknowledges the idea that cultural norms will affect the definition of that central case. Rather than spend so much time discussing Finnis's basic theories, it might have been better to get to this point more quickly, since this is central to the question. The author goes on to argue that the common good, as defined by Finnis, is subject to cultural quick to distance himself from the notion of 'an eye for an eye' in this theory, the implication of a principle of proportionality is nonetheless prominent. This begs the natural question of what is proportional, but no one natural answer can be given to this question. In one society or culture, for example, the central case of the law-abiding citizen would say that those convicted of petty theft should have to do community service to re-establish the common good, as this would best assure against a further deviation therefrom, whilst at the same time serving the purpose of re-establishing the equilibrium. By contrast, a different man in a different society, presented with the same case, may advocate a public flogging and a period of detension to serve the same purpose. The difficulty is decidint which one of these two systems is serving the common good best, and Finnis' theory seems unable to meet this problem with a concrete answer. A possible response to defend the theory against this criticism might be to say that in the second example the system is not working for the common good iin that the offender's good has been neglected, but this is only a possible defence, and its force is limited. In short, it is evident that the common good is a concept open to diverse interpretations, and that therefore there is no one answer about what law should contain in terms of values.

relativism, a conclusion that seems at odds with his earlier conclusion that Finnis does not purport to justify the status quo. This seeming contradiction is exacerbated by the absence of an overarching shape to the essay. While the author obviously has his structure in mind, it is not always obvious to the reader, leading to occasional confusion about the overall argument, even if individual points make sense on their own.

RESPONSE (paragraph six)

This seemingly formidable hurdle to the utility of the common good, however, does not seem such a grave defect in the theory of natural law ehen it is put into context with other legal theories. As has already been demonstrated, the common good is open to diverse interpretations because it is a relatively abstract concept. Yet if an account of

COMMENTS (paragraph six)

This paragraph is quite good. There are a few problems with antecedents (misplaced references to 'it') and typographical errors, but the author is making some very good points about Dworkin's work. Again, the best writing comes when the author ties his analysis specifically into the source material.

law is to be wide-ranging, departing from the source-based positivism of Austin, Kelsen and Hart to a lesser extent, surely it must follow that abstraction is necessary to embrace different values and conceptions. Indeed, Dworkin in 'Law's Empire' affirms that law is an interpretive practice, dependent very much on an interpretive attitude which contains subjective and objective dimensions. Like Finnis, the nearest that Dworkin can get to a universally applicable idea, or concept, is strikingly abstract, for he states that law is the best justification for coercion, and that the interpretive exercise must be embarked upon with this concept in mind. Dworkin's all-seeing judge, Hercules, may perhaps always be able to find a right answer, but he rightly acknowledges that two different judges in different jurisdictions may well give two different answers to the same question. All such material reinforces the point that if one is prepared to admit subjective interpretations into an account of law, different answers will be arrived at, and for the purposes of the present discussion this indicates that the significance of the objection that what is self-evident varies from culture to culture is not as weighty and fatal to the theory of natural law as first appears.

The passing references to other commentators (Austin, Kelsen and Hart) are less successful, precisely because they do not contain any detailed discussion of the commentators' work. Avoid name-dropping: either you have something important to say about these commentators (in which case you should say it explicitly) or you do not (in which case you should omit the reference). The one way that this discussion could be improved is if the author could link Dworkin's and Finnis's theories more explicitly. Right now, Dworkin's theory is presented but the connection to Finnis is left to the reader's imagination. The author has laid sufficient groundwork so that the connection can be implied, but it would be better for the author to state precisely what he means so that there can be no confusion.

RESPONSE (paragraph seven)

In conclusion it can be said that merely by adopting a framework which includes a possibility for exploration of what the law ought to be, Finnis convincingly rebuts the criticism that his theory of natural law is little more that a justification for the status quo, and as has been shown, it is in fact anything but this. The concept of the common good is, without doubt, open to the criticism provoked by cultural diversity, but the natural law theory is advocating an interpretive

COMMENTS (paragraph seven)

The author straightforwardly notes that this paragraph contains his conclusion, but he does not present his findings in anywhere near as straightforward a manner. Instead of slowing the pace and obscuring the meaning of this paragraph with numerous subordinate clauses, the author should be more direct in this paragraph and simply state his points.

approach for which diversity is an ally rather than an enemy. Naturally this may mean that the utility of the theory is sometimes limited, but no other theory has met the requirement of perfection. It is therefore most accurate to say that whilst self-evidence depends very much on cultural background, the natural law theory is nonetheless far more than a justification for the status quo, and provides scope for a perspective of what ought to be, leaving open the chance for reform.

This is a very good essay, and it's clear that the author has a wide ranging knowledge of key jurisprudential concepts. What is not so clear, however, is whether the author has adapted his knowledge sufficiently to answer the question as asked. The essay makes a number of very good points and relies on some esteemed commentators, but fails to give the reader an overarching structure. The discussion therefore reads as a series of possibly, but not necessarily, interrelated points. Some of the early points in particular don't seem to be related to the question at all, although the later discussion may make the appropriate connections. Still, much is implied where it could have been stated explicitly. Had the author done a slightly better job in explaining his argument, this could very likely rise to a first-class essay. As it currently stands, however, it is a very good 2:1.

Index